Base Camp Las Vegas

101 HIKES IN THE SOUTHWEST

Also by Deborah Wall

Base Camp Las Vegas: Hiking the Southwestern States

Great Hikes: A Cerca Country Guide

Access for All: Touring the Southwest with Limited Mobility

Base Camp Las Vegas

101 Hikes in the Southwest

Deborah Wall

IMBRIFEX BOOKS

IMBRIFEX BOOKS
Published by Flattop Productions, Inc.
8275 S. Eastern Avenue, Suite 200
Las Vegas, NV 89123

IMBRIFEX

Editor: A.D. Hopkins
Designer: Sue Campbell
Maps: Mike Johnson
All cover and interior photos by Deborah Wall, except as noted below:
p. 355, Mableen/iStockphoto; p. 358, Jeff Goulden/iStockphoto;
Author photographs: Sean L. Taylor

IMBRIFEX® is a trademark of Flattop Productions, Inc.

This publication is provided for informational and educational purposes. The Publisher assumes no liability for its use. No representations or warranties are made with respect to the accuracy or safety of the publication. Outdoor activities are always potentially dangerous. Awareness of local conditions, weather conditions coupled with good decision-making skills and astute judgment will help reduce potential hazards and risks. Preparing yourself with the proper equipment and outdoor skills will lead to an enjoyable experience. The information herein contained is true and complete to the best of our knowledge. However things can change after a guide book is published — trails are rerouted, trailhead signs are removed or damaged, jurisdiction changes in governmental management of an area can affect routes, seasonal impacts, etc. Corrections, updates and suggestions may be sent to the author at Deborah.Wall@basecampguides.com.

BaseCampGuides.com
Imbrifex.com

ISBN 978–0-9972369-4-1 (trade paper)
ISBN 978-0-9972369-8-9 (e-book)

Library of Congress Control Number: 2017932678
Second Edition: August 2017
Printed in Canada

Right: A hiker enters a narrow canyon along the White Domes Loop Trail. (See p. 117)

For my daughters Whitney, Olivia and Charlotte, who have brought me more love and happiness than I ever knew was possible.

CONTENTS

Foreword

Base Camp:

A place used to store supplies and rest, and as a starting point for activities, especially outdoor adventures.

WHEN DEBORAH WALL'S *BASE CAMP LAS VEGAS* WAS FIRST PUBLISHED IN 2010, IT immediately became the go-to guidebook for hikers interested in exploring the magnificent wild areas within easy reach of Las Vegas. The variety of hikes, the accuracy and clarity of directions, and the captivating photographs illustrating each destination made the book popular long after it went out of print. It's a pleasure to introduce this updated and expanded new edition, which not only reprises 61 great hikes from the first book but adds 40 new ones.

While many visitors to Las Vegas — and residents, too — revel in its man-made glories, more and more appreciate its unique location. In much of the United States, experiencing solitude — let alone wilderness — requires hundreds of miles of travel and a serious time commitment. But with Las Vegas as a starting point, a single day is enough to leave civilization behind and enjoy pristine world-class natural wonders.

Within sixty miles of Las Vegas, you can snowshoe four-foot drifts, swim in a lake, or photograph wildflowers — all on the same day. Ramble in Red Rock Canyon, hike in Valley of Fire, or enjoy crisp alpine air in the Spring Mountains. With a little more time, you can explore mysterious slot canyons, walk through hanging gardens of ferns watered by seeps in canyon walls, or stroll through lush groves of desert palms. Further afield, walk the Grand Canyon, soak up the glories of Zion, or marvel at the iconic formations of Monument Valley. This book tells how to make the most of your explorations.

While camping is always an option, and it's often pleasant to sleep under the stars without bothering to pitch a tent, using Las Vegas as your "base camp" is easier still. To enjoy many of the hikes in this book, you can pack only what you need for the day, then return to showers, fine food, and urban entertainment. A night or two in a rural motel makes longer excursions possible.

Deborah Wall is a recognized expert on the region's wild attractions. Her popular column on hiking and other outdoor adventures appears in the *View Neighborhood Newspapers*, published by the *Las Vegas Review-Journal*. For *Base Camp Las Vegas*, she has selected 101 of the best and most popular rambles for hikers with a variety of priorities and abilities.

The hikes are organized by geographic area, beginning with the hikes that are closest to Las Vegas. Wall provides an overview and directions for each area. She adds a detailed account of each recommended hike, along with directions to its trailhead, a difficulty rating, elevation, the best time of year to take the hike, and other relevant information specific to that trail. "Before You Hit the Trail" outlines advance preparations and precautions hikers should take when exploring in the wilderness.

With Deborah Wall as your peerless guide, I invite you to enjoy all the adventures so readily available within easy reach of Las Vegas. There's still a "Wild West" out there, just waiting for your footsteps!

— *A.D. Hopkins*

Before You Hit the Trail

Many who read this book will already be experienced and capable hikers. But if they got that experience and developed those capabilities elsewhere, they may still find it worthwhile to read some general observations about hiking in this particular region.

It's been one of my own experiences that while experience is famously the best teacher, she's rather a mean one. It's often less painful to get your lesson from somebody else's trials and errors. These things the author has learned, sometimes through her own pain, and sometimes, thankfully, that of others.

About Water

By definition, deserts are places where water is scarce. Furthermore, even where water sources are reliable, it's never safe to drink without the hassle of treating it.

For the latter reason I recommend carrying all your own water on day hikes. The easiest way to do this is by having a water hydration system in your backpack. If you are purchasing a new daypack many come with them already installed, but if not, you can buy the reservoirs or bladders separately. They come in various sizes from about thirty to one hundred ounces and each has a hose running from the top which lies on your chest with a bite valve on the end.

Experts recommend a minimum of one gallon of water per person, per day. Even on short hikes, I start with one hundred ounces of water — more than a gallon and a half. I might not use it, but in case of emergency where I am out longer than expected, or if someone in my group needs extra, it comes in handy. Once I had a mishap with my hydration pack many miles into a strenuous hike and lost just about all my water. On trips where it may be several hours to the next water source, I now carry two separate bladders with at least fifty ounces of water in each.

Water is heavy and weighs about eight and three-tenths pounds per gallon, but is worth the extra burden. And you can take some consolation in the fact that the more you drink, the less it weighs. However, relying on water alone to get you by is a danger in itself, so be sure to have lots of salty snacks and other types of food to eat.

Left: Desert bighorn sheep.
Above: Hydration packs are available even in small sizes, encouraging kids to drink enough water.

Flash flooding

ONE OF THE BIGGEST DANGERS OF HIKING THIS REGION IS FLASH FLOODING. EVEN A SMALL amount of rain can quickly become a raging torrent when the runoff of a large area is concentrated into a narrow canyon or wash, taking everything in that wash, including the occasional hiker, downstream with it.

Be aware that it can be a cloudless day where you are, but be raining upstream from your location. Having weather information is one of the most useful func-

Flash flooding can happen quickly and without warning in desert washes and canyons. Taking such signs seriously can save your life.

tions of visitor centers at state and federal parks; always ask there about the flash flood danger before setting out.

In this area the summer monsoon season is July and August, but storms and flash flooding can occur any month of the year. Since so many good hikes are up canyons and washes, form the habit of constantly looking for signs of past flooding episodes on their walls and on any trees growing in them. Sometimes you will have to look dozens of feet high up to see where water levels have reached in the past. Look for pieces of wood, twigs and other debris, which are often wedged into the cliff walls or stuck in tree branches, marking the past flood level.

As you travel along, keep a constant eye out for an escape route or easily accessed high ground that is above the highest water mark. Always be alert for rumbling sounds and, when hiking in sight of running water, be aware of subtle changes in the stream. Either of these could warn you of an impending flood, and is cause to seek high ground *that very moment*.

Never set up camp in a wash or in the low area of a canyon. And if you see water flowing in a dry wash or rising higher in a wet one, do not attempt to cross it. Climb to higher ground and wait it out. It usually doesn't take long for the water to recede.

Hypothermia and how to dress in cold weather

"But it was surprising, the rapidity with which his cheeks and nose were freezing. And he had not thought his fingers could go lifeless in so short a time. Lifeless they were, for he could scarcely make them move together to grab a twig, and they seemed remote from his body and from him. When he touched a twig, he had to look and see whether or not he had hold of it."
— *From Jack London's "To Build a Fire," 1908*

IN THIS CLASSIC SHORT STORY, LONDON REALISTICALLY DESCRIBES A CASE OF HYPOTHERMIA, frostbite, and other horrible consequence that can happen when an ill-prepared person faces prolonged exposure in freezing temperatures. These hundred years later, spending time outdoors can be safer, for we have much better weather forecasting, as well as more suitable equipment and clothing. But you'll need to take advantage of them.

Hypothermia can begin when the body's core temperature falls even a few degrees below its norm of about 98.6 degrees (this varies somewhat from person to person). What you might not know is that it doesn't even take freezing temperatures to make that happen. Spending a prolonged time outdoors on a rainy and windy day, even at temperatures in the fifties, can easily lead to hypothermia.

When heading outdoors for a winter hike or a snowshoeing excursion you probably know to bring the essential items including water, map, compass, sunscreen and sunglasses, extra food, extra clothing, headlamp, first-aid kit, fire-starter, and a knife. What is also crucial is to be well nourished and hydrated, to have the proper clothing, and to avoid getting wet or exposed to excessive wind.

Dress in layers of clothing and at all costs avoid cotton, which loses its insulating qualities if it becomes wet. A well-thought-out layering system for your body's core will keep you warm for even extended periods of time outdoors, even in freezing temperatures. Depending on the conditions you expect to encounter, choose the weight of these layers in light, mid or heavyweight fabrics.

Your first layer should ideally be a synthetic wicking fabric like Capoline, Coolmax, polypropylene, or some other man-made fabric; second best would be silk or wool. This layer is crucial in keeping you dry because these best fabrics won't absorb moisture from perspiration, but rather lift it out to evaporate.

The second layer should be something like a synthetic fleece jacket or vest; wool is the second-best choice. This is your insulating layer, which will hold in body heat. For extreme low temperatures, a down-filled jacket will also work well — as long as you can guarantee it won't get wet.

Your outer layer should be some sort of a shell jacket or coat. This serves two purposes: It keeps the wind, rain or snow out, but still allows moisture to escape.

Ideally find one that is a longer style so when you take that well-deserved break in some situation like sitting on a snow-covered rock, or while riding a ski lift, your derriere remains warm.

For winter hiking, snowshoeing or skiing, I have found the same layering system also works well for the lower body. In wet weather my outer layer is full-length side-zipped pants of Gore-Tex or other waterproof fabric. Side zippers are handy because if the weather clears up, you can take off the outer pants easily, without removing your boots. In heavy snow or rain, add some knee-high gaiters.

Don't forget good waterproof hiking boots and proper winter hiking socks — again, no cotton, but a polyester, acrylic, or wool blend that will wick moisture. Add good gloves that are insulated and waterproof.

Hikers head out on the slickrock in Zion National Park, Utah.

When you return home from the outdoors, store those gloves in your pack or in your jacket pockets at all times, because gloves are what people often forget. Top it all off with a warm fleece or wool hat, or even better, a balaclava.

I have seen even the most seasoned outdoorsmen neglect to bring some crucial layer, usually the outer shell, knowing they will warm up just minutes after beginning strenuous activity. It is best to at least carry along all the clothes you might need in an emergency. You might be carrying more bulk and a little more weight, but if some unforeseen event keeps you in the weather longer than you expected, it could save your life.

Consider how many ways that could happen: A day hike could take much

longer than expected and force an overnight bivouac; you could get lost; some member of the party might get sick or hurt, requiring that person and another to stay outdoors while someone else went for help; your friend who is to pick you up at the far end of a through hike might get delayed. These and more all happen.

Encourage all members of your group to learn the early warning signs of hypothermia, and watch for them in each other. Knowing the symptoms will help you take action before hypothermia advances past the early stages. Initial symptoms include shivering, numbness in limbs and some lack of coordination.

If you suspect even a mild case of hypothermia take it seriously. Find shelter and a heat source, remove all wet clothing and replace with dry, and help the person move around to warm his body. Offer the victim warm sweet drinks, non-alcoholic. If the victim begins to appear drunk, confused, or non-responsive, these are worse symptoms. You need to seek professional medical attention immediately, as the treatment changes in every stage of hypothermia. Hypothermia can rapidly become life-threatening.

No matter how prepared you are, a fall into cold water will bring on hypothermia even quicker. You will lose body heat about twenty-five percent faster than in cold air, and the longer you are in the water the lower your chances of survival.

It's worth knowing that disposable butane cigarette lighters will light even after being immersed several minutes in water, while traditional fluid-filled lighters, and of course matches, will not. And it's worth knowing that a two-inch stub of ordinary dining-table candle, placed inside a miniature teepee built of wet twigs and then lit, will dry the wood enough to ignite it. Your teepee fire will sustain itself even in steady rain, burning from the sheltered inside and drying its own fuel as you add even wet wood to the outside.

Many years ago I was part of a group of four, out for what was supposed to be about ten hours of midwinter canyoneering. We had to take an unplanned yet necessary ten-minute swim in a canyon pool complete with small icebergs. After this, things went downhill quickly.

One disoriented person in our party wandered away and simply vanished. Unwilling to abandon our lost friend, the rest of us used up the daylight looking for him, and had to spend the night huddled together, uncertain that we ourselves would survive.

All of us heard voices that weren't there, became delirious, and had trouble standing. If not for our essential emergency equipment, being properly dressed and in top physical condition, we probably wouldn't have lived through it.

With much difficulty the next morning, two of us were able to stumble out many miles to seek help, and the two others, including the one who had become separated from the group, were rescued the following day. Some of us lost toenails, which seemed uncomfortably close to losing toes, and one of the survivors said he couldn't feel the ends of his toes for years afterward.

Nowadays setting out on a hike, I'm no longer too shy to ask a casual acquaintance what kind of underwear she, or even he, is wearing

Rattlesnakes

When it comes to rattlesnakes, the world is divided into two groups; those who have a healthy fear of them, and those who become completely unglued even seeing a picture of one.

Since I moved to the West in the 1990s, I have come across a few dozen rattlers but only once, down by Lake Mohave, have I seen one try to attack. One of my daughters, who was twelve at the time, reached up on a

Mojave green rattlesnake.

rocky ledge, without looking first. This startled a rattlesnake, which lurched out at her without any warning.

To this day, I have never again seen my daughter fly, or felt the horror of seeing fangs come within an inch of a person's face. Not surprisingly, she is still terrified of rattlesnakes.

The most important rule to avoid getting bitten is to never put any part of your body anywhere that you haven't looked first.

Rattlers enjoy temperatures from seventy to ninety degrees, so in this region, late spring and fall are the times you're most likely to encounter them. By day, you might stumble upon a snake sunning itself on a boulder or in a wash. Once the sun goes down your worries are not over; these creatures hunt at night.

Learn to recognize the rattlesnakes in the area you will be hiking. If you ever did get bitten, the doctors would want to know what kind bit you. In the more

Red Rock Canyon National Conservation Area at sunrise.

likely event you just see one, you'll want to tell others what you saw, simply to share an outdoor experience.

Around Southern Nevada there are the sidewinder, Mojave, speckled and the western diamondback, but throughout the areas covered in this book there are many other varieties. Identifying the different types is easiest from photographs, or a book like the National Audubon Society's *Field Guide to North American Reptiles & Amphibians*.

Look at the unique patterns and colors, and keep in mind the adult size of each type. Of the four in southern Nevada the sidewinder is smallest, never more than a couple of feet long, but the western diamondback can grow to well over six feet. Mojave and speckled rattlers reach lengths somewhere in between.

Mojave rattlesnakes, which often have a green tinge to their skin, have a more dangerous poison than others, but are said to be more reclusive and therefore less frequently encountered.

Although people bitten by rattlesnakes sometimes die, most do not. One reason they don't is that most bites are not charged with a full dose of poison, because one fang or the other often fails to penetrate. About half of bites are entirely dry ones, meaning no venom has been released. And most bites are to legs or hands, giving victims time to seek treatment before the poison spreads to vital organs.

They have excellent chances of survival if they keep their heads and get to the nearest hospital promptly.

In getting there, however, they should avoid increasing blood circulation, because that will spread the venom quicker. That means the victim must not run a half-mile for help. Walk. Even better, if time and circumstance allow, is to bring a vehicle to the victim. Otherwise, if the person bitten is small enough, consider carrying him or her.

Never use the old-fashioned first-aid technique you see in Western movies — cutting the flesh and trying to suck the poison out. It's ineffective.

According to many experts the best method is to use constriction bands, like tight Ace bandages, between the area of the bite and the heart. Do not make them as tight as a true tourniquet, which would cut off all the blood flow and possibly lead to losing the entire limb. You just want to constrict the flow somewhat.

The majority of my rattlesnake encounters have been while hiking in desert washes. Most of the critters heard me coming and I watched as they slowly slithered away under a bush or other shelter. Some can be more stubborn and stand their ground, in which case I am happy to make a wide detour around them.

A few years ago while I was aboard a boat, also on Lake Mohave, a fellow passenger noticed a rattlesnake floating in the river. He had the bright idea of scooping up the dead snake with a paddle to show us what it looked like. This snake turned out to be very much alive. This is approximately how most snakebites occur — meddling with snakes. Leave them alone and they'll usually return the favor.

Petroglyphs and pictographs

Petroglyphs and pictographs, or "rock writings" as some call them, can be found on natural rock faces throughout our area.

Long ago, people pecked, carved or etched designs through the desert varnish, a dark coating that forms naturally on rock surfaces in dry climates. Where the varnish was scraped away, the lighter rock surface beneath showed through and made the design, called a petroglyph, visible at a distance. Pictographs were painted on rock and today, survive mostly in caves, alcoves, and other places sheltered from weathering.

Many of the images are easily recognizable as mountain sheep or human beings, but others seem less representational, perhaps standing for concepts rather

Pictographs were painted on rock.

than objects. Despite years of study, scientists understand relatively little of the writings' meaning and context. It is believed many were made by ancestors of the same Native American peoples, who have occupied the Southwest in recent history. But other writings in Nevada are as much as 6,000 years old, and are associated with cultures that vanished long ago.

Both petroglyphs and pictographs are very fragile and are irreplaceable. Never touch rock art as the natural oils on our hands will damage it. Also, don't climb or sit on boulders that contain rock art. Many boulders are unstable and could easily dislodge, not only displacing an important part of history but also endangering you and other visitors. If you want a closer look, bring binoculars.

Defacing a petroglyph, or taking one for a souvenir, is irresponsible and seriously illegal. Many were so lost in the past, but in recent years people have faced federal prosecution for such offenses.

Personally, I feel too reverent toward petroglyphs to even consider harming one. To look at some petroglyphs is to ponder a message from people who lived before the rise of Rome! What did they mean to tell those of us who came after?

Whatever the intended message, the one I always read Is this: That our culture is only a steward of this land, and not its owner. We are not the first, and perhaps may not be the last, to hold dominion here.

Hiking with Children
Giving your child an outdoor lifestyle

ONE OF THE GREATEST GIFTS PARENTS CAN GIVE THEIR CHILDREN IS AN APPRECIATION OF the outdoors, and one of the easiest ways to do this is taking them hiking. You won't put many miles on your boots, but you will be laying a foundation for a lifetime admiration of the natural world. The key is to go at their pace, allowing plenty of time to go short distances, so they can take pleasure in the details like wildlife, flowers, plants, and rocks.

Up to the age of three or so, hiking with kids is fairly easy. For the most part they'll walk a short ways on their own and get tired, whereupon you can put them in a child carrier-pack and be on your mutual way. Once they are too heavy to carry, the real work begins. You'll want to keep them moving and interested in their surroundings, so the trail becomes an exciting adventure.

Besides an eagerness to explore, children need a few things for hiking. Most you already own: comfortable yet rugged clothing that you can layer, a hat, sunscreen, sunglasses, a whistle to hang around each child's neck, and either hiking boots or sneakers, with good tread. Add their favorite snacks and water. Many kids will have more fun if you bring each one's favorite small stuffed animal or doll.

Parents have better luck when they select trails based on their children's interests and abilities. Best bets are short loop trails that have a variety of things to see, or hikes to some rewarding destination, such as a waterfall, a great view, or even a field of boulders to play on.

Desert tortoise.

Walking a quarter-mile trail could easily take an hour with kids who really like looking at rocks and lizards, but others just zip along, focused on the destination. Setting unrealistic goals is a mistake I have made many times, and I have paid for it by carrying a heavy and unhappy child miles back to the trailhead.

Boredom may kill any hike but can be beat with a few tricks. Older kids might want to learn how to use a compass or global positioning system, or read a map. All ages enjoy a contest such as seeing who can find the biggest cactus, rock, or tree; or who can spot the first jackrabbit, raven or lizard.

A laminated regional field guide to Southwestern desert life may have color pictures of familiar plants and animals in our area. No matter where you hike you will find at least one cactus, plant, or bird listed. When they identify something on the sheet, mark the date and location with a Sharpie and after just a few outings your child will have a simple diary. These field guides fold up flat and are available at park visitor centers and bookstores.

Consider buying your child one of the water hydration packs now used by nearly all seasoned hikers. If you're not already familiar with them, they include bladder-style reservoirs that are filled with water or some other liquid, and inserted either into a traditional backpack or a backpack built for the specific purpose. In either case a tube with a valve runs from the top of the pack over your shoulder and lies on your chest. You bite down on the valve and the water flows freely.

Children (adults, for that matter) will drink more often from the convenient drinking tube than if they had to unscrew a canteen lid, so they're less likely to become dehydrated. Furthermore, hydration systems keep your child's hands free for safer climbing, or to break a fall if the child stumbles. Hydration packs come in dozens of sizes and have pockets for extra items like binoculars, food, and extra clothing.

It's a good habit to repeat the family's standing safety rules, and announce any new ones for the specific hike, at the trailhead before taking the first step. Some good standing rules are always staying on the trail, no running ahead, always wearing a whistle, and never putting hands and feet into holes and crevices. In my experience, discussing rules with a child leads to better compliance than simply decreeing them. Ask the child why such-and-such behavior isn't a good idea, and the child will usually articulate a need for the rule.

The patience you'll need to hike with children is great but the payoff is worth it; before you know it, your child will be willing and eager to head out on the trail at the next opportunity.

Leaving no trace

VISITORS TO PUBLIC LANDS AND EVEN PRIVATE ONES ARE OFTEN ENCOURAGED TO FOLLOW the "Leave No Trace" principles designed to maintain, for future use, the same lands we enjoy. The author agrees with this trend and the principles are reprinted here (courtesy of *www.LNT.org*) for the reader's convenience.

The Leave No Trace Seven Principles

1. Plan Ahead and Prepare.
2. Travel and Camp on Durable Surfaces.
3. Dispose of Waste Properly.
4. Leave What You Find.
5. Minimize Campfire Impacts.
6. Respect Wildlife.
7. Be Considerate of Other Visitors.

The Southwest is famous for brilliant sunsets.

Red Rock

Canyon

National Conservation Area

Visitors to Southern Nevada are often surprised and delighted to learn that just outside one of the most bustling cities in the world, they can easily experience such a dramatically different landscape as Red Rock Canyon. Only seventeen miles west of the teeming and intentionally artificial Las Vegas Strip is a stunning display of natural beauty, offering pockets of solitude to those who seek it. If you don't live here or are a newcomer, not yet familiar with how lovely the outdoor West can be, Red Rock Canyon is where you should start to find out.

Looking toward the Calico Hills in Red Rock Canyon. Yucca, Joshua trees, and creosote coexist in this natural landscape.

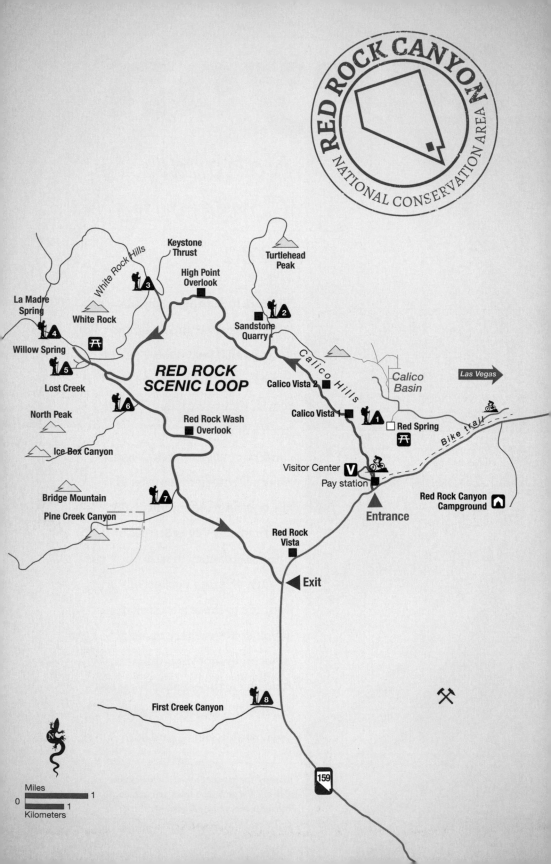

RED ROCK CANYON

NATIONAL CONSERVATION AREA

Keystone Thrust

White Rock Hills

High Point Overlook

Turtlehead Peak

La Madre Spring

White Rock

Willow Spring

3

Sandstone Quarry

2

Lost Creek

5

RED ROCK SCENIC LOOP

Calico Hills

Calico Vista 2

Calico Basin

Las Vegas

North Peak

6

Red Rock Wash Overlook

Calico Vista 1

1

Red Spring

Bike trail

Ice Box Canyon

Visitor Center

Pay station

V

Bridge Mountain

7

Red Rock Canyon Campground

Pine Creek Canyon

Entrance

Red Rock Vista

Exit

First Creek Canyon

8

159

Miles

0 —————— 1

Kilometers

—————— 1

Tucked into the eastern edge of the Spring Mountain Range, this is a land of red sandstone and gray limestone formations, amid open landscapes, narrow canyons, mountains, and springs. The park gets about six to ten inches of moisture a year although nearby Las Vegas usually gets only three to four inches. The canyon is moist enough to host eight major plant communities, which support a generous variety of wildlife.

Here are more than six hundred varieties of plants and three hundred of animals. Look for desert bighorn sheep in the rocky and steep terrain, mule deer in the foothills and even burros as you travel along the lower-elevation trails and roads. Gray foxes, coyotes, mountain lions, and desert tortoises also live here.

Fragile and non-renewable evidence of American Indian occupation, in both historic and prehistoric times, has been protected here. There are wonderful examples of agave-roasting pits, petroglyphs, and pictographs.

October through April is the best time to hit the trails. Summer's high temperatures can be unbearable unless you start (and finish) the trail first thing in the morning. There are no services in the park, but gasoline, convenience stores, and restaurants are available on West Charleston Boulevard, less than half an hour from the park's entrance.

In 1990 the area was officially designated Red Rock Canyon National Conservation Area; administered by the Bureau of Land Management (BLM), the park contains close to two hundred thousand acres.

The BLM has designated the park's thirteen-mile, paved, one-way scenic drive as a Backcountry Byway, recognizing its unusual level of beauty and interest. Most of the trailheads mentioned in this book are located along the byway, and are reserved for day use, which means the hours change according to the season. In October "day use" means 6 a.m.–7 p.m.; November-February, 6 a.m–5 p.m.; March, 6 a.m.–7 p.m.; April–September, 6 a.m.–8 p.m. The Red Rock Canyon Visitor Center is generally open 8 a.m.–4:30 p.m. daily. For visitor information: (702) 515-5350, or *www.redrockcanyonlv.org*.

Directions: From Las Vegas take Charleston Boulevard (Nevada Route 159) west. From its intersection with CC 215 (Las Vegas Beltway), continue west 5.8 miles and turn right for entrance station and Red Rock Canyon Visitor Center.

1 Calico Basin—Red Spring Interpretive Trail

CALICO BASIN OFFERS A MIXED GRILL OF THE RED ROCK AREA'S BEST, INCLUDING RIPARIAN habitat, meadows, springs, and even some cultural resources, all within the area's signature Aztec sandstone landscape.

An easy way to taste it all is to take the Red Spring Interpretive Trail, which starts directly behind the picnic area. This will take you up a small rise and to the grassy bench above. From here the trail makes a one-half-mile loop around the perimeter of the meadow. This trail is accessible for wheelchairs and baby strollers.

A boardwalk was installed in 2005 as part of a restoration project to protect the environmentally sensitive areas. This way, visitors can still enjoy the area without disturbing the fragile plant life. Outside the boardwalk there is a fence to keep burros and horses from trampling these areas.

As you travel along the boardwalk, stop and read the interpretive signs. Be sure and take time to sit quietly a while on one of the many benches along the way, listening and looking for wildlife. Because of a permanent supply of water, lush vegetation, and surrounding canyons, many animals thrive here. More than one

Calico Basin

A boardwalk was installed in 2005 to protect the Red Spring surroundings from being trampled.

hundred species of birds have been recorded, and the area is also home to mountain lions, kit foxes, coyotes, rabbits, ground squirrels, desert tortoises, and ringtail cats. I even had the good fortune of seeing a gray fox on one early-morning visit.

There are three springs in this vicinity. Ash Spring, Calico Spring and Red Spring provided reliable and vital water sources to humans for thousands of years. American Indians used this area and were followed by homesteaders and ranchers. As you make your way around the walkway and over to the sandstone cliffs, keep an eye out for rock art. There are two types in Red Rock Canyon, petroglyphs and pictographs. Here you will be seeing petroglyphs which have been pecked into the surface of rock, unlike pictographs, which were painted on the surface. Some of this rock art is thought to be more than five thousand years old.

Once you reach the far end of the boardwalk from where you started, you will see the waters of Red Spring itself, flowing from a small tunnel or cave. If you look carefully you will see many water-loving plants such as the stream orchid, watercress, Nevada blue-eyed grass and black-creeper sedge. The boardwalk protects not only these plants but also local inhabitants such as red-spotted toads and Pacific chorus frogs.

A few biologically sensitive species also call this area home. The Spring Mountain springsnail, *Pyrgulopsis deaconi,* is found only in four springs, all of them nearby. The alkali Mariposa lily, which grows in the surrounding riparian meadow, is found only in a few other places in Southern California and Nevada. The largest population in Nevada is said to be the one here.

If you visited this area before the boardwalk was installed, you might remember being able to drive almost up to the base of Red Spring, and park there. As you travel along the boardwalk it's worth a look in that area to see how it has been transformed. The old road has been covered over and replaced with native vegetation. It's on its way to restoration as original habitat.

Although this is an excellent place to go when your time is constrained, there are hiking trails just outside of the boardwalk area that are well worth exploring when you have more leisure. There is also a picnic area, with restrooms.

Calico Basin—Red Spring At A Glance

Best season: October–April.

Length: One-half-mile loop.

Difficulty: Easy boardwalk.

Elevation gain: Minimal.

Trailhead elevation: Thirty-six hundred feet.

Jurisdiction: Red Rock Canyon National Conservation Area.

Directions: From Red Rock Canyon's main entrance drive east on Charleston Boulevard (Nevada Route 159) for 1.4 miles. Go left onto Calico Basin Drive and drive about one mile to the signed parking area and trailhead.

⊋ Calico Tanks Trail

THE MAIN ATTRACTION OF THE CALICO TANKS TRAIL IS A LARGE *TINAJA* — A NATURAL waterhole or tank weathered into native rock. But the whole hike is interesting, taking you through a vegetated canyon within a white-and-red sandstone landscape.

Unless you arrive first thing in the morning you will probably find dozens of cars in the parking area. Although the hike is one of the most popular in the park, those cars did not all bring visitors to the tank. The parking lot also serves as the trailhead for Turtlehead Peak, and this is a popular area for rock climbers as well. It is also a favorite for those who come just to take a short and easy stroll around the colorful formations, and perhaps see the remnants of a historic sandstone quarry and an agave-roasting pit.

From the parking area head north along the wide and obvious trail. After about 140 yards you will want to head left across a wash, but first it's worth a look about twenty yards ahead at the large, square blocks of sandstone, said to weigh ten tons each. These are remnants from the quarry that operated here from 1905 to 1912.

After examining the blocks, backtrack and resume the main trail, swinging to the left of the blocks, which will take you down and over a usually dry wash. Start looking on your left for the BLM sign that marks an agave-roasting pit just a few yards off the trail. The hearts of agave, a kind of yucca which still grows hereabout, were a food highly prized by American Indians up to modern times. Continue north until you see the sign marking the right-hand turn for the Calico Tanks Trail.

Follow this spur trail which will take you up a small drainage surrounded by scrub oak, manzanita, and pinyon pines. If you take this hike in late March or early April you might be treated to the showy, bright pink bloom of the western redbud, a small tree that is a member of the pea family. There are only a handful in the canyon but they are a spectacular sight to see.

This hike is a good one for all ages except young children. There is cliff exposure in a few areas, while uneven terrain and elevation gain make it is too strenuous for little ones. Most of the trail is exposed to the sun, so this can be a warm walk, but there is shade to be found along the route, except at the tank itself. Along the way look off to the side of the trail, for areas with fine sand that captures the tracks of chipmunks and birds.

A hiker takes a break to admire the Calico Tanks.

As you continue up the canyon in the steeper sections, you will find hand-placed sandstone steps. There are a few areas you will need to do some route finding but it would be hard to get lost, for the right way is always up the main canyon.

The water level in the tank fluctuates greatly depending on rainfall. I have never found it completely dry, though I have never been there in summer. There is plenty of room to walk around the sandstone shoreline to the left, which affords a comfortable place to sit by water's edge. Be careful traversing the slope, though, for I have seen people lose their footing and slide in.

Another reason to watch your step is to preserve the easily damaged shoots of water-loving vegetation, especially in springtime and on the south shore. This waterhole is critical to the survival of the park's wildlife, but not good for humans; don't drink it or enter the pond.

Seasoned hikers looking for more adventure can head to the southeast corner of the pond and scramble twenty feet or so up a sandstone cliff. From here you can see the visitor center and the first parking area of the Calico Hills, which you passed on the way to the trailhead. If you travel farther, you can even get good, far-reaching views of Las Vegas. There are plenty of high drop-offs in this area, so only those who are sure-footed should hike here.

Calico Tanks At A Glance

Best season: October–April.

Length: 2.5 miles roundtrip.

Difficulty: Moderate.

Elevation gain: 450 feet.

Trailhead elevation: 4,310 feet.

Warnings: Cliff exposure, rock scrambling.

Jurisdiction: Red Rock Canyon National Conservation Area.

Directions: From Red Rock Canyon's main entrance, drive about 2.6 miles on the 13-mile Scenic Drive to the Sandstone Quarry parking area on right.

3 White Rock Hills/La Madre Spring Loop

THIS CIRCLE WILL TAKE YOU AROUND THE PERIMETER OF THE WHITE ROCK HILLS WITH excellent views of the surrounding La Madre Mountains. You'll see several agave-roasting pits and possibly bighorn sheep.

Furthermore, it's an unusually versatile trail with the opportunity for side trips to several springs. The entire loop is a bit long for children but there are no dangerous drop-offs if you stick to the main trail. Since it's a loop hike you can start in either direction but I recommend counterclockwise, which feels a little less strenuous because you'll encounter most elevation gain early in the hike, while you are still fresh.

From the signed trailhead, walk north. Look on your left, up a small rise, for a roasting pit. Little more than a century ago American Indians still used such pits to cook the hearts of agave plants, which grow in the surrounding hills and are marked by tall flowering stalks. Unfortunately this pit isn't well defined because people have trampled on it, but you can still see the faint mound shape, and the blackened rock and ash on the ground. This hiking route passes several more roasting pits in the Willow Springs area.

The trail is well worn and easy to follow except in a few places during the first one-half mile where it crosses a few small washes. Ordinarily there are obvious paths across the drainages, but after a heavy rain or flood you might have to scout upstream to find the trail on the other side.

Along the trail you will be in a pinyon-juniper plant community which includes scrub oak, Mormon tea, manzanita, Mojave yucca, and prickly pear cactus. In spring you'll see wildflowers. Keep an eye out for scrub jays and rock wrens.

From the trailhead it is a steady ascent of about 590 feet over about a mile and one-third, to a saddle, which marks the highest elevation of the hike. Vegetation becomes dense compared to that around the trailhead; up here pinyon pines and junipers grow higher than a person's head, and even provide some shade.

At the saddle you will find a spur trail on your left, marked by a cairn. Sure-footed adults willing to do some rock scrambling can take this path up the sand-stone bluff to points commanding spectacular views of the La Madre Mountain

The White Rock Hills route takes hikers through a pinyon-juniper plant community which also includes Mojave yucca and prickly pear cactus.

range to the north and west. These are great places to take a break and enjoy a snack, giving you more time to take in the views. Bighorn sheep frequent this area, so be on the lookout for movement in the steep parts of the landscape.

Once you backtrack down the spur to the saddle, the trail gradually descends into La Madre Spring Valley and the west side of the White Rock Hills. After about one and one-half miles you will reach a junction where the route turns left onto an old gravel road. But for an excellent side trip, go right instead, and follow the road less than a mile to La Madre Spring, which flows perennially.

The spring feeds a shallow pond, about the size of a large, portable wading pool, which was created by a dam built in the 1960s. Surrounded by Baltic rush, bulrush, reeds and other water-loving plants, it is beloved by area wildlife including bighorn sheep and mule deer. You can sometimes see them of a morning or evening.

If you're skipping the side trip, or after returning from it to the junction, follow the old road about one-half mile to Rocky Gap Road — main route to Pahrump in days of yore — and go left. Continue down the gravel road for about one-half mile to the Willow Springs Picnic Area.

A little below the parking area, look for the sign marking the point where the trail leaves the road and heads east. A little more than two miles farther along, you'll see another spur trail on your left that brings you down to White Rock Spring. There is a bench where you can relax, watch for wildlife and listen for birds before heading up the trail a mere one-tenth mile to the parking area where you started. That's one of the nicest and most unusual features of this hike. How many other opportunities are there to hike six miles, yet end the hike well rested?

White Rock Hills/La Madre Spring Loop At A Glance

Best Season: October–April.

Length: Six-mile loop.

Difficulty: Moderate.

Elevation gain: 885 feet.

Trailhead elevation: 4,875 feet if starting at upper White Rock Spring Trailhead.

Warning: Flash flood potential in washes.

Jurisdiction: Red Rock Canyon National Conservation Area.

Directions: From Red Rock Canyon's main entrance, follow the 13-mile Scenic Drive for 5.7 miles and go right. Follow this access road 0.5 miles to parking area. The trailhead for doing the loop in a counterclockwise direction is on the north side of the parking area.

4 La Madre Spring Trail

THIS ROUTE TAKES YOU DIRECTLY TO A PERENNIALLY FLOWING, SPRING-FED STREAM AND a small pond, manmade in the 1960s. Although many visit this spring as a side trip from the White Hills Loop Trail, this is a different, shorter route through sandstone and limestone hills.

It's a good hike for children, with no drop-offs or obstacles along the main route. Very young hikers, though, might struggle keeping balance on the uneven, rocky surfaces. And because it's very rocky in places, everybody will be more comfortable in sturdy-soled hiking boots instead of lighter-tread sneakers or trail-running shoes.

From the Willow Springs Picnic Area, which serves as the main parking area for this hike, walk up the rough, gravel Rocky Gap Road. This road was once called the old Pahrump Highway or the Potato Road, and was a major route to Pahrump for about fifty years starting in the early 1900s.

After one-half mile you will cross Red Rock Wash (usually dry, but a major drainage). After crossing the wash continue up the road about 130 yards and you will see the sign that marks the official La Madre Spring trailhead on your right.

From the signed trailhead head up the now-abandoned jeep road which will bring you high on the west bank of Red Rock Wash. You will be in a pinyon-juniper plant community which in this area includes scrub oak, Mormon tea, sagebrush, manzanita, Mojave yucca and prickly pear cactus.

About one-half mile after leaving Rocky Gap Road you will come to a signed junction. To the right is the White Rock Loop Trail that circles north around the White Rock Hills and back to the Willow Springs Picnic Area, about six miles in total. For the La Madre Spring hike, however, you continue straight ahead.

Travel about three-tenths miles farther and you will see an obvious and wide spur trail on the right. This fifty-yard side trip takes you to an old house foundation. I paced it out to be about fifty-five by thirty feet. There are still some remains of the old floor tile; very strong glue has held it in place through about four decades of desert heat and cold.

Off the main trail there is another short spur trail on the left where you can find another foundation about the same size.

Continuing up the main route about four-tenths miles you will arrive at the official end of the trail, marked by an interpretive sign. From here look down the embankment and you will see the pond and dam surrounded by Baltic rush, bulrush and other water-loving plants. La Madre Spring itself is located upstream.

This is a lovely place to have lunch or just relax on the wide flat areas and listen

for birds. Desert bighorn sheep and mule deer are often seen here in mornings and evenings.

Although this ends the official hike you can continue upstream on a well-worn, yet narrow path within a pretty canyon, and about one-half-mile farther will come to the remains of an old miner's cabin. This area was privately owned until 1975 when the Bureau of Land Management acquired it.

Along the way you will have to do many stream crossings but need not get wet, for the stream is usually only a couple of feet wide. The most pleasant part of hiking upstream is the sound of the water as it flows through the constricted drainage under a thick, low canopy of vegetation.

La Madre Spring Trail At A Glance

Best season: October–April.

Length: 3.6 miles roundtrip from Willow Springs Picnic Area.

Difficulty: Moderate.

Elevation gain: 715 feet.

Trailhead elevation: 4,580 at Willow Springs Picnic Area or 4,804 at official trailhead.

Warning: Flash flood danger.

Jurisdiction: Red Rock Canyon National Conservation Area.

Directions: From Red Rock Canyon's main entrance, take the 13-mile Scenic Loop Drive for about 7.5 miles. Go right and drive 0.6 miles, parking on the right at Willow Springs Picnic Area. If you have a high-clearance, four-wheel-drive vehicle you can drive 0.6 miles farther to the official trailhead.

A small dam creates a little pond, a haven for water loving plants. This area is frequented by mule deer and desert bighorn sheep in early mornings and evenings. La Madre Spring is upstream.

5 Children's Discovery Trail and Lost Creek

THIS IS A LOOP TRAIL WITH THE OPPORTUNITY TO TAKE A SHORT SIDE TRIP TO A SEASONAL waterfall in Lost Creek Canyon. Besides the waterfall, it accesses a creek, an agave-roasting pit, pictographs made by American Indians, and interesting plant life. With appealing elements for adults and children alike, it makes an ideal introductory hike.

The trip is easy but one must actually hike. Strollers and little ones' legs don't work well here because of uneven, rocky terrain, sandstone steps, stream crossings and slippery rocks near the water. Small children need to be in a child-carrier pack of some sort.

From the parking area, take the trail at the far right, well marked as the Children's Discovery Trail. After less than five minutes you will cross the broad Red Rock Wash. This is usually a dry stream, but if you happen to find a good flow of water here, or even if it rains when you visit, save this hike for another day. This wash is a major drainage, so flash flooding is common, and it is possible to walk across the wash dry-footed, yet be unable to return safely just a few minutes later.

On the other side of the wash, the trail narrows and begins an easy ascent up rocky terrain interspersed with smooth sandstone steps, into a plant community of manzanita, shrub live oak, juniper, and pinyon pines.

For the next quarter-mile the area contains important cultural resources — fragile and non-renewable evidence of prehistoric occupation. This area is known to have provided a seasonal camp for American Indians.

Look for the sign indicating the location of an agave-roasting pit, sometimes called a prehistoric kitchen, near a large pinyon pine. The native people created such pits by burying the basketball-sized hearts of the agave plant, along with rocks heated in a fire, which cooked this favorite food slowly and thoroughly. Vanishing elsewhere, the pits are still common around Red Rock Canyon.

You will find a signed spur trail on the right, to Willow Springs Picnic Area; the side trip is less than a mile one way. Continuing on the main loop, on your right you will notice sandstone cliffs that have many overhangs. Keep an eye out above and around these because sometimes you can see desert bighorn sheep, especially in the early morning.

There also are a few pictographs in this area. They are very faint so it might take you a while to spot them. But they're worth looking for, as pictographs are not common in our area. Unlike petroglyphs, the more common but equally irreplaceable form of rock writing, pictographs are painted. Pictographs tend to weather away, and both kinds are easily damaged by the touch of human hands, boots, etc.

About one half-mile from the trailhead take the unmarked spur trail on your right, towards narrow Lost Creek Canyon. You will need to make a couple of minor crossings over the creek. The trail also passes by a ponderosa tree, an unusual sight at this relatively low elevation. Because of the water and cooler temperature, a handful of ponderosas grow not only here but also in nearby Pine Creek Canyon. If you are unsure which of the large pines are ponderosas, smell the bark; its scent resembles that of vanilla.

Continue up the sandstone steps, which will bring you under the wedge where two giant boulders have fallen against each other, forming a roof over the trail for a few feet. The trail ends about fifteen yards from here inside a box canyon, highlighted by Lost Creek Falls. About fifty feet high, the falls are seasonal; the best time to see them is usually January through March.

On your return from Lost Creek Falls side trail, continue down the Discovery Trail and you will come to a wooden boardwalk. This walkway and deck serve a higher purpose than merely keeping your feet dry. This is a riparian restoration area, and the boardwalk protects all sorts of plants from getting trampled, including wild grapes, horsetails, watercress, grasses and rushes. It also protects critical habitat for the southeastern Nevada springsnail.

From the viewing deck you can see Lost Creek as it flows under the willows, which form a broad canopy over the creek. Benches are built into the walkway, making this a good place to stop for a while and listen to the gentle sounds of the creek and the local birds, who like this spot as much as we do.

Children's Discovery Trail At A Glance

Best season: October–April.

Length: 0.75-mile loop.

Difficulty: Easy to moderate.

Elevation gain: Two hundred feet.

Trailhead elevation: 4,460 feet.

Warnings: Flash flooding, uneven footing along rocky trail.

Jurisdiction: Red Rock Canyon National Conservation Area.

Directions: From Red Rock Canyon's main entrance, take the 13-mile Scenic Drive for about 7.5 miles and go right toward Willow Springs Picnic Area. Drive 0.2 miles and park on left at signed trailhead.

6 Ice Box Canyon

ICE BOX CANYON IS ALWAYS PICTURESQUE, ESPECIALLY FROM JANUARY THROUGH MARCH when you'll probably see the seasonal show of cascades, deep pockets of water, and possibly waterfalls among the colorful sandstone bluffs.

Of course, the moisture that makes those months so agreeable also brings the danger of flash flooding. On any canyon hike, get an up-to-date weather forecast before hitting the trail.

Although it's up to you how far you travel within the canyon, officially it is a two-and-one-half mile roundtrip with an elevation gain of a few hundred feet. You will encounter rocky and slippery terrain, so hiking boots with good treads and ankle support, never a bad idea, are especially in order here.

From the trailhead take the signed path and within minutes you will reach Red Rock Wash, a major drainage. The wash is about sixty yards across and during or directly after rain, can become a raging torrent. If rain threatens, yet the wash looks dry, do not be tempted to cross, for you might not be able to return safely if the weather isn't bluffing.

As you make your way across the drainage, look for the sandstone steps on the far side, which will take you up onto the natural bench. Travel along the obvious trail and after about two-tenths miles from the trailhead you will come to a signed junction. The trail to the right is called the Spring Mountain Youth Camp Trail, though the camp is now located elsewhere. It leads hikers over to the Lost Creek

Excellent rock scrambling skills can get you into Ice Box Canyon's upper reaches. A hiker is seen on a high cliff.

area. The one going left is Dale's Trail which leads to the Pine Creek area. For the Ice Box Canyon hike head straight, toward the mouth of the canyon.

As you continue you will find a plant community of scrub oak, desert willow, pinyon pine, and manzanita. There are quite a few social trails along the way, which can be confusing, but staying on the most-worn path and continuing up canyon will take you where you need to go. Some spur trails lead to the base of the steep cliffs and are used primarily by rock climbers. There are more than seventy climbing routes in this canyon alone, and more than two thousand in the park.

You might see white-tailed antelope squirrels, cottontails, jackrabbits, kit foxes, coyotes, or even a bobcat on this hike. Once inside the canyon look along the walls and you might see desert bighorn sheep. Birds here include Gambel's quail, mourning doves, white-throated swifts, and cactus wrens.

After about one mile the trail descends steeply into the boulder-filled drainage, which will serve as your route if you choose to continue. But this makes a good turnaround point if you have children along or others unprepared for some difficult rock scrambling. Those up to the task will not only get a good workout but also drink great gulps of the canyon's beauty.

It is a jumble of color with different-textured rocks from rough and jagged to slippery and water worn. There is no ideal route and you will have to find what works best for you. Be aware that many rock scramblers fall to their deaths each year. The most useful rule to avoid being one such is remembering that it's easier to go up a given slope than to descend safely. Before going up, figure out how to come down.

Ice Box Canyon At A Glance

Best season: October–April.

Length: 2.6 miles roundtrip.

Difficulty: Moderate.

Elevation gain: Three hundred feet.

Trailhead elevation: 4,285 feet.

Warnings: Rock scrambling in canyon. Flash flooding.

Jurisdiction: Red Rock Canyon National Conservation Area.

Directions: From Red Rock Canyon's main entrance, take the 13-mile Scenic Drive about 8 miles to the well-signed trailhead, located on the right.

7 Pine Creek Canyon

PINE CREEK CANYON HAS MUCH TO OFFER A DESERT HIKER, INCLUDING A SEASONALLY flowing creek, the remains of a homestead from the 1920s, dense vegetation, and plenty of opportunities to explore the upper canyon.

Children who can handle the distance will like this hike, but there are drop-offs in one segment. I wouldn't recommend allowing them into the upper reaches, because that requires too much rock scrambling.

From the parking area follow the well-defined trail south, down the bank and into Pine Creek Wash. Here the plants include blackbrush, Mojave yucca, and

The monolith called Mescalito towers over a meadow in Pine Creek Canyon.

Pine Creek is a seasonal stream, but waters vegetation that lasts all year.

cholla cactus. The trail then heads west toward the escarpment, and soon scrub oak, willow, and juniper join the habitat.

Look closely within the juniper trees and you will find plenty of desert mistletoe, a parasite with scale-like leaves and berries. Although the plant sucks nutrients and water from the host plant, sometimes killing it, the berries are a treat for some birds, especially the phainopepla.

To the south you will see the tops of trees marking Pine Creek itself. It's worth taking one of the many spur trails that lead over to its banks. Here you will find a riparian habitat mostly made up of willow and cottonwood trees. The creek area also supports old-growth ponderosa pines, pretty rare at this elevation.

Back on the main route, continue west toward the prominent red-capped monolith named Mescalito, which separates the canyon upstream. Along the way look for whitetail antelope ground squirrels, cottontails, jackrabbits, and wild burros. On the cliffs you might even see desert bighorns.

About three-quarter miles from the trailhead look on the left, for an unsigned, yet well worn spur trail. This will take you up a small rise where you will find the foundation of an old homestead. Back in 1920, Horace and Glenda Wilson settled in this scenic spot. They built a two-story house with fireplace, and planted an apple orchard and garden.

In 1928 they sold the property to businessman Leigh Hunt. They stayed on as caretakers for eight more years, then moved to Las Vegas. Once abandoned, the house fell victim to vandalism. In 1976 the Nevada Division of State Parks acquired the place.

There is still a lone apple tree in the grassy meadow west of the foundation, but it doesn't seem to bear fruit. An obvious path heads south through the meadow and over to the creek. If there has been rain recently, the path pools with water and it will be hard to avoid getting your feet wet. Don't wander off the trail, as there are very fragile plants throughout this area.

Once you have explored the homestead, return to the main trail. If you have kids along, an old hollow tree, on the left side of the trail, is perfect for a child to stand in. Continue on and soon you will come to a signed left turn. This marks the start of the hike's loop portion, which is only nine-tenths miles.

After you go left to begin this loop, it crosses the Pine Creek drainage and then makes a gradual ascent up its south side. After about one-tenth mile the trail forks and for this hike you will go right. (To the left is the Arnight Trail, a moderate hike which connects to the Oak Creek Canyon Trail at the parking area, a walk of one and seven-tenths miles from this junction.)

As you continue up the trail you will be in one of the most vegetated areas of the hike. Canyon grapes are very prolific here. As you reach the highest elevation of the hike you will be at almost the same level as the tops of the ponderosa trees. There are some drop-offs along this area so watch your footing. In a couple of places the trail is hard to follow so you might need to do some route finding.

The trail soon loses elevation and then loops around to the north where it crosses back over the creek and hooks up to the main trail for your return to the trailhead.

Those who can handle some demanding rock scrambling can travel up the forks on either side of Mescalito. Both are worth exploring but the south fork is easier to negotiate.

Pine Creek Canyon At A Glance

Best season: October–April.

Length: Three miles with optional extension.

Difficulty: Moderate.

Elevation gain/loss: Three hundred feet.

Trailhead elevation: 4,053 feet.

Warning: Washes subject to flash floods.

Jurisdiction: Red Rock Canyon National Conservation Area.

Directions: From Red Rock Canyon's main entrance, take the 13-mile Scenic Drive 10.2 miles to the well-signed parking area and trailhead, on the right.

8 First Creek Canyon

THE FIRST CREEK TRAIL PRESENTS A LITTLE OF EVERYTHING PEOPLE LIKE ABOUT RED ROCK Canyon, including open desert landscapes, riparian areas, a seasonal stream, and spectacular views of the sandstone Wilson Cliffs. Furthermore, it's an easy trail to access, for it doesn't lie on the one-way scenic loop.

From the trailhead start your trek west along the obvious well-worn path. For the first mile or so vegetation mainly consists of Joshua trees, banana yuccas, cholla cactus, and blackbrush. You might be lucky enough to see wild burros, coyotes, kit foxes, whitetail antelope ground squirrels, jackrabbits, or cottontails; you'll surely see evidence of their presence. You'll doubtless see a few lizards darting about, mostly the zebra-tailed, side-blotched, and desert spiny varieties.

About one mile from where you started, the trail veers right and tops an embankment of the First Creek drainage. There are a few spur trails along here that lead down into the creek bed, but most are pretty steep. Keep going, and you'll come to the main trail down — a much easier route.

Once in the drainage there are some boulders to sit on and enjoy the surroundings. If there has been rain recently, head upstream a short distance and you will be treated to a waterfall. Keep an eye out for hummingbirds, white-throated swifts, cactus wrens, mourning doves, nighthawks and Gambel's quail. Pacific chorus frogs and red-spotted toads also make homes here. Canyon grapevines grow profusely up many of the embankments and you will also find a variety of water-loving rushes and sedges. Flanking the streambed are willows, cottonwoods and single-leaf ash trees.

You won't travel too far within the drainage until you are confronted with dense vegetation, but this lush riparian area is a pleasant place to just relax a while.

Once they have seen the creek bed and waterfall, most hikers return to the trailhead. But those seeking more can continue west into First Creek Canyon. Along the way you will be entering the 24,997-acre Rainbow Mountain Wilderness Area which runs up and over the escarpment. This wilderness area is jointly managed by the BLM and the U.S. Forest Service.

As you continue up the canyon, the trail gets faint and harder to follow and eventually you'll have to do some rock scrambling. Within the canyon the vegetation changes dramatically due to more water and a cooler environment. Utah serviceberry, desert snowberry, and manzanita thrive here, and there are even Gambel's oaks and ponderosas scattered throughout.

First Creek Canyon At A Glance

Best season: October–April.

Length: Two to three miles roundtrip with opportunities to extend.

Difficulty: Easy to moderate.

Elevation gain: Three hundred feet.

Trailhead elevation: 3,645 feet.

Warning: Flash flood danger in canyon.

Jurisdiction: Red Rock Canyon National Conservation Area.

Directions: From Red Rock Canyon's main entrance head south on State Route 159 (Charleston Boulevard) about 4.2 miles. Parking area is on the right.

Right: A riparian setting along First Creek. Below: Low clouds at Red Rock Canyon National Conservation Area.

Mt. Charleston

Mt. Charleston Kyle
Canyon area.

Spring Mountains

National Recreation Area

Only an hour from the desert climate of
Las Vegas, winter snows can pile seven
feet deep and elk graze in lush meadows.
The Spring Mountains and particularly
their dominant peak, Mt. Charleston,
stand like green alpine islands in a sea of
sand and stone.

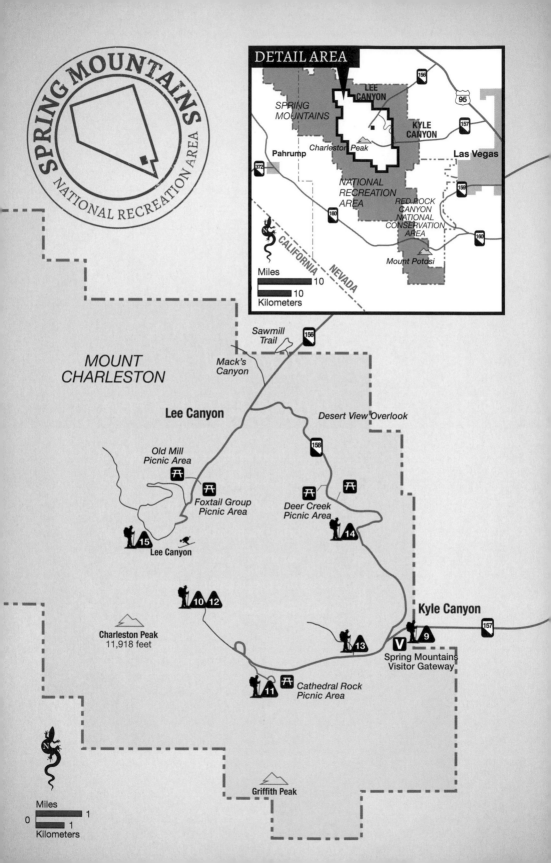

SPRING MOUNTAINS
NATIONAL RECREATION AREA

DETAIL AREA

SPRING MOUNTAINS

LEE CANYON

156

US 95

157

KYLE CANYON

Charleston Peak

Pahrump

Las Vegas

372

159

NATIONAL RECREATION AREA

160

RED ROCK CANYON NATIONAL CONSERVATION AREA

160

Mount Potosi

CALIFORNIA

NEVADA

Miles
10
10
Kilometers

Sawmill Trail

156

Mack's Canyon

MOUNT CHARLESTON

Lee Canyon

Desert View Overlook

158

Old Mill Picnic Area

Foxtail Group Picnic Area

Deer Creek Picnic Area

15

Lee Canyon

14

10   12

Charleston Peak
11,918 feet

13

Kyle Canyon

157

V

9

Spring Mountains Visitor Gateway

11

Cathedral Rock Picnic Area

N

Griffith Peak

Miles
0   1
1
Kilometers

Because of the heavy winter snows, late spring through early fall is the best time to hike these mountains. But because such a large population lives nearby, these months see heavy use, especially on summer weekends. If you desire solitude on popular trailheads, get there at first light.

Yet, there's a lot of outdoors to share here. The Spring Mountains National Recreation Area, established in 1993 as part of the Humboldt-Toiyabe National Forest, encompasses 316 thousand acres. Elevations range from about forty-five hundred feet up to 11,918 at Charleston Peak's summit.

In planning a hike it is important to factor in how altitude might affect your experience, for few of us are accustomed to such heights. At most of the trailheads you will be about five thousand feet higher than Las Vegas, so temperatures can easily be more than twenty-five degrees cooler. In the thin alpine air, hiking feels more strenuous, and it's easier to get sunburned.

There are no bears in the Spring Mountains but there is plenty of wildlife including wild horses, mountain lions, and desert bighorn sheep. In fact, with six different life zones, and ages of isolation from other high-country habitats, the Spring Mountains National Recreation Area has more than fifty species unique to the area.

In the upper reaches of this area you will probably come across Palmer's chipmunks, a species found only in these mountains and only where ponderosa trees are dominant, which is about eight thousand feet above sea level. A close cousin, the Panamint chipmunk, is found over a wider area. Most of us wouldn't notice the difference between the two unless they were standing side by side; then one might notice the Palmer's is a bit larger, and brighter in color. It's charming to know you're looking at a creature seen nowhere else in the world, but don't let that fact tempt you to feed them. They're trying to keep the wildlife wild around here.

Neither gasoline nor groceries are sold on Mt. Charleston, but there are restaurants at both the Mt. Charleston Lodge and Mt. Charleston Hotel in the Kyle Canyon area. There are some water sources on hiking trails, but not all are reliable, and all require thorough treatment to be potable, so it's best to bring plenty from home.

For visitor information: (702) 872-5486, *www.gomtcharleston.com*.

🄴 Spring Mountains Visitor Gateway

OPENED IN LATE SPRING OF 2015, THE SPRING MOUNTAINS VISITOR GATEWAY IN KYLE Canyon is the place to start any visit to the Mt. Charleston area. The complex features a new forty-five hundred-square-foot visitor center surrounded by 128 acres. The complex has something to offer all ages. Besides the visitor center, the Gateway includes an education building, two amphitheaters, a group picnic site, the nation's first Cold War Memorial, and the Nuwuvi (Southern Paiute) Seven Stones Plaza. Three hiking trails begin behind the visitor center.

Resting benches made of natural logs are found throughout the property, and there are stations to refill your water bottles or hydration packs, or maybe even draw water for your dogs. Great thought also went into choosing the native plants here. Look for aspen trees and evergreens, and for wildflowers blooming in summer.

Directly behind the visitor center is the USAF 9068 Memorial and Silent Heroes of the Cold War National Monument. As our nation's first Cold War Memorial, it

The Spring Mountains Visitor Gateway in Kyle Canyon opened in 2015.

honors veterans and those citizens who gave their lives in the national effort to maintain military readiness during almost fifty years of nuclear-armed tension.

On November 17, 1955, the highest peak of the Spring Mountains was the site of the USAF 9068 plane crash at 11,918 feet. The crash, which took place during a winter storm, cost the lives of fourteen men. They included Air Force personnel, scientists, engineers and CIA officials who were on a secret flight returning from "Area 51." The very existence of the Area 51 airbase and related facilities wasn't even acknowledged by the government until recent years, because their role is believed to be developing and testing secret weapons. The formerly secret U2 spy plane was tested there. Signs are present to interpret the memorial, and an airplane propeller, salvaged from the crash site, is on display

The Seven Stones Plaza acknowledges the Nuwuvi belief that their ancestors were created in the Spring Mountains. Here are seven boulders, one for each branch of the Southern Paiute people. These surround a center boulder with a hand print, which represents the Nuwuvi's creator, Ocean Woman.

If you have small children along they will be enchanted by the kid-friendly interpretive signs, wildlife tracks painted on the pathways, and the one-half-mile Pack Rat Trail, suitable for those who can't walk too far. In summer there are also ranger programs and other events.

The Spring Mountains Visitor Gateway is open 9 a.m.–4 p.m. Sunday through Thursday, and open till 6 p.m. Fridays and Saturdays. However, hours are subject to change, so always check before going. All the trails are open from dawn to dusk. For more detailed information go to *www.gomtcharleston.com*, or call (702) 872-5486.

Spring Mountains Visitor Gateway at a Glance

Best Season: May to mid-October, barring snowfall.

Length: Three trails ranging from 0.5 to 2.5 miles.

Difficulty: Easy to moderate.

Trailhead Elevation: Sixty-six hundred feet.

Jurisdiction: Spring Mountains National Recreation Area, Humboldt-Toiyabe National Forest.

Directions: From Las Vegas, take U.S. Highway 95 north about 17 miles. Go left on Kyle Canyon Road (Nevada Route 157). Drive about 16.5 miles and turn left to the Spring Mountains Visitor Gateway.

10 Mary Jane Falls

ALTHOUGH THERE ARE MANY EXCELLENT HIKES ON MT. CHARLESTON, RANGING FROM toddler-friendly trails to strenuous peak hikes, Mary Jane Falls might well be the best-all-around one, especially if those in your group vary by ages and abilities.

From its signed trailhead the route is obvious; just head up the wide and well-defined trail. Notice the rip-rap rocks set in place along the trail to help prevent erosion. Children find it irresistible to walk upon these, testing their balancing skills.

The trail starts as a pleasant stroll through a forest of ponderosa pines, white fir, aspens, and mountain mahogany, with an understory of thistle, elderberry, and willow. Along the lower part of this trail, you'll also find some rare wildflowers including a species called rough angelica (*Angelica scabrida*), which is also found in avalanche chutes in these mountains, yet nowhere else in the world.

After about seven-tenths miles the hike changes dramatically and you'll have to start doing some work. Here you'll begin the steady ascent up a steep slope, helped along by twelve switchbacks which make the walk longer but less steep.

If you have children along, this is a good place to teach them the importance of staying on official trails, and how shortcutting wreaks havoc, causing washouts, and destroying plant life that in many cases takes decades or longer to grow back. You'll notice where the U.S. Forest Service and various volunteer groups have placed jute netting, logs and branches along the slope to protect the area and help it recover from past damage.

Here, you have a chance to see the Palmer's chipmunk, a species unique to the Spring Mountains. It's usually found at an elevation of about eight thousand feet, where the dominant vegetation is ponderosa, as on this trail. The more abundant

Panamint chipmunk is also seen here, but has a wider range. They look almost identical except the Palmer's is slightly larger and a brighter color.

The final switchback leads you up to the base of limestone cliffs, where you will follow along the cliff base over a mix of natural and man-made steps, leading to the falls. The perennial water flow is from two springs located high on the cliff wall, well over one hundred feet above. During heavy run-off you will find three or more waterfalls. Watch your footing as the terrain becomes increasingly uneven, and extra slippery near the falls. Every time I have visited I have seen one or two people take a painful pratfall.

Tempting as it may be, resist climbing up inside the large overhang next to the falls, because of the fragile plant life. There are some natural steps though, by which you can climb up and take a good look into this natural shelter. From here you can look across the canyon to Big Falls, another great hiking destination, less known but a good one for those up to some route finding and rock scrambling.

On the far side of these falls, look for the well-worn spur trail which will lead you to a small cave, a good place to stop, relax, and take in the view. This is a popular hike so don't expect much solitude, but it is a good one to familiarize yourself with Kyle Canyon. And that will be a good idea, because most people like what they find here, and will soon be coming back to try its other trails.

~~~~~~~~~~~~~~~~~~~~~~~~~~~~~~~~

Mary Jane Falls At A Glance

Best season: May to mid-October, barring snowfall.

Length: Three miles roundtrip.

Difficulty: Moderate.

Elevation gain/loss: One thousand feet.

Trailhead elevation: 7,833 feet.

Warnings: Wet and slippery footing near falls. Ice is common.

Jurisdiction: Spring Mountains National Recreation Area, Humboldt-Toiyabe National Forest.

Directions: From the Spring Mountains Visitor Gateway take Nevada Route 157 west about 3.3 miles, staying right at the hairpin curve onto Echo Road. Drive 0.4 miles then go left on gravel road for 0.3 miles to trailhead.

11 Cathedral Rock

THE PLEASURES OF A HIKE TO CATHEDRAL ROCK INCLUDE WALKING THROUGH FORESTS, viewing seasonal wildflowers, crossing an open avalanche chute, and emerging atop the monolith, there to rest and enjoy breathtaking views of Kyle Canyon and beyond. There is also a side trip to a seasonal waterfall.

Older children will be able to handle this hike, but all hikers must keep in mind that once they arrive on top, there are severe drop-offs in all directions. Be extremely careful, as people have lost their lives by falling here.

Along most of the trail there is loose rock underfoot, so I recommend wearing hiking boots rather than sneakers or athletic shoes. Boot soles are usually thicker and have deeper treads, less likely to slip on loose rock.

The trail immediately starts ascending steadily through a forest of ponderosa pines and white fir in Mazie Canyon. Suddenly the landscape changes dramatically and you will be surrounded by young aspen trees. That's because this area is a major avalanche chute in winter, and aspen trees are among the few plants likely to survive the havoc. But in season you'll see wildflowers such as lupine, paintbrush, thistle, and penstemon.

After you cross to the other side of the chute and continue your ascent on the south side of the canyon, keep an eye out for a spur trail on your left. This short spur trail, only about one hundred yards long, is well worth the effort, for it ends at a series of three seasonal waterfalls. In spring they can pour quite spectacularly but in summer there is sometimes a mere trickle, except after storms. Trickle or torrent, it's a pleasant place to take a break.

Back on the main trail, continue up through the avalanche chute, which takes you around to the back side of Cathedral Rock.

Just before the trail reaches a saddle, you will come to a fork. Stay right and continue down a small dip, and you will hear the water flowing in a small creek on

Hikers walk along the avalanche chute at the base of Cathedral Rock.

your right. Continue on and then start up a series of switchbacks. You will notice manmade netting on the hillsides here, an attempt to stop erosion. The trail brings you up to the west side of the monolith and then swings north to the overlook.

The trail travels through fossil-bearing limestone. There aren't any vertebrate fossils in the formation, but you might find brachiopods, crinoids and horn corals.

Once on top you will have excellent bird's-eye views down into Kyle Canyon and the surrounding area. Below lie Mt. Charleston Lodge and the private homes that were built in this glorious setting. Looking down Kyle Canyon Road to the east you will have far-reaching views of the Sheep Mountains.

To the northeast is Mt. Charleston Peak, at 11,918 feet the highest in the Spring Mountains. If you're young and ambitious it may inspire you to bigger adventure on its slope. Or if you're middle-aged and out of breath, it may inspire you to rest on the laurels of a morning well spent.

Cathedral Rock At A Glance

Best season: May to mid-October, barring snowfall.

Length: 2.8 miles roundtrip.

Difficulty: Moderate.

Elevation gain/loss: 910 feet.

Trailhead Elevation: 7,680 feet.

Warning: Steep drop-offs.

Jurisdiction: Spring Mountains National Recreation Area, Humboldt-Toiyabe National Forest.

Directions: From Spring Mountains Visitor Gateway, go west on Nevada Route 157 about 5 miles to the Cathedral Rock Picnic Area, which is open 8 a.m.–8 p.m. Access trailhead from the first parking area.

12 Big Falls

THE BIG FALLS HIKE IS LESS KNOWN THAN SOME ON MT. CHARLESTON, YET OFFERS AS MUCH pleasure, including the sight of bristlecone pines, doubtless the oldest living individuals you're ever encountered.

From the trailhead follow the signed trail as if going to Mary Jane Falls. Immediately you will find yourself within a vigorous forest of ponderosa pines and white fir, mixed with aspens and mountain mahogany. At seven-tenths miles the well-worn Mary Jane Falls trail narrows and heads off to the right.

For this hike, though, you will go straight, on an abandoned gravel road. Follow this for about one hundred yards, then take the obvious left turn to the west. The trail will narrow and bring you over a couple of small washes, then arrive at the right or north side of the area's major drainage. You will follow this canyon upstream to Big Falls.

In this area look carefully at the conifers surrounding you, and you'll see a few of the famous bristlecones. You can recognize them by their branches, which have needles arranged in a pattern that resembles a bottle brush. Some along this trail are only about six feet tall, but they're close to a thousand years old. A few bristlecones in California have been scientifically estimated to be nearly five thousand years old — the oldest trees in the world, and perhaps oldest of all living things.

Follow the path until it drops into the drainage itself. From here just start heading up the canyon. There are many boulder-choked areas and small log jams that you'll have to maneuver around, but nothing very demanding until you get to the one large obstacle of the hike.

That obstacle is a very narrow section of the canyon, blocked by a fifteen-foot-high boulder wedged between the walls. You have two choices to get around this. If you have climbing skills, you can go directly up on the left side of the boulder using upended logs that have been placed there to aid you. The other option is backtracking about twenty yards and heading up the faint trail on the southeast side. Although there is also a clearly visible path on the northwest side, I can't recommend it. It's more strenuous, has more cliff exposure and is harder to negotiate safely.

After your ascent, drop back into the wash and continue upstream. Depending on recent rainfall, the rest of your route might be along a small stream, which

Left: It's a rugged route up to Big Falls.

disappears underground and resurfaces from time to time. You can easily skirt the water to the right. Continue up canyon until all progress is blocked by a one-hundred-foot pour-off, Big Falls. The water flow depends on snowmelt and recent rain, so the amount can change significantly from visit to visit.

Big Falls At A Glance

Best season: May to mid-October, barring snowfall.

Length: 2.7 miles roundtrip.

Difficulty: Moderate to strenuous.

Elevation gain: 850 feet.

Trailhead elevation: 7,833 feet.

Warnings: Route finding, rock scrambling and dangerous drop-offs.

Jurisdiction: Spring Mountains National Recreation Area, Humboldt-Toiyabe National Forest.

Directions: From the Spring Mountains Visitor Gateway take Nevada Route 157 west about 3.3 miles, staying right at the hairpin curve onto Echo Road. Drive 0.4 miles then go left on gravel road for 0.3 miles to trailhead.

13 Fletcher Canyon

IN THE KYLE CANYON AREA OF THE SPRING MOUNTAINS NATIONAL RECREATION AREA, Fletcher Canyon offers a moderate hike through a dense evergreen forest, past a small spring-fed stream and through a narrow limestone canyon.

This hike is safe for children as there are no high drop-offs or major obstacles. There will be a little rock scrambling, and fallen logs across the trail in its upper reaches. And keep in mind there is an elevation gain of 880 feet, which might prove too strenuous for some.

Since the trailhead elevation is at about seven thousand feet, expect temperatures much cooler than in Las Vegas. When I last hiked there, it was eighty-seven degrees in Las Vegas, but only sixty-one at the Fletcher Canyon trailhead. Such a difference is typical.

From the signed trailhead, pick up the obvious trail which heads up a small hill. Here you will find ponderosa and pinyon pine trees, mountain mahogany, manzanita, and oak. After a few hundred yards the trail curves around to the left and you will be walking next to a wide, but usually dry, wash.

The trail is well-worn and easy to follow. You will cross the main drainage three times. About one and one-quarter miles from the trailhead you will cross the drainage once more but this time you will find a small spring-fed stream.

From here on the canyon has more vegetation; in summer you will find plenty of thistle, red columbine, and penstemon.

Steller's jays, recognized by their dark blue color and a prominent crest, love

this canyon, as do a few broad-tailed hummingbirds. This is mountain lion territory, so keep an eye out for tracks in the damp or muddy areas.

Once you cross the stream, the trail becomes a little more strenuous over the next fifty yards or so, then drops into the drainage itself where you will head left. If thunderstorms threaten, stay out of the wash for fear of flash floods. From here on up, there is no easily accessible high ground for refuge.

Even days after rain, you might find pools of water in this part of the canyon. Be careful hopping from rock to rock. They are slick and can twist an ankle, or worse.

As you head up the rocky canyon, the wash itself will serve as your trail most of the time. In a few areas, paths take you up and around small obstacles.

Hiker heads into a narrow section of Fletcher Canyon.

When the canyon narrows even more, you will come to a boulder jam blocking easy progress. Although you will see a faint path heading up the terrain to the right, it is easier to climb up to the left of the boulder.

After this, the walking is easy except for crossing a few fallen logs. In the canyon's narrowest section, the walls rise some one hundred feet, yet are so close in places that a long-armed person could probably touch both sides at once.

The narrows continue for about fifty yards, and mark the hike's end for most. But it's worth climbing up above the ten-foot boulder to the right and seeing what the upper canyon offers. Here the canyon forks. To the right is a small canyon worth exploring. It's short and ends after only thirty yards or so, at a dry fall.

Good climbers with more adventure in mind can continue up the canyon along the left fork. Be prepared for intense rock scrambling, as the path is choked with boulders. Once above these obstacles, the terrain is easier.

Fletcher Canyon At A Glance

Best season: May to mid-October, barring snowfall.

Length: Three to four miles roundtrip.

Difficulty: Moderate.

Elevation gain: 880 feet.

Trailhead elevation: 6,920 feet to 7,800 feet.

Warnings: Flash flooding. Equestrians share trail in lower portion. Rock scrambling in upper portion.

Jurisdiction: Spring Mountains National Recreation Area, Humboldt-Toiyabe National Forest.

Directions: From the Spring Mountains Visitor Gateway drive west about 1.1 miles to a parking pullout on left. Trailhead is directly across the street.

14 Robbers Roost

ROBBERS ROOST IS THE DESTINATION OF A SHORT, APPEALING HIKE, IDEAL FOR THOSE NEW to hiking or who have children along. Even spending some time exploring, adults and older children can do this in an hour, but younger children who want to walk on their own will need more time.

Local legend asserts this small canyon was used to hide contraband, and even stolen animals, after thieves raided travelers along the old Mormon Trail during pioneer days. Whether that's truth or fiction, the cave-like overhangs and canyon setting would have made an ideal hideout.

From the well-signed trailhead, the obvious trail first crosses the old road built in the 1930s and 1940s by the Civilian Conservation Corps, a public works agency formed during the Great Depression, to connect Kyle and Lee Canyons. This road just looks like a wash nowadays. As the trail heads west, you will be in a woodland of pinyon pine and white fir, which also contains mountain mahogany. You'll pass a few ponderosa pines as well.

As you continue your ascent the trail gets a little steeper and small children might find it more difficult going. Rocky terrain and man-made stone stairs create uneven footing, especially hard to maneuver with small legs.

Once you arrive at the base of a giant sloping rock, about five or ten minutes from the trailhead, you will be able to catch a glimpse into the overhang on the right. Although it looks tempting to head off trail and climb directly up here, just continue a bit farther and you'll find easier access.

After exploring this overhang, and maybe looking for some hidden cache, continue up canyon. In about thirty yards the canyon becomes very narrow and all further progress is blocked. This is a box canyon where you will find yourself at the base of a dry fall. During rainstorms this can become a heavy-flowing waterfall, and the canyon bottom may turn onto a watercourse, so if rain threatens leave this hike for another day.

In the upper canyon look along the canyon walls for evidence that rock climbers also enjoy this area. There are dozens of routes. The most obvious are on the right where you'll note a series of fixed climbing anchors, called chain draws, heading up the vertical canyon wall.

As you descend from the narrow section, stay to your right and pick up the spur trail which will take you back down to your vehicle, forming a loop. As soon as you get on this path look for another trail directly on your right that will bring you to another overhang or small cave, where children love to play.

Beyond this point the lower loop becomes just narrow enough that it's awkward to hold a little one's hand while walking. Yet you'd really need to do so, for there are potentially dangerous drop-offs. So, if small children are among your companions, it's best to head back the way you came.

Wildfires are a constant threat in the Spring Mountains. Below: Robber's Roost is a good choice for children.

Robber's Roost At A Glance

Best season: May to mid-October, barring snowfall.

Length: 850-yard loop.

Difficulty: Moderate.

Elevation gain/loss: Two hundred feet.

Trailhead elevation: 7,870 feet.

Warnings: Flash flooding, drop-offs.

Jurisdiction: Spring Mountains National Recreation Area, Humboldt-Toiyabe National Forest.

Directions: From the Spring Mountains Visitor Gateway, drive west on Nevada Route 157 for 0.5 miles and go right onto Nevada Route 158 (Deer Creek Road). Drive 3.4 miles to parking pullout on right. The signed trailhead is directly across the road.

15 Bristlecone Trail

WHEN YOU JUST WANT TO GET SOME MILES UNDER YOUR BELT AND SOME CITY COBWEBS out of your head, the Bristlecone Trail is good medicine. It's especially good in crisp fall weather after quaking aspen leaves have turned to gold. Even in summer, it offers a chance to enjoy a forest and possibly see some wildlife, and can be done either as a loop or an out-and-back of whatever distance you choose. The latter is particularly useful for families with small children.

There are two trailheads — upper and lower — and almost a mile of paved road between them is part of the complete loop. Most loop hikers park at the lower

Right: Bristlecone pines of Mt. Charleston are among the world's oldest living things.

trailhead and start by walking the road to the upper one. That gets this uphill part out of the way before they get tired. It also brings them past the Las Vegas Ski and Snowboard Resort (also known as Lee Canyon) early in the day, when they have a better chance to see wild horses on its grassy slopes.

From the upper trailhead the well-defined path goes up the ridgeline to the north and right side of the ski area. A spur trail heads off to your left at the beginning, which can be confusing, but it quickly rejoins the main trail. You'll be in a forest consisting mostly of ponderosa pine, bristlecone, white fir, and mountain mahogany mixed with aspen. Shrubs include gooseberry currants, recognized in fall by their red berries.

Among healthy conifers stand dozens of dead ones, called snags, stripped of bark and leaves, yet essential habitat for insects, birds and small animals. Look and listen for birds, which may include northern goshawks, woodpeckers, chickadees, bluebirds, jays, and warblers.

You might see deer or even elk. You probably won't see the stealthy bobcat or mountain lion, but you might find footprints or other proof they're around.

As the trail loops around to the southeast, views open up and you see the west side of Mummy Mountain. Continuing, you'll reach an exposed point where you will be able to see down into Lee Canyon and far-reaching views of the Sheep Mountains, part of the Desert National Wildlife Range.

Conifers are sparse on these rocky slopes, but it's here you'll find tough, wind-blown bristlecone pines. The oldest trees alive are bristlecones, and some on this very trail are pushing birthday number five thousand. Increasing in girth less than one one-hundreth inch per year, a five-foot-tall bristlecone might be two thousand years old.

The trail goes west and narrows as it reaches its highest elevation, then heads around a rocky slope to Scout Canyon Road. Graveled but now abandoned, the road serves as a trail for the rest of the hike.

About halfway through the hike you'll reach a saddle and a sign identifying the Bonanza Trailhead. This little-known trail is beloved by backpackers seeking solitude in the nearby Mt. Charleston Wilderness Area.

Continuing down the road you'll find excellent views of the ski slopes; above them, evidence of past avalanches. Not long after that, you'll pass a large grove of aspens — one last sweet sight before the road levels out and offers an easy descent into the lower trailhead parking area.

Bristlecone Trail At A Glance

Best season: May to mid-October, barring snowfall.

Length: 6.2 miles when done as loop.

Difficulty: Moderate.

Elevation gain/loss: 918 feet.

Trailhead elevation: 8,680 at upper trailhead, 8,462 at lower.

Warnings: Mountain bikers share entire trail and horseback riders the lower segment.

Jurisdiction: Spring Mountains National Recreation Area, Humboldt-Toiyabe National Forest.

Directions: From the Spring Mountains Visitor Gateway, drive west on Nevada Route 157 for 0.5 miles and go right onto Nevada Route 158 (Deer Creek Road). Follow for about nine miles. Go left onto Nevada Route 156 (Lee Canyon Road). For lower trailhead follow 2.55 miles and go right onto gravel side road for 130 yards to lower parking area and trailhead. For upper trailhead continue 0.8 miles farther along Nevada 156 to upper parking area of Las Vegas Ski and Snowboard Resort (also known as Lee Canyon), or 3.4 miles from the Nevada 156/158 junction.

Lake Mead

National Recreation Area

The name of Lake Mead National Recreation Area calls up visions of boating and fishing, but outdoor folk also cherish its canyons, fiery red sandstone formations, high mountain peaks, desert washes, springs, riparian areas, scenic backcountry roads, and historic areas. The park encompasses nearly one and-one-half million acres including lakes and both shores of the Colorado River in Southern Nevada and Northwestern Arizona. Its diverse habitats support about nine hundred kinds of plants, and 240 bird species have been recorded here. More than sixteen hundred archaeological sites have been recorded to date.

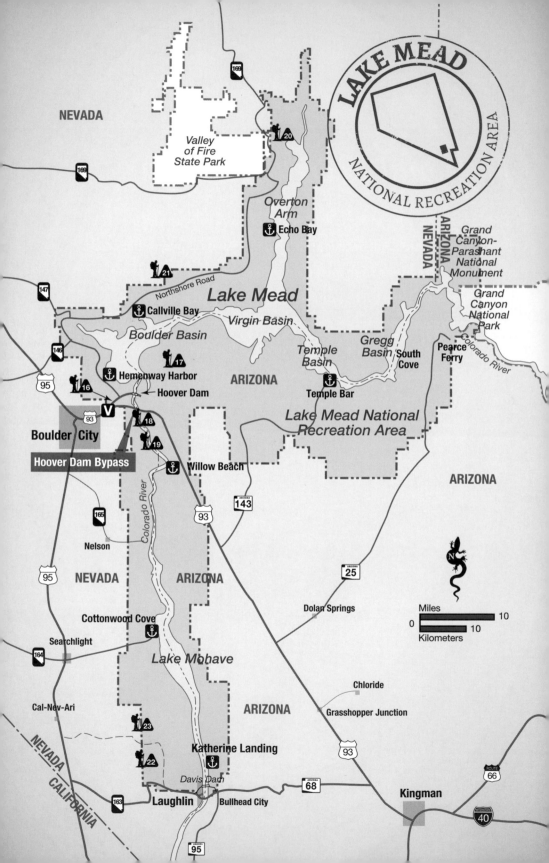

LAKE MEAD NATIONAL RECREATION AREA

NEVADA

Valley of Fire State Park

Overton Arm

Echo Bay

Northshore Road

Callville Bay

Lake Mead

Boulder Basin

Virgin Basin

Temple Basin

Gregg Basin

South Cove

Pearce Ferry

Grand Canyon-Parashant National Monument

Grand Canyon National Park

Colorado River

Hemenway Harbor

ARIZONA

Hoover Dam

Temple Bar

Lake Mead National Recreation Area

Boulder City

Hoover Dam Bypass

Willow Beach

ARIZONA

Nelson

Colorado River

NEVADA

Cottonwood Cove

ARIZONA

Dolan Springs

Searchlight

Lake Mohave

Chloride

Cal-Nev-Ari

Grasshopper Junction

ARIZONA

Katherine Landing

Davis Dam

Laughlin

Bullhead City

Kingman

Miles
0   10
Kilometers
10

This was a desolate area until 1931 when the U.S. Government embarked on the largest construction project in modern history, building Boulder Dam (now called Hoover Dam). Completed in 1935, the project created Lake Mead. Davis Dam, about sixty-seven miles downstream, was completed in 1953 and formed Lake Mohave. In 1964 the region was designated the country's first national recreation area, which now includes both lakes.

The best times to hike the park's lower elevations are from October through March, but you can extend the season by limiting outings to early morning. Be advised that almost all trails are fully exposed to the sun, so hats, sunscreen, and protective clothing are in order.

The park is open year-round, twenty-four hours a day, yet some beach areas are designated for day use only. The Alan Bible Visitor Center, just outside Boulder City, Nevada is generally open 9 a.m. to 4:30 p.m. daily, except major holidays. Hours are subject to change so always call ahead. Lodging, grocery stores, gasoline and medical service are available not only in Las Vegas but also more nearby in Boulder City, Henderson, Laughlin, and Bullhead City, Arizona, at the park's southern end.

For information, call the Alan Bible Visitor Center, (702) 293-8990, or go to the Website: *www.nps.gov/lake*.

Directions to the Alan Bible Visitor Center: From Las Vegas take U.S. Highway 93 about 20 miles south through Boulder City to Lake Mead National Recreation Area. Go left on Lakeshore Road for 0.4 miles and go right into parking area.

16 Railroad Tunnel Trail

THE HISTORIC RAILROAD TUNNEL TRAIL IN LAKE MEAD NATIONAL RECREATION AREA IS A triple treat, offering not only history but also stunning views of Lake Mead and the inherently interesting experience of walking through five tunnels.

Furthermore, it's easy. Because steam railroads were built with the most gradual elevation gains the terrain allowed, the hikers who inherited retired roadbeds need not huff and puff like "The Little Engine That Could."

Surrounded by volcanic cliffs, this wide gravel hiking trail is also suitable for

Tunnel-filled stretch of construction railroad for Hoover Dam became a popular hiking trail with almost-level terrain.

bicyclists, or for those pushing a jogging stroller. But if you take along ambulatory children or uncoordinated adults, beware of the severe drop-offs along the route.

A roundtrip through all five tunnels and back is less than five miles, but if time allows you can easily continue all the way to Hoover Dam. This will add an additional two and one-half miles.

From the trailhead go west a few dozen yards up the wide and obvious paved trail. Go left onto the signed gravel trail and this will head you southeast for a hundred yards or so, to join the old railroad bed. Here you will head east for the rest of the hike.

The roadbed's original purpose was to assist in the huge construction project that became Hoover Dam. The government and six large contractors, collectively known as Six Companies Inc., built three rail segments, totaling almost thirty miles. Standard-gauge track with ninety-pound rails connected cement mixing plants, quarry pits and other facilities. When in full operation the special-purpose railroad required nine steam locomotives and four that ran on gasoline, and more than seventy workers.

The segment you will be hiking ran from Boulder City down to Hemenway Wash, and then to the Himix, a concrete mixing plant at the rim of Black Canyon. After the dam was completed in 1935, many parts of these tracks were either flooded or highly damaged. This segment, though, was still used occasionally until 1961, when one final delivery was made, of a generator to the dam's power plant. The following year the tracks were removed and sold as scrap.

About one-half mile into the hike you will come to the first of a series of benches installed by the park service. These are located here and there all the way to the fifth tunnel. If you look up the volcanic cliffs from this first bench you will see a boulder big as an auto. If this should ever fall, which could be thousands of years from now, I would imagine this boulder would happily roll or bounce its way down to land exactly where this bench is located.

A few minutes' walk from here you will notice a narrow and unmarked spur trail on your right, which heads up the left side of a steep ravine. This path accesses the trail's alternate starting point in the Hoover Dam Lodge's east parking lot. This part of the railroad trail was used in *The Gauntlet*, a 1977 Clint Eastwood film. An assassin in a helicopter was chasing Eastwood and Sandra Locke, who were on a motorcycle.

Continuing around a bend, look down the embankment on your right and you will see an enormous pile of broken cement. These are concrete plugs that were removed from the dam to install turbines.

About one mile from the trailhead you will reach the first tunnel. Each is approximately three hundred feet in length and about twenty-five feet in diameter. They were built bigger than standard tunnels to accommodate the large equipment and penstock sections that were being brought to the dam. Droppings on the ground and walls show that birds, as well as bats, make homes here.

I have also heard a rattlesnake was spotted near the entrance of the third tunnel but I haven't seen one. In spring or fall snakes might be out sunning themselves during the day. They seem to enjoy the temperatures from seventy to ninety degrees.

As you approach the fifth tunnel look high above the entrance and you will see a stone wall, and maybe even people. This is the parking area for the Lakeview Scenic Overlook. This tunnel was sealed in 1978 after being burned by arsonists but was reopened in 2001. This tunnel is unique because you can't see the exit point when you first enter, so it is very dark.

Most people turn around at the fifth tunnel and return to the trailhead, but some continue to the dam. The rest of the path is well-graded and makes its way past Bureau of Reclamation buildings and the new dam bypass highway, winding up at the dam parking garage. It's mostly downhill.

Remember that the part of the trail after the fifth tunnel is designated for day use only, with a locking gate to make the designation meaningful, so be sure to leave the area before somebody locks it.

Directions: Take U.S. Highway 93 south past Boulder City to Lake Mead National Recreation Area. Go left on Lakeshore Road and drive 0.4 miles, then turn right into the parking area. This will be 0.1 miles past the Alan Bible Visitor Center.

Railroad Tunnel Trail At A Glance

Best season: October–April.

Length: 4.28 miles roundtrip to east end of the fifth tunnel. Opportunities for extending the trip to Hoover Dam.

Difficulty: Easy.

Elevation gain: Thirty-five feet to east end of fifth tunnel.

Trailhead elevation: 1,567 feet.

Warnings: Steep drop-offs. Shared with mountain bikers and runners.

Jurisdiction: Lake Mead National Recreation Area.

Directions from Las Vegas: Take U.S. Highway 93 south through Boulder City to Lake Mead National Recreation Area. Go left on Lakeshore Road and drive 0.4 miles and go right into parking area. This will be 0.1 miles past the Alan Bible Visitor Center entrance.

From the Alan Bible Visitor Center: Pick up the trail at the east end of the parking area and walk 300 yards. Go right for Railroad Tunnel Trail or continue straight for 100 yards for official trailhead.

17 Fortification Hill

FORTIFICATION HILL IS A FLAT-TOPPED MESA TOWERING ABOUT TWO THOUSAND FEET ABOVE Lake Mead on the Arizona side of the lake, not far from Hoover Dam. Though its appearance, and hence its name, suggest a man-made fort, it's a natural formation resulting from hundreds of volcanic episodes between five and six million years ago. Those steep cliffs facing the lake are insurmountable, but on the hill's southeastern side, reachable by a rough gravel road, you will find a trail to the top.

One short stretch requires a tough and potentially dangerous scramble up a break in the basalt cliffs. There's also a scree slope, not too difficult going up, but hard to get down without a painful and possible hazardous fall on your derriere.

Because of these challenges I wouldn't recommend this hike for most children. But if you have older children and are confident in their climbing abilities, and have a strong, able adult both below and above each child at all times, then it shouldn't be a problem.

From the trailhead walk up the rocky wash and then immediately go right, picking up the worn footpath that leads up the ridge. There isn't much vegetation here except for barrel cactus and creosote bushes. Travel along this trail as it undulates about a mile, and then up to a well-defined saddle. You will know you are in the correct place when you see the large pile of three- to four-foot basalt boulders that look completely out of place.

From the saddle the work begins, as you head up the steep slope towards the base of the cliffs. Once at the base go right and travel fifty yards or so looking closely for the break in the cliffs. Sometimes there is a cairn — a clearly man-made pile of rocks — marking the spot, but cairns often get knocked down. If the trail starts to descend for more than about twenty feet, you have gone too far. Turn back as this area has extreme drop-offs.

Once you find the correct entry route head up through the cliffs, following cairns that mark the easiest way. On top, an obvious trail heads southwest and then west. Vegetation is more diverse here, with Mojave yuccas and silver cholla, besides the usual creosote and barrel cactus.

Your destination will be an observable rocky outcropping. When you get there you will also see a large cairn and wooden pole marking the spot. Look around for the steel ammunition box that contains a hiker's register. Be sure to enter your info, and if you have the time read some of the notes written by people who came before you.

Views from this summit are some of the best in the park. Just below you are the Paint Pots, colorful formations of red, pink, and orange, resulting from geothermal activity. The nearest part of the lake is Boulder Basin and to the southeast you also can see part of Hoover Dam.

Looking northwest you can see the Las Vegas Strip, and beyond that, the Spring Mountains and their tallest peak, Mt. Charleston. To the north you can see the Muddy Mountains and directly east, Arizona's Black Mountains. To the southwest and flanking the Colorado River are the Eldorado Mountains, and beyond them the McCullough Range.

This is a fully exposed hike with no shade along the entire route. Wear a hat and bring more water than you think you would ever need, in case some emergency proves you wrong. Start on the trail early in the morning, as close to sunrise as possible. This way you will be happily on your way home before the mid-day heat hits.

In climbing these cliffs, long pants of sturdy fabric are worth their weight in human skin. And on this trip, a pair of hiking poles will earn their price, if only by keeping you upright when descending the steep scree section on your return down to the saddle.

Be advised that air traffic, from scenic flights to the Grand Canyon, is constant and extremely annoying. Otherwise, this hike is a classic rendezvous with unspoiled nature.

Fortification Hill At A Glance

Best season: October–March.

Length: 3.4 miles roundtrip.

Difficulty: Strenuous.

Elevation gain: 1,360 feet.

Trailhead elevation: 2,326 feet.

Warnings: Steep drop-offs. Route finding is required. Rough access road requires high-clearance vehicle, and is subject to flash floods.

Jurisdiction: Lake Mead National Recreation Area.

Directions: From Las Vegas drive south on U.S. 93 over the Hoover Dam Bypass Bridge into Arizona. Continue about 1.1 miles and exit right to Kingman Wash Road (Approved Road 70). Drive 5.2 miles on the well-maintained gravel road to Kingman Wash. Turn right on Fortification Road (Approved Road 70 C), where a four-wheel-drive vehicle is recommended, and high clearance required. Continue 2.5 miles to the parking pullout and signed trailhead. Neither of these gravel roads should be driven during rain or threat of rain, because of flash flood danger.

18 Liberty Bell Arch

THIS IDEAL WINTER HIKE OF ABOUT 5.5 MILES ROUNDTRIP TAKES YOU BY REMNANTS OF AN old magnesium mine, to the natural arch itself, and to a great viewpoint overlooking the Colorado River in Black Canyon.

From the parking area, located at about 1,550 feet in elevation, walk down into White Rock Canyon, then go right and pass under the highway. Continue downstream using the sandy area of the wash as your trail. Keep an eye peeled, as desert bighorn sheep frequent this area.

After about 0.6 miles from the parking area, the canyon narrows and you will be walking on a hard surface briefly. About 0.2 miles farther and just after a narrow section of the wash, look for the right-hand turn and trail to access a side canyon.

Follow the path for about 0.4 miles from where you entered White Rock Canyon and you will find yourself at the junction with the Old Liberty Bell Arch Trail, an abandoned gravel road. The first part of this original trail is no longer used because of changes made in widening U.S. 93 to a four-lane highway in 2010.

From this junction you will hike about two hundred yards west up the hill to the ridge, then downhill, and then up to another ridge where you will arrive in the old mine area. Look on the north side of the trail and you will find a structure about twenty feet long, which appears to have been a chute for loading ore trucks. This is one of the many remnants of a magnesium mine that operated in the 1940s. In this area you will find many spur trails to explore more of the mining operation and its left-over artifacts, if you are interested.

From the mine area, the main trail heads down steeply about one hundred yards and into a wash where you will go left. Travel in the

Liberty Bell Arch

The Colorado River in Black Canyon can be seen from an overlook just after visiting Liberty Bell Arch.

wash for about 250 yards and look for the cairn that marks the place to go right, where you will pick up the trail for the final hike to the arch. This final section is about one-third mile long, heading first northwest and then southwest, and finally to the south side of the arch for the best viewing. The arch resembles the shape of the famous Liberty Bell in Pennsylvania, and I would estimate that the opening is about thirty feet high.

Although the arch is the highlight of this hike, it is also well worth your time to hike about one-half mile farther along the trail, heading southwest to the Black Canyon Overlook. About one thousand feet above the Colorado River, this is a great place to look for bald eagles, great blue heron and other water-loving birds, or to look down and spot kayakers enjoying the Black Canyon National Water Trail.

Liberty Bell Arch At A Glance

Best Season: October–April.

Length: 5.5 miles.

Difficulty: Moderate.

Elevation gain: 550 feet.

Trailhead elevation: 1,550 feet.

Warnings: Due to excessive heat the trailhead is closed May 15–Sept. 30. There are steep drop-offs near the mine area, as well as at the Black Canyon Overlook.

Jurisdiction: Lake Mead National Recreation Area.

Directions: From Las Vegas, drive south on U.S. 93, through Boulder City, and over the Hoover Dam Bypass Bridge into Arizona. Just after mile post three, turn left at the White Rock Canyon sign, carefully crossing the two north bound lanes of U.S. 93. Follow the access road to the large parking area and trailhead.

19 Black Canyon National Water Trail

LOCATED ALONG THE COLORADO RIVER, STARTING BELOW HOOVER DAM, THE THIRTY-MILE Black Canyon National Water Trail is one of about twenty national water trails in the United States. Designated in 2015, this river corridor was the first in the Southwest to earn the distinction.

Although it is more often accessed by kayaks, canoes, paddleboards, and motorboats, there are numerous short hiking trails you can take to see hot springs, caves, historic sites, and other nifty locations on both sides of the river. The east bank is in Arizona and the west in Nevada, as the river constitutes the state line.

The water trail is a smooth-water experience and has no whitewater rapids. Its most popular section is Black Canyon, the 11.7 miles between Hoover Dam and Willow Beach, Arizona. If you prefer human-powered craft, as many do, Sundays and Mondays are the best times to go. Private motorboats are not allowed in that section on those days, and you'll have a quieter experience, perhaps with a greater chance of spotting wildlife.

Depending on how much time you have, you can go downstream from the base of Hoover Dam or upstream from Willow Beach.

The excursion from Hoover Dam takes a full day. It also requires that you use an outfitter authorized by the National Park Service, because you will need to be transported through the dam's security zone. The outfitter will acquire permits and transportation for you to launch a self-guided tour. If you don't have your own kayak, canoe, or paddleboard, they can rent you one. At the end of the trip at Willow Beach, they will pick you up and transport you back to your vehicle or hotel, if needed.

However, if it is your first time on the river, I recommend signing up for a fully guided trip, either from Hoover Dam or traveling upstream from Willow Beach. This will give you more bang for your buck, because your unfamiliarity with the canyon won't cause you to miss any of its charms. The professional river guides will point out and stop at the most pertinent places, and they also are very knowledgeable on the flora and fauna.

For a trip upriver from Willow Beach, one authorized outfitter, River Dogz, offers not only kayaks and paddleboards, but hydrobike rentals and tours.

Right: A hiker heads down the ladder after a visit to the Arizona Hot Springs in Black Canyon. Below: Hydrobikes are an alternate mode of seeing Black Canyon.

Hydrobikes have two pontoons with a bicycle-like mechanism mounted on the top. When you pedal, the power goes to a propeller rather than a tire. You steer just as you would a bike, and this controls the vessel's rudder. Hydrobikes are best suited to people at least four-feet-eleven tall. But they are great for people who might be out of shape, as they offer low-impact cardio exercise.

For groups, it often increases the fun if you organize a mixture of kayaks, paddleboards and hydrobikes, so everybody can take turns and try each kind of craft.

If you're not part of a tour group, just paddle or pedal upstream as far as you feel comfortable, then return. Even a mile or two upriver from Willow Beach is worth doing.

Authorized outfitters in Lake Mead National Recreation Area include River Dogz Adventure Tour Company at (702) 901-1060 or *riverdogzlv.com*; Desert Adventures at (702) 293-5026 or *kayaklasvegas.com*; and Desert River Kayak at (928) 754-5320 or *desertriveroutfitters.com*.

For more information on the Black Canyon National Water Trail and a full list of authorized outfitters, contact Lake Mead Visitor Center at (702) 293-8990 or *nps.gov/lake*.

Black Canyon National Water Trail At A Glance

Best Season: Year round.

Length: Thirty miles one way, but often done as a two-to-four-mile roundtrip upstream trip from Willow Beach, or a one-way 11.7 mile downstream trip, from Hoover Dam to Willow Beach.

Difficulty: Easy to moderate.

Trailhead elevation: 646 feet at Willow Beach.

Warnings: Excessive heat in summer, cold water all year, and can be windy.

Jurisdiction: Lake Mead National Recreation Area.

Right: The smooth waters of the Colorado River below the Hoover Dam. Kayaking is one of the most popular ways to enjoy the river.

Directions: From Las Vegas drive south on U.S. 93 over the Hoover Dam Bypass Bridge into Arizona. Continue south for 14 miles and go right onto Willow Beach Road. Follow for about four miles to Willow Beach.

20 St. Thomas

IN THE OVERTON ARM OF LAKE MEAD NATIONAL RECREATION AREA, NOW HIGH AND DRY, lie the remains of a once-thriving Mormon pioneer settlement. The town of St. Thomas was founded in 1865 but lasted only until 1938. That's when the waters of Lake Mead, created by the construction of Boulder Dam (the one now called Hoover Dam) rose so high they drowned the town.

Although the waterline has dropped enough a few times since then to allow a glimpse of this miniature Atlantis, the water levels are now at a historic low, making a trip to St. Thomas the easiest it has been since 1938, and the driest.

It wasn't very long ago that the remains of this settlement were more than sixty feet beneath the surface of the lake, where they were seen only by aquatic life forms and an occasional SCUBA diver. Now, even children — at least those who can handle a pedestrian roundtrip of two-and-a-half miles — can also enjoy the historic site.

Mormon settlers built the town near the confluence of the Muddy and Virgin Rivers. A couple hundred residents mostly farmed or mined, and occupied homes in the shade of cottonwood trees they planted themselves. St. Thomas had a hotel, a restaurant, and a reliable garage, so in the early days of the automobile, it became a welcome stop along the Arrowhead Trail, the main motor route from Salt Lake City to Los Angeles. In 1912 there was even a railroad branch built to the town.

When the waters receded more than a decade ago, eager visitors made their way here to claim bragging rights as first to revisit the resurrected town site. Under the muddy conditions, though, only those wearing high rubber boots maintained dry feet. After a decade baking in the sun, however, the neighborhood is now definitely terra firma, with a well-worn and easy loop trail.

Right: Now dry once again, the ruins of St. Thomas lay seven decades beneath the waters of Lake Mead.

Standing on the bluff, look east from the trailhead and take time to get your bearings. The low area before you, where the town site is located, is the Overton Arm of Lake Mead. Looking across the arm you can see, running north to south, a faint green ribbon of vegetation within the sea of tamarisk. This is where the Muddy River makes its final journey down through Moapa Valley and south to Lake Mead. Looking slightly to the southeast, to your right, you will also be able to see another tributary, the Virgin River, which is ending its journey as well.

From the trailhead, descend the worn trail to the old lake bed. The trail from here on out is, for the most part, hard-packed mud dotted with shells. You will be trekking through a tangle of tamarisk, a non-native pest plant which grows about five feet high, on both sides of the trail. This limits your view to the path before you.

There are no interpretive displays and just a few trail signs for guidance, so it can be confusing where to go and which trail to take. If you take one of the many spur trails, be sure to head back to the main one before continuing. It is mazelike, and you could easily get turned around and confused as to where you are.

But do take a few of the less-worn spurs, for the fun of exploring is worth the risk of confusion. You'll see the remains of personal residences, a schoolhouse, the hotel, and hundreds of small artifacts such as rusty metal, broken china, and colored glass. Some foundations have stood the test of time and water better than others. Large stumps of mature cottonwood trees can still be found, remnants of thousands that once grew here.

When the Hoover Dam project began, evacuation notices were posted, but most people didn't leave until water became visible. The last resident left June 11, 1938. Hugh Lord had waited so long he had to make his exit by boat.

This is a day-use area only. Do not climb on any of the ruins, move any artifact, or otherwise disturb the site. Some people waited seventy years to see this place again, so don't spoil it. Save this trail for another day if it has rained recently or threatens to, as the trail becomes muddy. Heavy rains often wash out the access road, so after such events it would be prudent to check with the park service website, *www.nps.gov/lake*, or call (702) 293-8990, to inquire about road conditions.

St. Thomas At A Glance

Best season: October–March.

Length: Two miles roundtrip, depending on route.

Difficulty: Easy.

Elevation loss: Twenty-four feet.

Trailhead elevation: 1,227 feet.

Warnings: Flooding, route finding.

Jurisdiction: Lake Mead National Recreation Area.

Directions: From Las Vegas take Interstate 15, north about 30 miles to exit 75. Drive east on Nevada Route 169, passing through Valley of Fire State Park, for about 25 miles. Cross directly over Northshore Road onto St. Thomas Road. This route is well-marked and usually well-maintained but sometimes washes out. Drive 3.2 miles, staying right at the fork for St. Thomas Point and trailhead.

21 Bowl of Fire

BOWL OF FIRE, PART OF THE MUDDY MOUNTAIN WILDERNESS AREA, IS A LANDSCAPE OF red sandstone outcroppings surrounded by gray limestone hills and mountains. Its hiking and exploring opportunities are almost endless. The trip can be as simple as strolling in a little more than a mile, sitting down, and just basking in the beauty surrounding you. Or it can be a strenuous long adventure, exploring the very wrinkles of the landscape.

Any version is an exposed hike, so if you are hiking off-season try to arrive at the trailhead early — by sunrise, if possible. That way you'll not only get more hours of moderate temperature, but also the thrill of seeing these formations glow in the low morning sun like so many miles of mesquite embers.

From the parking area head north toward the end of the prominent limestone ridge which lies a few hundred yards directly northwest of the trailhead. There is no marked trail at this point, but as you get closer to the ridge you will see a footpath worn up its northern end. Follow this up and then down the other side. Here, to the northwest, you will get your first look at the red sandstone outcropping in the Bowl of Fire.

Vegetation through this segment of the hike is mostly creosote bush and blackbrush, but you will also find a few barrel and beavertail cactus.

On the other side of the ridge, the route follows the left side of a small drainage and then seems to just end. But follow the narrow wash about thirty yards more and look for a cairn on your right. It marks the very faint route that takes you directly to Bowl of Fire.

Although it might seem easier to just gallop across country, it's worth scouting out the trail through the entire hike, so you don't trample any plants or disturb the fragile cryptobiotic soil found in a few areas. This soil supports the sparse vegetation, so to damage any is to damage the gemlike location.

From here on you will cross a couple of broad gulches including Callville Wash. It's usually dry, but it is the main drainage of this area and therefore subject to flash flooding. You might see tire tracks. This is Lake Mead NRA's Approved Backcountry Road 94, Callville Wash North Road. For an alternate starting point

Given enough time, wind and blowing sand can cut a hole through sandstone.

on this hike, you can access the trailhead and parking area just south of here. You will need a high-clearance, four-wheel-drive vehicle to get there. Approved Road 94 starts near Mile Marker 16 on Northshore Road.

After passing over Callville Wash, continue northwest until the trail ends at the bank of another smaller drainage. Drop down the short, yet steep bank into the wash and go right to continue upstream. This area receives a bit more moisture, so you will see desert willow growing. Follow the wash a hundred yards or so until all easy progress is blocked by a cluster of large conglomerate rocks. The easiest way up this obstacle is to the left, a scramble of about fifteen feet. Once on top you have arrived in Bowl of Fire.

In spring you might see wildflowers including blue Mojave

Blue Mojave asters bloom in Bowl of Fire area.

aster, orange desert mallow, purple phacelia, and even a few white desert primrose.

These outcroppings were sand dunes back in dinosaur days. After time turned them to stone they were further shaped by complex uplifting, faulting, and erosion. The red and orange colors result from oxidized iron in the rock. Some spots are lighter shades because groundwater percolated through and leached out some color.

Once in the Bowl of Fire the route is up to you. A good one to follow, as far as you feel comfortable, is the small wash up to the left. Explore some of the many small arches, windows, holes, and overhangs along the way. There are many places that you can easily climb up the outcroppings themselves. But to fully explore all the unique formations, viewpoints, and peaks in Bowl of Fire would take months, if not years. Yet so enchanting is this landscape, some people probably plan to do it.

Bowl of Fire At A Glance

Best season: October–March.

Length: 2.25-mile roundtrip, with plenty of options to extend.

Difficulty: Moderate.

Elevation gain: One hundred feet or more, depending on distance.

Trailhead elevation: 1,933 feet.

Warnings: Rock scrambling, no shade.

Jurisdiction: Lake Mead National Recreation Area.

Directions: From Las Vegas, take U.S. Highway 93/95 south to Lake Mead Drive. Go east on Nevada Route 146 for about 10 miles to the Lake Mead National Recreation Area's entrance station. Drive 0.3 miles and go left onto Northshore Road (Nevada Route 167). Follow for 18.2 miles. Just after mile marker 18, look for parking pullout on left side of road, which serves as the trailhead.

22 Grapevine Canyon

GRAPEVINE CANYON IS ONE OF THE BEST PLACES IN OUR REGION TO SEE PETROGLYPHS. Prehistoric American Indians pecked these symbols into the desert varnish on cliffs and boulders, exposing the lighter-colored rock beneath.

This is an especially great place to visit if you have children in your group or others who can't hike very far, as the finest petroglyph panels can be found a mere quarter-mile from the trailhead. But for those willing and able to do some rock scrambling, this canyon also rewards exploring upstream.

Bighorn sheep are depicted in this petroglyph panel at Grapevine Canyon. Below: Abstract concepts are seen on this rock art panel.

From the parking area, follow the path west along the sandy bench of the broad, and usually dry, Grapevine Wash. Once you reach the mouth of the canyon, start looking on the boulders and cliff faces for the rock art. There are panels on both sides of the canyon, inside and out, but those on the north side are more concentrated.

You will see all sorts of designs and figures. Some, such as bighorn sheep and lizards, are easy to decipher, but most are abstract symbols whose meanings remain mysteries. Research has shown that the age of the etchings varies by centuries; some are more than eight hundred years old and some as young as 150.

Prehistoric American Indians spent time in this canyon starting somewhere around A.D. 1100. This canyon is considered sacred ground for the Yuman-speaking peoples of the lower Colorado region. Spirit Mountain, just a couple of miles to the north, is said to be the spiritual birthplace of the tribes. You'll probably recognize the sacred mountain, for its 5,639-foot summit is the highest peak in the Newberry Mountains.

This is an excellent place to impress upon your children, or others in your group, the importance of caring for our cultural resources. Teach them to never touch rock art, as the natural oils on human hands will damage them. Also, they should not climb or sit on boulders that bear petroglyphs. Many boulders are unstable and could easily dislodge, not only displacing an important part of pre-history but also endangering children or other visitors. So nobody will be tempted to climb for a closer look, bring binoculars.

As you walk upstream, the rock art becomes less concentrated. For those with small children along, the hike will end only thirty yards or so from the mouth of the canyon, where you will reach a jumble of boulders and then a dryfall. Take a look below the dryfall as there is usually some water, thanks to a natural spring.

For those up to the scramble, exploring farther upstream will be well worth it. The easiest route is up to the right side of the dryfall, but be advised, even this way is steep and the granite is very slippery.

Once up above the dryfall, follow the drainage as best you can, in and around the thickets of canyon grapes and other dense vegetation. For the most part, staying to the north side is the easiest. You will find some worn paths sporadically, but none last the entire route. Continue upstream and you will find pockets of cottonwood and willow trees thriving in the moist soil, thanks to small seeps and springs. In some places there are even some cattails and rushes. In places where you need to cross the wash, be sure to watch your footing as there are deep wet areas that might catch you off guard.

About one mile from the mouth of the canyon, just when you think there isn't much more to see, the wash curves north and you will enter a short but sweet slot canyon — a small, extra pleasure marking the turn-around point of an already pleasant hike.

Grapevine Canyon At A Glance

Best season: October–March.

Length: About .25 mile with options to explore up canyon.

Difficulty: Easy to moderate in upper reaches.

Elevation gain: Fifty to three hundred feet.

Trailhead elevation: 2,385 feet.

Warnings: Rock scrambling and route finding if exploring upper reaches.

Jurisdiction: Lake Mead National Recreation Area.

Directions: From Las Vegas take U.S. 95/93 south for about 23 miles. At Railroad Pass go right onto U.S. 95 south for 53 miles. Go left onto Nevada Route 163 toward Laughlin and drive for 12.9 miles, then make another left onto Christmas Tree Pass Road. Follow this well-maintained gravel road for 1.8 miles and go left. Drive 0.1 miles to parking area and trailhead.

23 Spirit Mountain

IF LOOKING FOR A CHALLENGE, MOST HIKERS WILL FIND A SUFFICIENT ONE ON SPIRIT Mountain Peak. You'll have to pick your own route, over rocks that won't be kind to exposed skin. But those who reach the summit will enjoy some of the best views available in Southern Nevada, taking in mountain ranges of four states.

Located in the extreme southern end of Lake Mead National Recreation Area, Spirit is the highest peak in the Newberry Mountains, a prominent range that runs southeast of Searchlight between U.S. 95 and Lake Mohave.

Be prepared to do lots of rock scrambling, some of it over loose rocks.

There is no official trail; these are merely general directions. The trick is to start on the southeast side of the mountain and make your way northwest. From the unsigned trailhead, walk north around a large rock outcropping and start ascending the steep terrain. Though there is no trail, just select the section that looks least intimidating.

Once up on this first ridge, there is a nice flat area to take a break. Turn around for the first great view of this hike, including parts of Davis Dam, Laughlin, and across the river into Arizona, Bullhead City, and the Black Mountains.

As you resume climbing, your route-finding skills will be tested. There are many boulders and ledges, and you won't be able to see very well where you're heading. Keep in mind that if you're faced with any tricky, dangerous move, it's time to backtrack. Finding the safe route may be tedious, but except for the rock scrambling, the hike shouldn't be hazardous.

Keep an eye out for a cairn that indicates you'll need to head right. If you miss it, you'll find out soon, as further progress is blocked by a tremendous drop-off into a canyon. Just backtrack and then go north. Here you will traverse another flat area, reaching the base of another steep slope, which you'll need to climb to a wide saddle. If you look closely from below, you'll see a green marker pole at the top. When you reach the saddle, you will see your first views to the west, especially stunning ones into the Mojave National Preserve.

Next, follow the obvious path to the right, or north, toward another saddle separating two peaks. The official peak is to the left, and accessing requires more route finding and rock scrambling. You'll know you have reached it when you see the wooden survey post and find the army surplus metal ammunition box containing a hikers' logbook.

There isn't much room to wander the summit, and the footing is uneven. But a few of the rocks are comfortable enough to sit on, rest, write in the logbook, and take in the fabulous panoramas.

On a clear day you can easily see more than a hundred miles, northwest to Mt. Charleston and even as far as southern Utah. Closer up and to the east, you will see Lake Mohave as it flows south from Cottonwood Cove. You'll also see the Colorado River as it makes its way south of Davis Dam, past Laughlin and Bullhead City and on towards Needles. It's fun to bring a regional map up here, unfold it, and identify real-life sights that correspond to the mountain ranges and other landmarks depicted on paper.

Spirit Mountain is a culturally significant and sacred place to all the Yuman-speaking people of the lower Colorado region. The Mojave people call it Avikwame, and the Hualapai, Wikame. They believe it to be the birthplace of their first ancestors.

Bring plenty of water, bring gloves, and wear long pants of heavy-duty fabric. Be prepared to remove some cactus needles: A fine-tooth comb, tweezers, or even pliers usually do the trick. If it's been raining or rain threatens, save this hike for another day.

Spirit Mountain At A Glance

Best season: October–March.

Length: About four miles roundtrip, depending on route.

Difficulty: Strenuous.

Elevation gain: 2,344 feet.

Trailhead elevation: 3,296 feet.

Warnings: Route finding, cliff exposure and rock scrambling.

Jurisdiction: Lake Mead National Recreation Area.

Directions: From Las Vegas, take U.S. 95/93 south for about 23 miles. At Railroad Pass, exit right and follow U.S. 95 south for about 50 miles, passing through Searchlight. Go left on Christmas Tree Pass Road and drive 10.2 miles to the parking pullout on left, which is the unsigned trailhead.

Nevada

State Parks

Nevada's state parks are as diverse as the state's extraordinary landscapes, and each was set aside for special attributes. You can learn about all of them at *www.parks.nv.gov*. But the following five are favorites in the lower-middle half of the state.

Spring Mountain Ranch State Park is located within Red Rock Canyon National Conservation Area, just west of Las Vegas. Once a working ranch, it has many historic buildings and sites. At an elevation of about thirty-eight hundred feet, it is also ten to fifteen degrees cooler than Las Vegas. Hours at the main ranch house are generally 10 a.m.–4 p.m., and a little later in spring or summer. Hiking trails are usually open from 8 a.m. until one hour before the park closes. For the exact current schedule, check at (702) 875-4141 or *parks.nv.gov/parks/spring-mountain-ranch-state-park*. No services are available in the park.

Directions: See Spring Mountain Ranch, p. 110.

Valley of Fire State Park was Nevada's first state park, dedicated in 1935, and is its largest, containing almost thirty-six thousand acres. The park's main attraction is its vibrant red sandstone landscape. Those fiery colors result from traces of iron that have oxidized, and the dramatic formations from millions of years of uplifting and faulting, followed by erosion. The park also features excellent panels of ancient rock art, historic sites, and areas of petrified wood. There

Horses graze at Spring Mountain Ranch State Park.

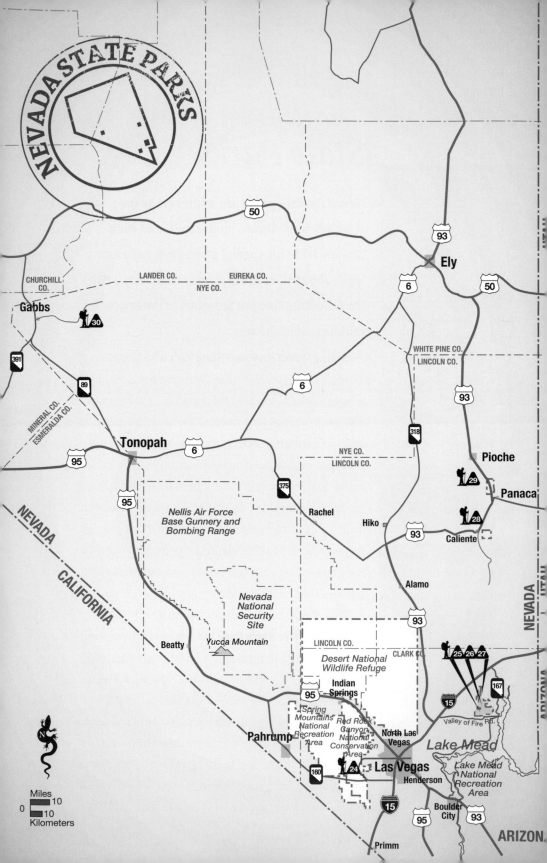

are no services in the park, but gasoline and restaurants can be found at Moapa Valley Travel Plaza, which you will pass when entering from Interstate 15, and in nearby Overton to the north. The visitor center is generally open from 8:30 a.m. to 4:30 p.m. (702) 397-2088, *parks.nv.gov/parks/valley-of-fire-state-park*.

Directions: From Las Vegas take Interstate 15 north about 30 miles to exit 75. Drive east on Nevada Route 169 for about 18 miles into the park and go left to the visitor center complex.

Kershaw-Ryan State Park is just south of Caliente in Lincoln County. The main area of the park lies in a highly vegetated, narrow valley, surrounded by high canyon walls. Elevations run from 4,312 to 5,175 feet, so it is a pleasant place, even in summer, to picnic or splash in the spring-fed wading pool.

This was once a homestead, first settled in 1873, and features mature landscaping including canyon grapes, fruit trees, and shade trees in the main area of the park. For questions, contact (775) 726-3564, or *parks.nv.gov/parks/kershaw-ryan-state-park*. Caliente has gasoline, a convenience store, a restaurant, and basic motels.

Directions: See Kershaw-Ryan, p. 122.

Cathedral Gorge State Park, established in 1935, lies just west of Panaca in Lincoln County. The park is primarily composed of whimsical looking formations of buff-colored siltstone and clay shale. Narrow canyons and gullies were formed by erosion of its cliffs. Trails are fully exposed to the sun, so the best hiking can be found from early fall through late spring. For further information, check *parks.nv.gov/parks/cathedral-gorge*. There is a regional visitor center at the park's entrance, (775) 728-4460, generally open from 9 a.m. to 4:30 p.m. A gas station and convenience store is near the entrance of the park on U.S. 93.

Directions: See Cathedral Gorge, p. 125.

Berlin-Ichthyosaur State Park was established in 1957 to protect Nevada's state fossil, the ichthyosaur. These prehistoric marine reptiles ranged in size from about two to more than fifty feet in length and the ones here were the largest specimens found in the world.

The park also protects the Berlin Townsite, a small, well-preserved mining town that flourished in the late nineteenth and early twentieth centuries. The park is a good destination from late spring to early fall, as its elevation ranges from 6,840 to 7,880 feet. For more information, visit *parks.nv.gov/parks/bi*.

Directions: See Berlin-Ichthyosaur, p. 127.

24 Spring Mountain Ranch State Park

SPRING MOUNTAIN RANCH STATE PARK IS THE IDEAL PLACE TO INVEST ABOUT HALF OF A perfect day. That's all the time it takes to hike its short network of trails, tour its historic buildings, and relax a while in the shaded picnic area.

Lying within the Red Rock National Conservation Area at the base of the multi-colored Wilson Cliffs, the park's main area is about thirty-eight hundred feet above sea level, so temperatures on a given day are some ten degrees cooler than in Las Vegas. The 520-acre park encompasses four plant communities: desert scrub, blackbrush, pinyon-juniper, and riparian.

The main ranch house is the best place to start; besides taking a self-guided tour of the historic residence, you can pick up a brochure about the entire property. Park docents are usually on hand to answer questions. The main ranch house is generally open from 10 a.m. to 4 p.m.

Be sure to look at the old photographs on display around the house, depicting interesting people who were part of the ranch's rich history. The first to file claim to the land were an army sergeant based at Fort Mohave, James B. Wilson, and his partner George Anderson, in 1876. Anderson soon left for good, but Wilson stayed until his death in 1906, rearing Anderson's two half-Paiute children as his own. These sons took their stepfather's name and were known as Jim Wilson Jr. and Tweed Wilson.

In 1929 Willard George, a prominent furrier from Hollywood, acquired the ranch and even raised chinchillas here, but left most other operations in the hands of the Wilsons. The next owner was Chet Lauck, who had won fame as "Lum" on the popular radio program, *Lum & Abner*. The comedy was about the owners of a general store in backcountry Arkansas. Lauck was responsible for the 1948 construction of the ranch house you see today. In 1955, German movie actress Vera Krupp purchased the ranch and stayed on until 1967. The reclusive billionaire Howard Hughes also owned the ranch before the Nevada Division of State Parks took it over in the 1970s.

It is well worth your time to take the guided tour of some of the property's

Above: Main dwelling at Spring Mountain Ranch was built by Chet Lauck, the actor famous for playing "Lum" of the popular radio show Lum & Abner.

other historic buildings, which include such curiosities as a blacksmith shop and the chummy two-hole outhouse.

Another great place to begin a visit is the Overlook Trail, a short and easy loop hike that starts directly across from the parking area. The trail heads up to a natural bench at the base of the sandstone cliffs and offers a birds-eye view of much of the property including the ranch house, other historic buildings, and the surrounding verdant meadows. Look for wildlife such as a variety of lizards and snakes, antelope ground squirrels, jackrabbits, and cottontails. You might see a coyote or, if fortunate, even a charming little kit fox.

From the overlook continue your loop by following the trail downhill to the west. Here you will have views of the park's Harriet Reservoir, a pond built in the late 1940s to irrigate the pastures and provide water for the owners' household. After that you will pass the fenced cemetery, which holds the graves of three generations of Wilsons, the family that owned the property in the early twentieth century. Stay left at the fork and descend to another, smaller reservoir, which is

A hiker climbs past cholla cactus and yucca on a well-marked trail.

often occupied by a variety of ducks. Cross the bridge and then continue to the gravel road where you will go left, back to where you started.

This trail is open from 8 a.m. until one hour before park closure. The park also offers guided night hikes to Sandstone Canyon and Ash Grove.

~~~~~~

Spring Mountain Ranch State Park At A Glance

Best season: October–April.

Length: Network of short loop trails.

Difficulty: Easy.

Elevation gain: 210 feet.

Trailhead elevation: 3,750 feet.

Jurisdiction: Nevada Division of State Parks.

Directions: From Las Vegas, take Charleston Boulevard (Nevada Route 159) west. From West Charleston's intersection with CC 215 (Las Vegas Beltway) drive 5.8 miles, to Red Rock Canyon Visitor Center. Continue past it about 5 miles to Spring Mountain Ranch State Park's access road on your right.

~~~~~~

25 Atlatl Rock, Valley of Fire State Park

IN THE WONDROUS LANDSCAPE THAT IS THE VALLEY OF FIRE, A VISIT TO ATLATL ROCK IS the quintessential experience. The rock itself is one of the valley's dramatic formations, a very large boulder sitting atop an even larger outcropping of red sandstone. Much of the stone is covered with natural dark desert varnish. Prehistoric American Indians pecked hundreds of designs through this varnish, making the underlying colors show up as petroglyphs, or rock writing.

Ancient artists climbed perilously high to make the designs, but visitors can get a close look from the safety of modern metal stairs installed for that purpose.

One of the most unusual petroglyphs, which gave the location its name, depicts the ancient weapon called an atlatl. Hunters and warriors used the atlatl to add force and range when throwing light spears. It was a carefully-shaped stick about two feet long, with a handhold on one end, and on the other a notch or hook to engage the butt of a spear. The spear lay atop and parallel to the atlatl, the spear's sharp end extending forward over the user's hand. He would bring both atlatl and spear back over his shoulder, then whip them forward toward the target in much the same way as if throwing a full-sized spear or javelin. But the atlatl remained in his hand, in effect lengthening the user's arm, and imparting much more velocity to the spear before it parted company with the atlatl. Although the atlatl is thought to predate the bow and arrow, it was better for certain purposes and some hunter-gatherers still used it in the twentieth century.

Human history in the park dates back to 300 B.C., when people called the Basketmakers lived here, and continued through about A.D. 1150 with the Ancestral Puebloans. The desert tribes of later centuries did not leave so many traces, perhaps because the climate became harsher and they spent less time there.

Once you come down the stairs, instead of returning to the parking area, head south around the base of the outcropping. Look around for the boulder that is packed with more petroglyphs. Behind this you can head up the outcropping and take in some excellent views. On your way up, look for the naturally formed water tank or *tinaja*, sometimes filled with rainwater and an important drinking spot for area wildlife.

From here you can extend your outing with a two-mile scenic drive which loops around and back to the main road, but exploring afoot is much more rewarding.

There are plenty of interesting formations along the road but the crème de la crème is Arch Rock, located about one and one-half miles into the loop. The arch is visible on the left side of the road on top of a sandstone outcropping. To access it, walk around to the left of the outcropping and behind the arch, then head up the sandstone. Never climb on top of the arch itself. The park asks visitors to limit their group size to no more than ten.

In the sandy areas beneath your feet, take time to look for animal tracks. White-tailed antelope ground squirrels, black-tailed jackrabbits, kit foxes and spotted skunks make their home here, as do thirteen species of lizards and fifteen of snakes. Resident birds include the raven, house finch and roadrunner, and in winter there are occasionally bald and golden eagle sightings.

Atlatl Rock's petroglyphs can be seen close up at the top of the metal stairs. Atlatl Rock's main petroglyph panel features the atlatl, an ancient weapon, seen at the top of the panel.

Arch Rock, found along the scenic drive near Atlatl Rock.

If the idea of the atlatl caught your interest, the World Atlatl Association holds an event here each spring. Although there are seriously competitive events, there are also events for those lacking confidence, competence, or competitive personality. Even children are welcome to try; and if you don't happen to own atlatls and spears, somebody will loan you equipment.

When visiting here, or any other rock art site, remember to never touch petroglyphs (or the rarer pictographs, which are painted on the rock), as natural oils from our hands will damage them, and they're irreplaceable. And of course, don't climb on or near them.

Atlatl Rock At A Glance

Best season: October–April.

Length: One hundred yards roundtrip with opportunities to extend.

Difficulty: Easy.

Trailhead elevation: 2,234 feet.

Jurisdiction: Valley of Fire State Park.

Directions: From the visitor center, return to Highway 169 and go west for 1.9 miles. Go right and follow for one-half mile and go left into parking area.

26 Mouse's Tank, Valley of Fire State Park

IF YOU HAVE TIME ENOUGH IN VALLEY OF FIRE STATE PARK TO HIKE ONLY ONE TRAIL, MOUSE'S Tank should be your destination. Not only does it allow you to explore a mysterious canyon associated with prehistoric rock writings and with a regional legend based in historical fact, but it also is a particularly versatile trek. You can make it a quick trip to the natural water tank itself, or turn it into a half-day adventure exploring rock formations, peaks, and side canyons, and trying to read the stories in hundreds of petroglyphs lining the canyon walls.

Just a few steps from the trailhead, you will already be in a canyon, and in minutes you'll see the first petroglyphs. The most striking panels seem to be on the left. Occupation of the area is thought to have taken place from 300 B.C. to A.D. 1150. starting with the Basketmaker culture, followed by Ancestral Puebloan. (The latter is the same culture once called the Anasazi by archaeologists, but that name is now considered derogatory.)

As you travel along you'll also find thousands of holes, windows and pockets in the sandstone, formed by natural erosion. They are all shapes and sizes, many so small you might not even notice them, while others could easily accommodate many adults. The park allows you to explore and climb around the formations; just don't touch or climb anywhere near the petroglyphs. Crawl into one of the holes rounded out by wind erosion, and find the place where the natural stone hollow just exactly fits your back. On a cool afternoon, with the sun-heated stone radiating warmth into your body from every direction, you can feel comfortable as a kitten in a hatbox.

If you have children along, this canyon will easily become an educational experience. A stop at the visitor center, which is on your way to the trailhead, offers kid-friendly exhibits and interactive displays on the geology, wildlife, prehistory, and history of the area.

Once you reach the trail, encourage your children to travel back in time, imagining where the Indians might have slept, hunted and prepared their food. Did they enjoy the small holes and canyons as a place to play? Which small peak might they have sat on to enjoy a spectacular sunrise, sunset, or full moon, or to spy enemies or game to hunt?

Once you reach the tank you'll have to lean over between two rock walls and twist your body in a peculiar fashion to get a good look. I wouldn't let a child try it without a firm adult hand holding her belt to prevent a tumble into the tank.

Such natural tanks or *tinajas* were critically important water sources to human travelers even into the twentieth century, and remain so to desert wildlife. Mouse's Tank is not the largest in the park but because of its deep bowl shape and shaded location, it holds water the longest.

Sometimes you will find plenty of water, while at other times it is bone dry with the sandy bottom visible. Unlike some desert water basins that are easily accessible to wildlife, this one is hard for some to take advantage of. It is about eight feet deep, has no easy access except just dropping into it, and could be difficult to get out of.

Mouse's Tank gets its name from a Paiute who lived in the region in the 1890s. There are several versions of Mouse's story, but it's generally agreed that he ran afoul of white man's law and became a much-feared fugitive. The official park story says that Mouse was able to evade posses for an extended period because

Just driving through The Valley of Fire is a feast for the eyes.

he knew about this natural water supply, and could therefore survive in what was a very dangerous desert when walking or riding horseback remained the only means of travel. By most accounts Mouse never surrendered and was killed by a posse in 1897.

Look carefully in the sand along the sides of the trail and you might see evidence of those who still live here. You might see small tracks made by kit foxes, chuckwallas, and zebra-tailed lizards, and the distinctive continuous trails made by snakes. Before you place your feet or hands in any holes, take a quick look inside; the park boasts thirteen species of lizards, and fifteen species of snakes, a few of them venomous. All of them find these holes in the rock just as appealing as we do.

Most of the wildlife, of course, is completely harmless. On the canyon floor you may see white-tailed antelope ground squirrels, black-tailed jackrabbits, and even the less-usual cottontails darting to safety. Keep an eye to the sky for red-tailed and rough-legged hawks and even an occasional golden eagle. Few sights in Southern Nevada can compare to the sudden appearance of a soaring raptor, outlined on the bluest skies the West affords, framed by the blood-red rock of the Valley of Fire.

Mouse's Tank At A Glance

Best season: October–April.

Length: 0.6 miles roundtrip.

Difficulty: Easy.

Elevation loss: Forty feet.

Trailhead elevation: 2,070 feet.

Warning: Sandy terrain.

Jurisdiction: Valley of Fire State Park.

Directions: From the visitor center head northwest along White Domes Road about one mile, to signed parking area and trailhead on right.

Wind hollowed holes big enough for an adult to take a nap inside, on the way to Mouse's tank.

27 White Domes Loop Trail, Valley of Fire State Park

ALTHOUGH JUSTLY FAMOUS FOR ITS SIGNATURE FIERY RED SANDSTONE, VALLEY OF FIRE State Park incorporates a multi-colored landscape, and the rest of the spectrum is especially noticeable on a visit to its most northern area.

The White Dome Loop trail is short and easy, only one and-one-quarter miles, yet one of the park's best for diversity. You will walk through sand dunes, the remains of a movie set, and a narrow slot canyon. You'll see hundreds of sandstone formations in more fantastic shapes than one can readily imagine.

Children will especially like this hike, and except in a couple of short sections that have minor drop-offs, they can safely play to their hearts' content.

As you drive up to the trailhead, it won't be hard to figure out you are at the correct place. The white domes are obvious as giant scoops of ice cream on the colorful surrounding landscape.

Blazing reds and oranges on every side are the result of trace iron minerals that have oxidized. The white domes' contrasting light color was created when groundwater leached out the rusted iron. On closer inspection you will see the domes are not completely colorless. Look toward the peaks and you will see muted hues of yellow, gold, and purple. The dome on the right has a four-foot-wide ribbon of pink that runs almost horizontally across the formation.

From the trailhead the route heads up the sandy trail between the two prominent domes. Notice the creamy tan color of the sand along this section. As you hike this trail you will notice many different colors of sand, from light coral all the way to a dark orange.

This first section is much like walking on a sandy beach, so it can be tiring, but after about five minutes the terrain becomes firmer when you reach the top of a rocky slope. Here the trail descends a series of man-made and natural sandstone steps into a large, open and flat area.

Around this flat you will find several sandstone block walls, the remains of a movie set built in 1965 to film *The Professionals*. That action Western starred Burt Lancaster, Lee Marvin, Jack Palance, and Claudia Cardinale. The park's unique landscape has been used for scenes in many other movies, including a few Westerns as early as the 1920s. Some more recent and well-known films partially shot here include *The Electric Horseman*, *Star Trek: Generations*, and *The Good Son*.

Valley of Fire still serves as the backdrop of about fifty commercial shoots yearly, but because of today's strict rules for leaving the landscape unchanged, you'll never find any evidence of the filming unless you happen to be in the park while it's going on.

From the movie set, pick up the trail which heads south. After about twenty yards it drops into a drainage called Kaolin Wash. The official trail will go right, or west, but if you have time, there is also a nice canyon well worth visiting to the left.

Continuing right, in less than a minute or two you will reach the narrow slot canyon. The walls of the narrows don't reach very high, perhaps fifty feet at most, but they do canopy much of the sky. It's a tight slot, so even young children will be able to reach out and touch both sides at the same time.

Once out of the narrows, the trail goes right and gains some elevation, but still isn't strenuous. When it reaches the next flat area, there are unusual sandstone

Groundwater has leached out the rusted iron creating the lighter color on the White Domes, seen here at trailhead.

formations in great variety, inspiring all ages to play in the holes, windows, and overhangs. You might see small animals searching for food in this area.

As you continue, keep an eye out for some large open areas, where it is not vegetated. This is especially noticeable on your left, where the terrain is very flat. Look closely at the ground here, and you will see small round balls, mostly about one inch in diameter. Called "Indian marbles," these occur naturally when sandstone forms around some harder mineral.

White Domes Loop Trail At A Glance

Best season: October–April.

Length: 1.25-mile loop.

Difficulty: Easy.

Elevation gain/loss: One hundred feet.

Trailhead elevation: 2,015 feet.

Warning: Sandy terrain at the beginning.

Jurisdiction: Valley of Fire State Park.

Directions: From the visitor center head north on White Domes Road about 5.5 miles to the end of the road for parking area and trailhead.

28 Kershaw-Ryan State Park

KERSHAW-RYAN STATE PARK, IN LINCOLN COUNTY, IS A DESERT OASIS WHICH HAS BEEN made even more enjoyable by man's improvements.

Only a few miles drive south of Caliente you will find a lovely canyon with lush vegetation, picnic areas, volleyball courts, horseshoe pits, a couple of backcountry hiking trails, and a spring-fed wading pool.

Kershaw Canyon was named for homesteaders Samuel and Hannah Kershaw, who lived here in the 1870s. Other early settlers followed and from 1892 to 1904 there were even enough people to support a post office. In 1904 the Kershaws sold their land to cattle rancher James Ryan of Caliente.

The property was then known as "Kershaw Gardens," and Ryan kept it until 1926 when he and his wife donated the land to be used as a public park. Things really got going during 1934-35 when the Civilian Conservation Corps added picnic spots, campsites, a caretaker's cabin, toilets, and the wading pond.

This used to be a fairly small park of only 240 acres until recently when about fifteen hundred acres were transferred from the Bureau of Land Management.

The spring-fed pool is perfect if you have children in your group. Only two feet deep and about the area of a large backyard swimming pool, it's deep enough for an adult to soak, or rediscover the joy of sitting on the edge and dangling feet in the coolness.

Manicured lawns and rose bushes are flanked by canyon grapes and deciduous trees. Nine springs, occurring mostly along natural fault lines and flowing through the park, provide all the landscaping water. Water also carved deep channels into the volcanic rock of the surrounding cliffs.

The most dominant trees in the main area of the park are cottonwoods, willows, dogwoods, and Gambel's oaks, but there also are fruit trees including apples, pears, and plums, remnants of an orchard the Kershaws planted.

Natural plant communities in the park number four: desert scrub, mountain brush, riparian and, in the higher elevation areas, a pinyon-juniper community. Spring flowers include four o'clocks, Palmer's penstemon, firecracker penstemon, and phacelia.

Habitats and plants so varied naturally support a rich variety of wildlife including mountain lions, coyotes, bobcat, and foxes. In the main area of the park, I once saw a male summer tanager, rare for this region. Look for canyon wrens, warblers, towhees, lazuli buntings, hummingbirds, western tanagers, Bulloch's orioles, canyon jays, hawks, and occasionally a golden eagle.

As yet there is only a small network of interconnecting trails. They are the one-mile Canyon Overlook Trail and the Horsespring and Rattlesnake Canyon Trails, each a half-mile long, that spur off from the main trail.

Because the park is located in a canyon it has been affected by severe flash

The former ranch that became Kershaw-Ryan State Park still has a homelike setting of grassy lawn, fruit trees and rose bushes. Below: The Elgin Schoolhouse State Historic Site, about 18 miles south of the park, became part of Kershaw-Ryan for administrative purposes, in 2005. The rural school was used from 1922 through 1967.

flooding. The most devastating floods were in 1984, causing such bad damage the park had to be closed. Through a parks-and-wildlife bond issue approved by voters in 1990, the park reopened in 1997.

The Elgin Schoolhouse State Historic Site, about eighteen miles south of the park, became part of Kershaw-Ryan for administrative purposes in 2005. The rural school was used from 1922 through 1967. It is accessed by driving Nevada Route 317 (Rainbow Canyon Highway), south of Kershaw-Ryan. Tours are available by appointment only; to arrange one, call Kershaw-Ryan State Park at (775) 726-3564.

Kershaw-Ryan State Park At A Glance

Best seasons: May–June, September–October.

Length: Network of three trails ranging from 0.5 to 1.1 mile roundtrip.

Difficulty: Easy to moderate.

Elevation gain: 260 feet.

Park elevation: 4,312 feet to 5,080 feet.

Warning: Flash flooding.

Jurisdiction: Nevada Division of State Parks.

Directions: From Las Vegas take Interstate 15 north about 21 miles, exiting onto U.S. 93 north, the Great Basin Highway. Drive about 128 miles to Caliente. Take a right onto Nevada Route 317 and follow for about 3 miles going left into Kershaw-Ryan State Park entrance road.

29 Cathedral Gorge State Park

CATHEDRAL GORGE STATE PARK IS FAMOUS FOR ITS BADLANDS OF CLIFFS, SPIRES, AND TIGHT CANYONS. Made up of soft bentonite clay, these formations offer a great natural playground for adults and children alike.

The badlands terrain was created by erosion. Around one million years ago this area was a freshwater lake. With climate change, uplifting and faulting, the lake dried up and sediments on the lake bottom were exposed. The hardened clay is still soft by geological standards, so rain, snow, freeze-and-thaw cycles, heat expansion and wind helped carve small gullies. Gullies naturally widened and weathered over the years and still are doing so. This is a constantly changing landscape.

The park encompasses about sixteen hundred acres. Elevation of its main area is about forty-eight hundred feet, and some of the trails are exposed to sun, so it's best avoided in the hottest time of year.

The ideal way to visit the park is spending a couple of days here, but if you have limited time, the short trail to Miller's Point will take you by some of the best formations and to the finest overlook. The one-mile roundtrip route travels along the valley floor at the base of the park's eastern escarpment. It is easy except for the last segment, where you will need to climb a series of man-made stairs, overall about one hundred feet, to reach the overlook.

At first glance the park's colors may appear drab, but in different lighting,

The Badlands of Cathedral Gorge State Park, seen from Miller's Point.

especially at sunrise and sunset, the buff-colored cliffs become multi-hued in pinks, blues, and grays.

As you travel this trail, turn aside and poke around the landscape. You will be pleasantly surprised to find small canyons leading to other more narrow ones. Some of these areas are often called caves, because the cap rock on the two sides meets at the top, creating a cave-like feeling.

Stay off the clay if it is wet, as it becomes slippery enough to be hazardous, and so soft that walking on it can change the natural patterns of erosion.

Area residents have enjoyed the gorge for more than a century. In the 1890s, Mrs. Earl Godbe, a resident of the nearby silver mining camp of Bullionville, was a frequent visitor. She thought the spires and formations looked like European cathedrals, and she named it Cathedral Gulch. The name was changed later to Cathedral Gorge.

Others who spent time here included the Edwards family of nearby Panaca. They would let their children explore the hard clay formations, and in the 1920s were the force behind preserving and protecting their natural playground. The gorge became a state park by act of the Nevada Legislature in 1935.

On the clay cliffs and formations themselves you won't find any vegetation. This is because constant erosion denies roots any opportunities to take hold. On the valley floor though, soil is loamy and some desert plants grow. You will find narrow-leaf yucca, juniper, sagebrush, greasewood, shadscale, and four-winged salt bush.

These provide a good habitat for the park's wildlife. In the sand or dried mud, look for tracks of black-tailed jackrabbits, cottontail rabbits, coyotes, and gray foxes. During fall and winter deer can also be found here.

Ravens, American kestrels, and hawks are often spotted in the park and many migratory birds pass through. Toward the end of September look for cedar waxwings, which stop by for a treat from the Russian olive trees. In October and November ruby-crowned kinglets are often seen around the visitor center. Others that make brief stopovers include tanagers and a variety of hummingbirds.

The Depression-era Civilian Conservation Corps built the campground, stone water tower, and restroom as well as the ramada at Miller's Point.

The Regional Information Center is at the entrance of the park and provides answers about all of eastern Nevada, including the area's seven state parks.

Cathedral Gorge State Park At A Glance

Best season: September–June.

Length: Network of six trails ranging from 220 yards to seven miles roundtrip.

Difficulty: Easy to moderate.

Elevation gain: Minimal to one hundred feet.

Trailhead elevation: 4,760 feet at visitor center.

Warnings: Flash flooding, clay becomes slippery when wet.

Jurisdiction: Nevada Division of State Parks.

Directions: From Las Vegas take Interstate 15 north for about 21 miles. Exit right onto U.S. 93/Great Basin Highway and follow north for about 142 miles through Caliente. One mile north of the intersection of U.S. 93 and Nevada Route 319 at Panaca, go left into access road for Cathedral Gorge State Park.

30 Berlin-Ichthyosaur State Park

BECAUSE OF ITS REMOTE LOCATION, MOST PEOPLE WILL NEVER SEE BERLIN-ICHTHYOSAUR State Park. On the western edge of the Shoshone Mountains, it's a couple of hours north of Tonopah, itself remote from Nevada's population centers. But those who make the trek find it well worthwhile, and indeed, unique. The 1,540-acre park highlights two very different features: the well-preserved mining town of Berlin, and the remains of our state fossil, the ancient ichthyosaur (pronounced ICK-thee-o-saur.)

When you first arrive in the park you will be in the Berlin Townsite area where you can hit the trails and take a self-guided tour of more than seventy historic points. It is a pleasant way to spend a couple of hours outdoors on a network of easy hiking trails while learning about the rich history of the area.

Prospectors in 1863 discovered the first major ore body in the immediate area surrounding the park in Union Canyon, and one year later the Union Mining District was formed. The Berlin Mine wasn't added until 1896. Berlin thrived a few years but in 1908, with labor disputes and lower yields, miners moved on to other places. By 1911 it was a mere ghost town.

More than a century later, you can still find some wonderfully preserved buildings including the most prominent structure, the Berlin Mill. Inside you can see remains of a bank of stamps for crushing ore, and other artifacts. It once housed five boilers, four steam engines, a crusher, and thirty stamps.

Once you have seen Berlin you can either hike or drive 1.7 miles up to the Ichthyosaur Quarry site. Along the way be sure to stop at the site of Union, a town which once boasted a school, town hall, a mill, a saloon, and private dwellings. You can poke around the town's ruins on short trails and read the interpretive signs.

If you thought the mining towns were old, you'll find the ichthyosaur site has them beat by about 200 million years! Ichthyosaurs were ancient marine reptiles that inhabited the ocean waters which once covered central Nevada. Scientists believe they evolved from land reptiles, much as modern whales and dolphins are thought to have evolved from land mammals. Indeed, the skeletons of ichthyosaurs, whales, and dolphins rather resemble one another. Ichthyosaur fossils have been found on every continent except Antarctica.

While the first fossils here were discovered by a professor from Stanford University in 1928, excavation didn't begin until 1954. But the specimens found here show these creatures reached fifty feet in length, and are some of the largest in the world. About forty have been discovered in the park.

The shelter site is only accessed by tour but there are viewing windows if you

Ichthyosaurs, depicted here, were marine reptiles that inhabited the ocean waters which covered central Nevada in ancient times.

cannot be there during a regularly scheduled tour. The tour site contains the remains of nine ichthyosaurs and you can see skulls, jaws, backbones and other segments including a well-preserved ribcage.

The forty-minute tours usually run from Memorial Day to Labor Day, daily at 10 a.m. and 2 p.m., with a noon tour added on Saturday and Sunday. From late March to Memorial Day and from Labor Day to late October, tours are only available on Saturday and Sunday at 10 a.m. and 2 p.m. (775) 964-2440, www.parks.nv.gov/parks/bi.

The 1,540-acre park preserves the mining town of Berlin. The Berlin Mill is seen here.

Berlin-Icthyosaur State Park At a Glance

Best season: April–October.

Length: Varies, depending on trails taken.

Difficulty: Easy.

Park elevations: 6,840-7,880 feet.

Warning: No services in park.

Jurisdiction: Nevada Division of State Parks.

Directions: From Las Vegas, take U.S. 95 north for about 287 miles, passing through Tonopah. Go right onto Nevada Route 361 and follow for about 28 miles to Gabbs. Take a right onto Nevada Route 844 and drive about 16 miles to park.

Nevada's

Other Public Lands

The hikes in this section, except for the River Mountain Hiking Trail in Boulder City, are on lands administered by the Bureau of Land Management. The bureau looks after 264 million acres of our nation's public lands, primarily in the West. Of that amount, nearly 48 million acres are located in Nevada.

The Bureau publishes good backcountry maps, as well as other information of interest to hikers and backroaders.

The Bureau of Land Management Southern Nevada District Office is located at 4701 Torrey Pines, Las Vegas. Office hours are 8 a.m. to 4:30 p.m., Monday to Friday, (702) 515-5000, *www.blm.gov/nv/*.

Well-preserved petroglyphs in Sloan Canyon.

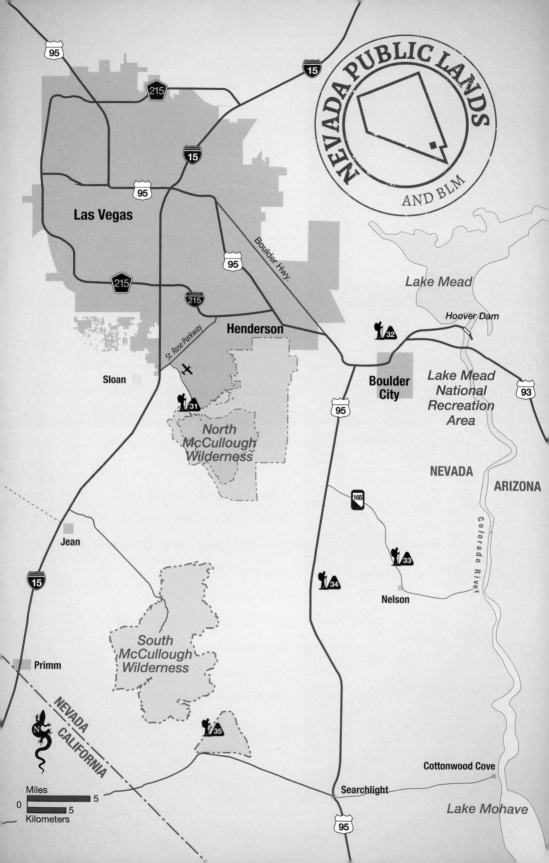

NEVADA PUBLIC LANDS

AND BLM

Las Vegas

Henderson

Sloan

North
McCullough
Wilderness

Jean

South
McCullough
Wilderness

Primm

NEVADA
CALIFORNIA

Miles
0   5
                     5
Kilometers

Lake Mead

Hoover Dam

Boulder City

Lake Mead
National
Recreation
Area

NEVADA

ARIZONA

Colorado River

Nelson

Cottonwood Cove

Searchlight

Lake Mohave

Boulder Hwy.

St. Rose Parkway

31

32

33

34

35

165

95

15

215

93

N

31 Sloan Canyon's Petroglyph Trove

SLOAN CANYON NATIONAL CONSERVATION AREA OFFERS PLENTY OF SOLITUDE AND DIVERSE desert scenery, in easy reach of Las Vegas. But the gem in this precious setting is the Sloan Canyon Petroglyph Site. Few petroglyph sites are so rich, few so unspoiled.

Designated by Congress in 2002, the 48,438-acre conservation area, south of the hamlet of Sloan, overlaps the 14,763-acre North McCullough Wilderness Area, which contains the petroglyph site. Petroglyphs are symbols engraved or pecked into the desert varnish or patina of rock surfaces, which exposes the light color underneath. Here are more than seventeen hundred designs on about three hundred panels. Experts believe the earliest of these were made by Ancestral Puebloans in the archaic period, generally considered to have ended more than three thousand years ago, but other peoples may have continued to add petroglyphs into the historic period after contact with European cultures.

Some of this rock art depicts recognizable forms such as bighorn sheep, lizards, and humans, while others remain a mystery. A couple of human figures appear to wear broad-brimmed hats, leading to speculation they depict travelers or settlers of European cultures.

The hike to the prime viewing area is about one mile from the trailhead, with an elevation gain of about two hundred feet. It is mostly an easy walk, along a gravel and sandy wash, but in a few sections you will have to do some rock scrambling.

Children will enjoy this hike, and it makes a good opportunity to teach them how to respect archaeological sites such as this one. Our best chance of preventing vandalism and careless misuse, which have compromised so many of our cultural sites, lies in teaching ethics early. This is especially important for children growing up in places like Las Vegas, where there is easy access to fragile sites on public land.

The conservation area is managed by the Bureau of Land Management, and they have a temporary contact station on the Nawghaw Poa Road, at the parking area and trailhead.

The first three-quarters miles is just walking up a wide gravel wash with sparse vegetation, mostly creosote bushes. When you arrive at your first obstacle, a rocky area that goes across the wash, look for the worn trail on the left. This is the easiest route, especially for children, but it isn't very challenging to just head up the terraced rock itself.

Over the next quarter-mile, canyon walls begin to rise along the edges of the wash. As the canyon heads southwest, you will come to a series of four obstacles. The first three are small and can be climbed without much trouble. The forth is a ten-foot-high chockstone wedged between the canyon walls. This obstacle is best passed by backtracking about fifteen feet and taking the route which skirts it on the left, then rejoins the wash farther up.

After the canyon bears left, the majority of the rock art is along the right side over the next one hundred yards or so. In a few areas, every boulder has petro-glyph panels. Some boulders just have one or two symbols, while on others, every available space has been inscribed.

In one part of Sloan Canyon nearly every boulder bears rock art. Below: Bighorn sheep on boulders.

Stay in the wash itself so the boulders don't get disturbed. To get a closer look at higher panels, bring binoculars. Most of the art here is still intact, and responsible use will keep it that way. It shouldn't need to be said in the twenty-first century, but apparently does need to be: Taking such an artifact for a souvenir is irresponsible and seriously illegal.

As you continue farther upstream, the petroglyphs are less concentrated but there are still many worth seeing, and it is a pleasant place to hike.

The only thing I found disconcerting about this hike was constant air traffic, mostly from private planes, which I assume were heading in or out of Henderson's Executive Airport located northeast of the canyon.

Keep hiking groups as small as possible, and confine visits to the daytime. Such easily damaged areas are inappropriate for camping, mountain biking, or ATV use. This is an exposed hike with very little shade, and the enclosed canyon gets hotter than its surroundings, so do this hike no earlier than October and no later than April, unless in very early mornings.

Contact station hours are 8 a.m.–4:30 p.m. In summer the contact station is open only Friday through Sunday. From October 1 through May 31, it normally will be open every day, but hours and days are subject to change. Call (702) 515-5350.

Sloan Canyon At A Glance

Best season: October–April.

Length: Two miles roundtrip to prime viewing area.

Difficulty: Easy, with moderate rock scrambling in a few areas.

Elevation gain: Two hundred feet.

Trailhead elevation: 2,895 feet.

Warning: Moderate rock scrambling.

Jurisdiction: Bureau of Land Management.

Directions: From Las Vegas take Interstate 15 south and turn onto St. Rose Parkway East (Nevada Route 146). Drive about 2.4 miles and go right onto Executive Airport Road. (Alternately, from the downtown Henderson area, take Interstate 215 West about 5.5 miles and take Exit 16, St. Rose Parkway, go left and drive 4.1 miles and left again onto Executive Airport Road.)

Once on Executive Airport Road drive about 1.7 miles and go straight onto Via Inspirada. Continue 1.4 miles on Via Inspirada, then turn left on Bicentennial Parkway. After about 0.5 miles go right onto Via Firenze. Follow another 0.5 miles and go left on Savello Avenue for 100 yards, then go right, back onto Via Firenze and follow south about 0.4 miles to Democracy and go right. Follow for about 0.2 miles (currently a short section of gravel road) and turn left onto access road (Nawghaw Poa Road,) and follow 0.6 miles for parking. (This route is subject to change because of ongoing construction projects.)

32 River Mountain Hiking Trail

Built by the Civilian Conservation Corps in the late 1930s, the River Mountain Trail in Boulder City remains one of the best-loved hiking trails in the area. Although the entire route will hold your interest as it travels over a variety of terrain, the crème de la crème of this hike is the summit. From there you will be treated to far-reaching panoramic views including Las Vegas, the Spring Mountains, Lake Mead, and Boulder City.

Children might struggle on this hike because it's more than five miles roundtrip with an elevation gain of about one thousand feet, but for adults it is a moderate one. There is one area of switchbacks that will be more strenuous but it's a short segment and the rest of the elevation gain is spread fairly evenly throughout.

The trail starts directly behind the signed kiosk on the north side of the parking area. Follow the wide and clear path, which skirts to the left of a man-made drainage between the Lakeview subdivision and St. Jude's Ranch for Children.

Follow the trail around north of the subdivision and into the desert. Along the first mile, the trail crosses a couple of old gravel roads and lower sections of Bootleg Canyon's mountain bike trails, but the route remains obvious and easy to follow.

Creosote is the dominant shrub along the entire trail, but in early spring the landscape is dotted with wildflowers such as orange globe mallow, pink beavertail cactus, blue Mojave aster, and yellow brittlebush. Those are what I see, but my daughters say I am color blind sometimes.

The trail serpentines toward Red Mountain through some small washes and canyons, and then to the north of a small hill. After about one mile the route heads north and into a wide canyon between mountains locally called "Red" and "Black." While in the canyon, stop and take a minute or two to scan for movement along the rugged cliffs, because desert bighorn sheep are commonly seen here.

Other wildlife you might see include coyotes and desert tortoises, and maybe even a rattlesnake or two.

About two miles from the trailhead you will reach the top of the switchbacks, which take you up and out of the canyon and to a wide saddle. Here you will go right. For about fifty yards or so you might be sharing the trail with Bootleg Canyon mountain bikers, but they will go north to continue on the Boy Scout Trail, while hikers will head east and up a small rise. From here continue along the meandering trail for about one-half mile to reach the summit.

The views are some of the best in Boulder City. To the east is Lake Mead's Boulder Basin and behind that the prominent landmarks of Fortification Hill and Wilson Peak in Arizona. To the south and spread out below is Boulder City; to the southwest, Eldorado Valley and the McCullough Mountains. To the northwest you can see Las Vegas and beyond to the Spring Mountains, including Mt. Charleston.

The five-mile roundtrip trail first heads up the canyon between Red and Black Mountains, then follows switchbacks up to a saddle for your final summit on Black Mountain.

River Mountain Hiking Trail At A Glance

Best season: October–March.

Length: Five miles roundtrip.

Difficulty: Moderate.

Elevation gain: 1,082 feet.

Trailhead elevation: 2,430 feet.

Jurisdiction: Boulder City.

Directions: From Las Vegas take U.S. 93 south about 25 miles to Boulder City. At the second stoplight (corner of Nevada Highway and Buchanan Boulevard) go left, continuing on U.S. 93. Drive about 0.7 miles and go left at the sign identifying "River Mountain Trail Parking." This is immediately before the main entrance of St. Jude's Ranch for Children.

33 Bridge Spring Trail

THE ELDORADO MOUNTAINS FLANK THE WESTERN SIDE OF THE COLORADO RIVER'S LAKE Mohave, just south of Boulder City. Its four-wheel driving opportunities are well-known, but the area also contains roadless stretches that are a hiker's paradise, unspoiled and rarely explored. Yet most of it is within easy reach, even if your only transport options are low-clearance sedans and shoe leather.

A good way to familiarize yourself with this area is hiking to Bridge Spring. This is a fairly easy journey of less than two miles, roundtrip. If you take the main route, the travel distance and elevation gain are minimal, so it is appropriate for children, but they will need to do some rock scrambling, and you'll have to beware some drop-offs once you near the bridge.

Natural bridges are rarer than arches, because the former, by definition, span or at one time spanned a waterway, the water being in some way responsible for forming them. In this case, a spring-fed stream runs only a short distance, and breaks up into occasional pools and puddles. But it waters plants and creates animal habitat that otherwise wouldn't be present, adding to the interest of the place. Just going to the bridge and back makes an excellent outing, but for more adventure you can easily turn a trip here into a full day of exploring.

From the trailhead, head east up the faint trail to the ridgeline. From here you'll be able to catch a glimpse of Nelson, a colorful old mining town which lies about a mile south. Continue on, making many gentle ascents and descents along various ridges. After about a quarter-mile the trail drops into a well-defined wash, which serves as your route for the remainder of the hike.

This natural bridge can be found near the town of Nelson, Nevada. Bridges, formed by water, are rarer than arches in the Southwest.

Hiking this drainage is pretty straightforward, although occasionally you will have to skirt some obstacles, such as pour-offs and rocky areas. Keep an eye out for interesting formations, like windows in the rocks and one stunning twenty-five-foot corkscrew run-off.

If you have the time on your return, take side trips up the spur canyons, all well worth the trip. Some are just short and box-like, where without good climbing skills your progress will eventually be blocked. Others are passages so tight that if you reach out, you can easily touch both sides at the same time, which makes them especially fun to walk through,

After about one-half mile, on the right side of the drainage, you'll come to a boulder about twenty-five feet tall and fifteen wide, which seems to balance there as if defying gravity. It appears as if you leaned against it might fall. After this, the wash becomes more lushly vegetated, mainly with vigorous scrub oaks, some of which grow as tall as twenty feet.

A little farther on, look up to the high cliff on your left and you'll see the large entrance to a cave. It is accessible, but requires a one-hundred-yard climb up a tricky scree slope, and the unstable scree makes for a dangerous return descent. The inside of this cave is about twenty yards long and the ceiling in places rises to about fifteen feet. At the far end it has a natural opening just big enough to fit a human or large animal, which could make a handy escape route if some danger came in the front door.

Because of the nearby spring, this is an important area for wildlife. Some of the more interesting creatures that call this area home are bighorn sheep, chuck-walla lizards, bats, rattlesnakes, and even the elusive Gila monster. This monster, actually a one- to two-foot-long poisonous lizard, should be hibernating in winter, but come springtime you might encounter one. If you're so fortunate, you'll recognize its colorful pattern of black with prominent splotches of orange, pink, or yellow. The habitat here is an ideal one, for they prefer damp, rocky, desert areas. Poisonous though it is, this species is protected.

As you continue down the wash, the vegetation becomes dense; lichen and moss colonize on many boulders, and you'll notice more water along the route. Keep an eye out for the well-worn wildlife trails that run up the grassy areas leading to a broad canyon on your right.

As you get closer to the bridge you'll find a few obstacles in the way — boulders that you have to carefully scramble down — and thickly vegetated areas. Once the bridge comes into view, stay left against the canyon wall, for the easiest way to reach its base. The bridge spans about thirty feet, joining the two canyon walls with a fifteen-foot-thick rib of rock. There's plenty of room to stand underneath; the clearance seems about as high as the bridge is thick.

If you continue downstream past the bridge, the canyon becomes steep and is choked with boulders. Here though, is one of the few places that afford passage up to the top of the left cliff. You won't find it an easy climb but for those who can make their way up, there are incredible views. You'll be able to see down Eldorado Canyon about seven miles to Lake Mojave, and as far as Mount Tipton, forty miles away, just south of Dolan Springs, Arizona.

Bridge Spring Trail At A Glance

Best season: October–March.

Length: Two miles roundtrip.

Difficulty: Moderate.

Elevation loss: 203 feet.

Trailhead elevation: 3,510 feet.

Warnings: Route finding skills needed. Flash flood danger.

Jurisdiction: Bureau of Land Management.

Directions: From Las Vegas take U.S. Highways 93/95 south 23 miles to Railroad Pass. Turn south on U.S. 95 for 9.8 miles and turn left on Nevada Route 165, toward Nelson. Drive 9.4 miles and go left onto the unsigned gravel road. You may park here, or high-clearance vehicles may go 0.2 miles farther and park at the base of the hill.

34 Keyhole Canyon

THE CRAVING FOR NATURAL BEAUTY RESPECTS HUMAN SCHEDULES NO MORE THAN DOES craving for chocolate. Just as many folks keep a candy bar hidden but handy against inconvenient hunger, so a devoted hiker mentally stashes a quick but satisfying hike, to be done when life affords only a few hours outdoors.

One of the best such emergency hikes is up Keyhole Canyon, south of Boulder City on the western foot of the Eldorado Mountains. It's so near town that little equipment is required: just plenty of water, seasonal clothing, binoculars and emergency supplies. Furthermore, it's easy, suitable for whatever companions you must entertain — even people who are a little lame, a little lazy, or just plain little. Hiking Keyhole end-to-end will only take ten to fifteen minutes, but admiring the canyon's petroglyphs and pictographs can enrich as much time as you choose to invest.

Depending on where you park, follow the fence line to the mouth of the canyon where you will find a log-and-wire hikers' gate. Upon entering stop and take a look around at the boulders and cliff faces, and you'll see the first of many petroglyphs associated with this canyon. Prehistoric American Indians pecked these symbols into the dark desert varnish on the rock surface, exposing lighter-colored rock underneath. Here, the rocks are mostly quartz monsonite.

Don't forget to look high on the walls, because that's where you'll find some of the most interesting panels. They are especially concentrated on the left side going in. Never attempt to climb up for a closer look; the climb is steep, dangerous, and can damage the art. The best way to see these panels really well is with those binoculars you brought.

Below: A rare pictograph among hundreds of petroglyphs, at Keyhole Canyon. Right: A visitor comes to a dryfall at the end of the Keyhole Canyon hike.

Most of the glyphs are abstract, ranging from simple lines to more complicated symbols and designs. There are also plenty of recognizable forms, though, and children will especially enjoy finding the depictions of bighorn sheep, lizards, and humans.

As you proceed farther into the canyon keep an eye out underneath the overhangs and unexposed surfaces for pictographs. Pictographs are painted on the rock surface and are a treat to see since they are far less common in our area than are petroglyphs. Typically they survive only in protected places like rock shelters and caves. These were painted with red ocher, a natural clay pigment.

There are also some cupules here — manmade circular depressions in the rock, which are thought to have been used for Indian ceremonies.

The canyon ends at the base of a dry waterfall.

Keyhole is popular among rock climbers, who use it primarily for traditional climbing, but there are some bolted routes. If you plan on climbing, please stay one hundred feet from any rock art.

You will need a high-clearance vehicle once you get off the highway and onto the gravel roads. Because of flash flooding, don't enter the canyon or even attempt the access roads if rain has occurred or is forecast.

Keyhole Canyon At A Glance

Best season: October–March.

Length: 350 yards roundtrip.

Difficulty: Easy.

Elevation gain: Minimal.

Trailhead elevation: 2,854 feet.

Jurisdiction: Bureau of Land Management.

Directions: From Las Vegas take U.S. Highways 95/93 south toward Boulder City. After about 23 miles, at Railroad Pass, exit on U.S. 95 south toward Searchlight. Drive 15.7 miles and go left through the median on the paved crossover. (This will be 5.9 miles after the turnoff to Nelson.) Follow this gravel road 2.1 miles and go right at the power lines. Follow the power line road for about 1.8 miles and then go left just after power line tower 23E3. Continue about 0.3 miles to parking area.

35 Wee Thump Joshua Tree Wilderness Area

For those of us not raised in the desert, the sight of a Joshua tree, its armored arms snaking off in every direction, is a romantic reminder we're not in Kansas anymore. Perhaps to congratulate ourselves for making a home in such a beautifully different place, many of us like to look at Joshuas up close and often. An excellent place to do this is the Wee Thump Wilderness Area, just west of Searchlight near the California border. While you can visit any time of year, spring is especially good because you catch spring flowers, yet miss the summer heat.

Designated by United States Congress in 2002, and managed by the Bureau of Land Management, the 6,050-acre wilderness area lies in Paiute Eldorado Valley, between the southern sections of the McCullough Mountains and the Highland Range.

Wee Thump means "Ancient Ones" in the Paiute language. And many of the Joshua trees you see are indeed old growth, towering thirty feet high. Average life span of Joshua trees is 150 years, but they can live more than five hundred.

Joshua trees are unique to the desert Southwest and occur at elevations from about two thousand to six thousand feet. Wee Thump is about forty-one hundred to five thousand.

The wilderness area is pretty much triangular with the northern corner cut off. The easiest place to enter is at the southeast boundary.

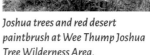

Joshua trees and red desert paintbrush at Wee Thump Joshua Tree Wilderness Area.

Once off the pavement you will see the large Bureau of Land Management sign identifying the Wee Thump Joshua Tree Wilderness Area. You can park here and start exploring, but for more solitude and quiet, you can drive up the gravel road a ways, unless recent rain has made that road doubtful.

It heads north over a cattle guard and in 0.2 miles you reach an open area, where you will find a windmill, a large wooden corral, and a cement water tank, all old and no longer in use. Here you will bear left to continue along the preserve's southeast boundary.

When you are ready to start hiking, park in one of the handful of pullouts on the right, or east, side of the road. There are good spots about one and one-half miles from the pavement, and others about three miles. From there, walk along the road and select one of the small sandy washes heading west. These are ideal hiking routes because you won't be treading on sensitive plants or soils, yet the greater moisture that collects in them gives the potential to see a greater variety of plants.

The relatively soft floor of a wash is also the best place to look for wildlife tracks. Besides the famous coyote, the ubiquitous rabbit, and a variety of rodents, snakes, and lizards, you might find evidence of kit fox and desert tortoise.

If you hike in the western part of the wilderness area, keep an eye out for old mines and stay away. Wherever you intend to hike, bear in mind that Joshua trees provide almost no shade, so bring enough water, sunscreen, and hat for exposed conditions. You might want to use a compass; a Joshua forest is one of the few environments in the Mojave Desert where it would be possible to lose your bearings.

In late April there are usually beavertail cactus in bloom, pockets of red desert paintbrush, and desert sage, a one-to-two-foot high rounded shrub, easily recognized by its deep blue, two-lipped flowers. The woodland also supports buckhorn cholla, Mojave yucca, and banana yucca.

Many types of birds live here, including the great horned owl, loggerhead shrike, cactus wren, and Scott's oriole. Bird watchers might get a special treat and see a gilded flicker. Once considered an accidental tourist in this area, this woodpecker is now known to live here.

Despite their name, Joshuas are not true trees but a kind of lily; some experts classify them further as part of the agave family. The leaves are slim, spine-tipped and rigid. Joshuas start growing as one trunk and are often more than five feet tall before they even start to branch out. Growth is slow — only one-half to three inches per year.

Not only birds, but mankind and moths have had special relationships with Joshua trees. American Indians made footwear and strong cord from the plant. Some used the plant for food; petals from the conspicuous, football-sized bloom clusters, if properly cooked, are said to please even the picky palates of modern city folk.

The yucca moth enables the plant's sex life. Because the pollen is sticky, it is not readily carried to other plants by the wind. Yucca moths, seeking to lay eggs on the plant, carry the pollen from one to another. Joshua trees can also propagate by sending out shoots from their roots or crown.

Because the branches twist themselves in snaky growth patterns not seen in more familiar trees, some find the appearance of Joshua trees a little scary. But pioneer Mormons found in them an echo of faith. To these pilgrims, the trees suggested a wild-haired warrior-prophet Joshua, praying or pointing the way toward the Holy Land, which Israel's children were destined to conquer.

Once you cease to fear their strangeness, and recognize their suitability for the life they lead in their place, you will be ready to enjoy one of the most stunning sights the Mojave affords — the word-defeating wonder of a dense Joshua tree forest on a moonlit night.

In late April you can usually find beavertail cactus in bloom while at Wee Thump.

Wee Thump At A Glance

Best season: October–April.

Length: Depends on route.

Difficulty: Easy.

Elevation gain: Minimal.

Trailhead elevation: 4,150 feet.

Jurisdiction: Bureau of Land Management.

Directions: From Las Vegas drive south on U.S. 95 about 60 miles to Searchlight. Go right onto Nevada Route 164 and drive west 8.2 miles, turning right into the gravel parking area. This will be the signed southeast boundary of the Wee Thump Joshua Tree Wilderness Area.

Desert

National Wildlife Refuge

The Desert National Wildlife Refuge was established in 1936 to preserve desert bighorn sheep and their native habitat. But it also preserves the sanity of humans who need occasional experiences in unspoiled nature. At 1.6 million acres, it's the largest National Wildlife Refuge. Even though entry is prohibited to the 846,000 acres that are shared with the military's Nellis Test and Training Range, there's a lot of space left for the sheep and us. Very limited hunting is allowed, but target shooting, off-road driving, and other activities which might interfere with the range's mission, are not, so it is uncrowded.

Elevations range from about three thousand feet near the main entrance, twenty-eight miles north of Las Vegas at Corn Creek, to almost ten thousand feet in the Sheep Mountain Range. Summers are extremely hot in the lower elevations, and winter brings heavy snow to the upper reaches.

Except for the visitor center, there are no services in the refuge, and once you head out on the gravel roads beyond Corn Creek it is extremely remote. You will need a high-clearance vehicle with good off-road tires. Carry plenty of water, food, and other supplies in case you are stranded by some misfortune. It can be several days or longer before another visitor comes along, and cell phones are unreliable.

The modern, ten-thousand-square-foot visitor center is well worth checking out. There are wonderful interpretive displays about wildlife and the history of the original ranch and the refuge. Its gift shop has a good selection of maps, wildlife guides, and books.

The center has been recognized and received awards for its sustainable de-

Man-made bridges are found over the perennial creeks throughout Corn Creek.

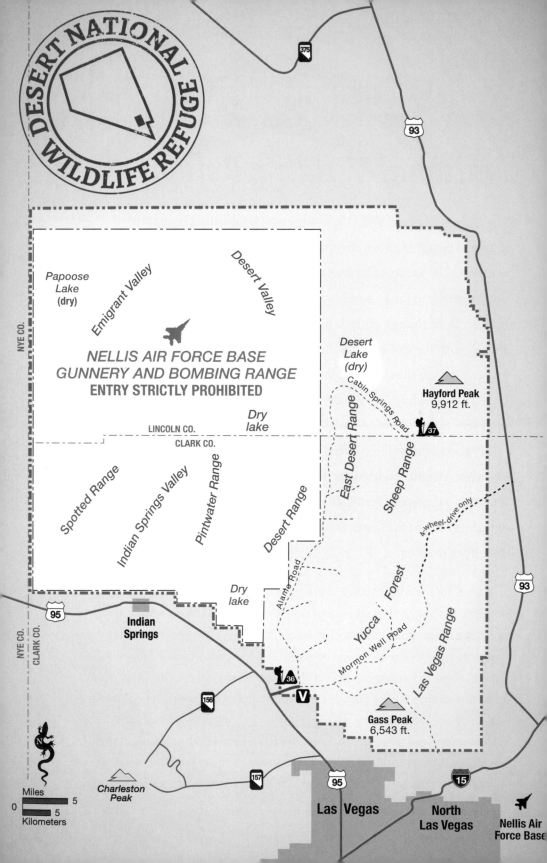

DESERT NATIONAL WILDLIFE REFUGE

375

93

Papoose Lake (dry)

Emigrant Valley

Desert Valley

NELLIS AIR FORCE BASE GUNNERY AND BOMBING RANGE ENTRY STRICTLY PROHIBITED

Desert Lake (dry)

Cabin Springs Road

Hayford Peak 9,912 ft.

37

Dry lake

LINCOLN CO.

CLARK CO.

NYE CO.

Spotted Range

Indian Springs Valley

Pintwater Range

Desert Range

East Desert Range

Sheep Range

4-wheel-drive only

93

Alamo Road

Dry lake

95

NYE CO.

CLARK CO.

Indian Springs

Yucca Forest

Mormon Well Road

Las Vegas Range

36

V

Gass Peak 6,543 ft.

156

N

Miles
0   5
5
Kilometers

157

Charleston Peak

95

15

Las Vegas

North Las Vegas

Nellis Air Force Base

sign and the technology used in building it. The building includes solar photovoltaic arrays, recycled materials, natural light to minimize electric usage, low-flow plumbing fixtures, and is surrounded by native Mojave Desert landscaping. It was certified platinum, the highest rating under the U.S. Green Building Council's LEED (Leadership in Energy and Environmental Design) program.

The refuge is open all year, twenty-four hours a day. Its visitor center is generally open Friday through Sunday, from 8 a.m. to 4:30 p.m. Days and times are subject to change so always call ahead: (702) 879-6110, *fws.gov/refuge/desert/*.

36 Corn Creek Visitor Center

THIS IS A SPECIAL TREAT FOR VISITORS WHO LIKE TO TASTE a smorgasbord of outdoor pleasures, or for family groups who must accommodate the varying appetites of different ages and personalities. Within about one and one-half miles there are tree-lined trails, spring-fed ponds, and a perennial stream. You can also visit a rare fish in its refugium, see an historic and unusual cabin, and glimpse some of the many birds that love the lush habitat.

Hikers read one of the many interpretive signs found at Corn Creek, pictured here at the junction of Bighorn Loop and Whispering Ben Trail.

The five trails are interconnected by loops, three of which are ADA accessible, and all run over fairly flat terrain. Each bend brings some new point of interest. There is no right or wrong direction to hike at Corn Creek. There will be many spur trails, which don't go anywhere in particular, but it would be hard to get lost.

About 320 species of birds have been recorded at Corn Creek. Although the best hours for serious birding are early morning and evening, you can count on seeing a feathered multitude even at midday. If you are here before the visitor center is open, an outdoor kiosk offers brochures with the refuge's bird list, breaking it into categories of common, uncommon, occasional, and rare birds, and according to what season you might see them. Bring along binoculars and a guide to Western birds, and you will be off to a good start.

There was a ranch at Corn Creek from 1916 until the federal government bought the land in 1939. Be sure to check out the Railroad Tie Cabin, located on a spur trail off of the Coyote Loop. This was probably built in the 1920s. The ties composing it came from the old rail line that ran from Las Vegas to Beatty from 1906 to 1918. After the railroad stopped operating, steel rails would be removed for reuse, but wooden ties were left behind. In Southern Nevada ties were commonly seized for building material, but this cabin is one of the few tie buildings left.

After visiting the cabin, be sure to look into the windows of the Pahrump pool-fish refugium, located near the cabin. The man-made building provides habitat much like the spring where this species originally lived. That spring has since gone dry. This holds some of the last remaining fish and keeps them protected from predators such as bullfrogs and crayfish, non-native species that were illegally introduced into Corn Creek.

From here you could head west and pick up the one-half-mile Bird Song Loop.

Clockwise: A great blue heron takes flight above the pond behind the visitor center. More than 300 species of birds have been identified here. A visitor on the Coyote Loop passes by the grassy meadow and fruit orchard. Telescopes for bird watching can be found along the Coyote Loop.

Look for desert mistletoe, a parasite making its home in a variety of host trees. The plant has scale-like leaves with a profusion of pink to red berries. The phainopepla, a crested, black bird commonly seen at Corn Creek, especially favors these berries. From this loop you will also enjoy fine views of the Spring Mountains to the west.

The Coyote Loop is in between the two outer and larger loops, Bighorn and Birdsong. Being highly vegetated, it is the favorite for birders. Mature cottonwood trees, large cattails and other water-loving plants thrive here and provide a safe haven for a variety of wildlife. Because of the natural cover, you probably won't see too much at eye level or near the ground, but if you stop for a while and listen, you will find it riotous with sounds from birds and other creatures rustling around.

Along the trail are a perennial stream and a serene meadow, with a grassy orchard that includes pecans, almonds, pomegranates, and other fruit trees.

Corn Creek Visitor Center At A Glance

Best season: September–May, or early mornings.

Length: One and one-half miles of interconnecting loops.

Difficulty: Easy.

Elevation gain/loss: Minimal.

Trailhead elevation: 2,926 feet.

Jurisdiction: Desert National Wildlife Refuge.

Directions: From Las Vegas go north on U.S. 95 about 26 miles. Go right onto the paved Corn Creek Road for 3.7 miles to Corn Creek Visitor Center.

37 Hidden Forest

HERE IS AN ENCHANTING HIKE TO A REMOTE CABIN DEEP IN A PONDEROSA PINE FOREST. You can stay overnight in the cabin, basking in its historic and romantic

Agave-roasting pits can be found throughout the park. They were used by pre-historic Native American people to slow cook meats and vegetables.

associations, and in winter the adventure is often enhanced by requiring snowshoes. Yet this rare experience is yours less than fifty miles from Las Vegas.

The trailhead lies in an isolated part of the Desert National Wildlife Refuge. Weather here seems to head in fast, furious and without warning, and in winter, even if the trailhead is bare of snow, there still could be a foot or more up canyon.

From the trailhead drop into the broad wash and head upstream and onto an abandoned road. For the first mile or so the terrain is mostly loose gravel, which makes slow walking, but it becomes more forgiving as you travel farther up and into Deadman's Canyon, in a little more than a mile.

The trail is easy to follow and has a steady elevation gain, spread out evenly along the way. It's not a tough trek but might be on the return, if you end up snowshoeing or plodding bare-boot through deep snow.

Near the trailhead you'll be in a blackbrush plant community with small Joshua trees and yuccas. After that you'll walk through an area mostly vegetated with single-leaf pinyon, Utah juniper, and big sagebrush. After about four miles you'll start to see dispersed stands of ponderosas and white fir; farther along, this will turn into the fully mature Hidden Forest.

In this area a few downed trees are minor obstacles, but it's easy to climb over them. Once, while traveling through here in winter, I heard a loud crackling behind me, turned around and watched as a thirty-foot pine, laden with snow, fell directly onto the path I had just traveled, seconds before.

The cabin sits on a small rise in the open, so you shouldn't have trouble finding it. As you travel up the canyon it will be on your left, at the mouth of an unnamed side canyon. This cabin is on the National Register of Historic Places. Details on the nomination form are fairly vague but it does indicate that the cabin is thought to have been built by a cattleman or miner at the end of the nineteenth century, and is made of hand-hewn wood. Like many cabins off the beaten track, this one was also known to be used by moonshiners during Prohibition.

Wiregrass Spring is about 250 yards up the side canyon, north of the cabin. The water may be contaminated, so treat before drinking. For those of you who are making this trip an overnight excursion, the cabin is available on a first come, first served basis, but you probably would have to share it with small creatures in any case. A better overnight choice is dispersed camping, which is allowed, except near the spring. The cabin has a wood stove, pots and pans, various tools, and some emergency supplies.

Whether you go for a day trip or for camping adventure, it is imperative, on your way to the trailhead, to stop at the Corn Creek Visitor Center and sign in at the self-registration box by the parking lot. This might save your life, and also lets the preserve know that people are using the area, which might mean funding to maintain it for many more years of enjoyment.

Hidden Forest At A Glance

Best season: April–October.

Length: Ten miles roundtrip.

Difficulty: Moderate.

Elevation gain/loss: Two thousand feet.

Trailhead elevation: 5,860 feet.

Warning: Snow in winter. Pack snowshoes, trekking poles, and winter gear for an emergency bivouac.

Jurisdiction: Desert National Wildlife Refuge.

Directions: From Corn Creek Visitor Center, go left onto Alamo Road and drive about 15 miles to Hidden Forest Road. Go right 3.6 miles to parking area and trailhead. All roads in Desert National Wildlife Refuge are worn gravel passages, requiring a high-clearance vehicle with off-road tires.

Basin

& Range

National Monument

Basin and Range National Monument was created in 2015 and encompasses about 704,000 acres. Especially rich in American Indian cultural history, it also preserves evidence of ranching, mining and pioneer settlements of the nineteenth century. It is the first national monument in Nevada to be managed by the BLM.

Basin and Range National Monument.

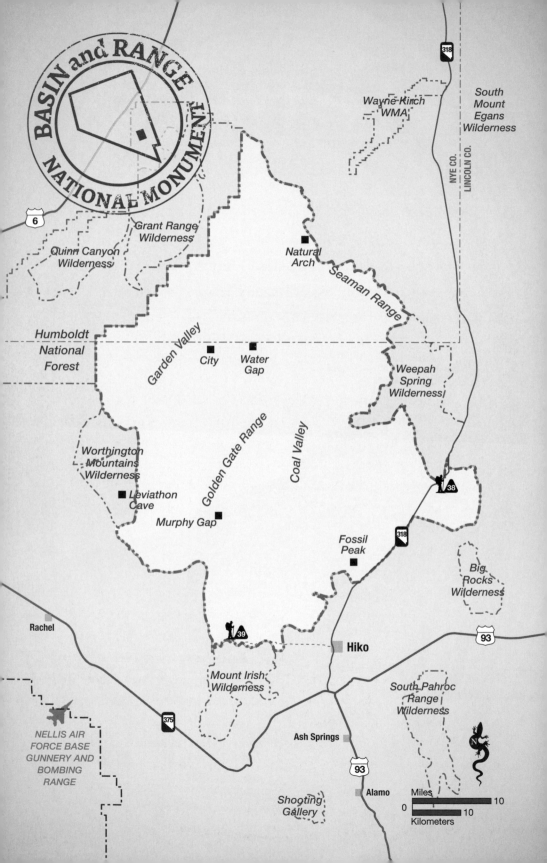

BASIN and RANGE NATIONAL MONUMENT

318

South Mount Egans Wilderness

Wayne Kirch WMA

NYE CO.
LINCOLN CO.

6

Grant Range Wilderness

Quinn Canyon Wilderness

Natural Arch

Seaman Range

Humboldt National Forest

Garden Valley

City

Water Gap

Weepah Spring Wilderness

Worthington Mountains Wilderness

Golden Gate Range

Coal Valley

Leviathon Cave

Murphy Gap

38

Fossil Peak

318

Big Rocks Wilderness

93

Rachel

39

Hiko

Mount Irish Wilderness

South Pahroc Range Wilderness

375

NELLIS AIR FORCE BASE GUNNERY AND BOMBING RANGE

Ash Springs

93

Alamo

Shooting Gallery

N

Miles

0   10

10

Kilometers

Lying across parts of both Lincoln and Nye counties in Central Nevada, the monument takes its name from the geographic term for an even larger area. The Basin and Range Province refers to the region lying between the Sierra Nevada Mountains and the Colorado Plateau, where mountain chains commonly stretch from north to south, with level valleys called basins lying between the ranges. The basins are primarily salt pans, dry lakes, and sinks. Nevada has some 150 named mountain ranges, more than any other U.S state. Clarence Dutton, a geologist and army officer who helped map the region, suggested one should visualize the country as "an army of caterpillars marching toward Mexico."

Because it is extremely remote, the monument is a very special place to explore on your own, as long as you are well prepared. It is good for camping, hiking, and especially for backroad rambling. Access is mainly by gravel roads, turning off a few main highways northeast of Rachel, north of Alamo, and south of Ely.

The monument protects thousands of years of culture including the White River Narrows Archaeological District and the Mt. Irish Rock Art and Archeological District, both of which were established prior to the national monument. Both these districts are located off State Route 318, north of Alamo on the way to Ely, and feature large concentrations of prehistoric rock art. Some of the petroglyph panels date back four thousand years. Climbing over rock art to get a closer look is damaging and dangerous, so bring binoculars to view those which are inconveniently located.

You can visit both these sites in a single day, but you'll need a high-clearance vehicle with good off-road tires, or a good mountain bike to take the access roads. I start with the White River Narrows, as it is farther from Las Vegas, and then I work my way back south twenty miles or so to the Mt. Irish area, which is the more isolated.

While neither of the sites is too far off the main road, they are nevertheless lonely places, and visitors must be self-sufficient to assure their own safety. There is no safe drinking water, and neither cell phones nor GPS devices are reliable here. Nor is there currently a visitor center in the park, so you must plan accordingly: Do all your trip research, obtain your maps, tell some responsible person where you are going and when you'll be back, and buy your supplies, all before going there. If you are coming from Las Vegas you will presumably travel through Alamo and Ash Springs, the last convenient places to obtain gasoline, food, water, or lodging.

Because the monument is so new, at this time there are no officially designated trails, but that could change once a complete resource management plan has been implemented. Camping is allowed, but there is a fourteen-day limit in any location and some places are off-limits. For instance, never camp near an archaeological site. Before you set out, be sure to contact the BLM at *www.blm.gov*, the Ely District Office (775) 289-1800, or the Caliente Field Office (775) 726-8100. For more information on the rock art sites go to *lincolncountynevada.com*, choose the menu option "Exploring" and then drop down to "Rocking." This website will also help you find a place to camp, lodging, dining, and other services in the area.

Famously, the monument also contains one of the largest earth sculptures ever created, but it is not yet open to the public and no opening date is certain. "City" is the work of artist Michael Heizer and a team who push and carve the earth with heavy construction equipment. It is about one and one-quarter miles long, eighty feet high in places. Begun in 1972, it was still unfinished in 2016. The son of an archaeologist, Heizer in his childhood and youth visited monumental works built by ancient civilizations, and has said he took his inspiration partly

Detailed petroglyphs from both pre-historic and historic times at the "Amphitheater." Below: A very well-defined petroglyph. Man or beast?

from them. The sculpture is built on private land in Garden Valley and cannot be viewed without illegal and unwelcome trespassing.

38 White River Narrows

THE FOUR-THOUSAND-ACRE WHITE RIVER NARROWS ARCHAEOLOGICAL DISTRICT WAS first placed on the National Register of Historic Places in 1976. The highlight here is the "Amphitheater" where you will find panel after panel of petroglyphs, which span a few hundred yards along the cliff walls of rhyolite.

From the parking area, sign the register, walk up the old jeep road and then toward the cliffs on your left. The grass is high, and I have seen a rattlesnake here, so try to stay on the spur paths and watch where you step.

The rock art can be found along the entire cliff area, very concentrated in some places and very sparse in others. Most images were created by American Indian peoples, but there are also some carved by pioneers of European descent. One etching says "Carl Williams, Sept. 18, 1926" directly below some intricate petroglyphs that seem to depict an arrow and many abstract designs.

The American Indian rock art consists of two main styles, one associated with the hunter-gatherers (Basin and Range tradition), and one with Fremont culture, whose members relied not only on wild foods but also on farming, and who made pottery and built villages in the Southwest more than a thousand years ago.

One panel in the Amphitheater stretches almost sixteen feet and features dozens of petroglyphs. Some are abstract and some obvious wildlife such as bighorn sheep. Above the panel is etched "NO HORSES."

When you leave this site and are returning to the main road, after about one mile, look on your left for a spur road going to another cliff face. Here, all by itself, you will find an unusual glyph, referred to as a "calendar fence." No one knows for sure, but the vertical lines might indicate a person's life, or a time of waiting. This one contains almost eighty such lines.

Despite the area's name, don't look for an actual river here. While the White River is significant to the geology of the region, it flows underground for nearly its entire length.

Very intricate designs are found in this panel at the "Amphitheater."

White River Narrows At a Glance

Best Season: October–May.

Length: 0.4 miles roundtrip.

Difficulty: Easy.

Elevation gain: Minimal.

Trailhead elevation: 4,560 feet at White River Narrows Amphitheater.

Jurisdiction: Basin and Range National Monument.

Directions: From Las Vegas take Interstate 15 north and drive 21 miles, exiting onto U.S. 93 north, the Great Basin Highway. Follow U.S. 93 north for about 85 miles, traveling through Alamo and Ash Springs and go left onto Nevada Route 318. For the White River Narrows, drive about 23 miles north on Nevada 318 to the gravel entrance road located on your right. Drive in about 2.1 miles (staying left at the forks) to the register and Amphitheater.

39 Mt. Irish Petroglyph Site

THE MT. IRISH PETROGLYPH SITE CONSISTS OF ABOUT 640 ACRES WITHIN THE SOUTHERN boundary of the main monument. This district has been little visited, and for the time being you are on your own to explore the three major rock art locations: Paiute Rocks, Shaman Knob and Shaman Hill. Currently there are registers at these main sites, so please be sure to sign in.

Besides the major sites there are other petroglyphs panels scattered about, via short hikes on both sides of the access road, but the largest concentrations are in the aforesaid areas. There are footpaths, but most are not very well defined. It is an exciting place to explore, and almost like a treasure hunt, seeing what you might discover on every twist and turn, on cliff faces and boulders. There is a wide variety of rock art, from abstract, to zoomorphs such as bighorn sheep and deer, to anthropomorphs, or figures that resemble human bodies.

Plan on spending at least a few hours to enjoy this area and discover to your heart's content. Scientists, after studying chipped and ground stone, rock shelters, and petroglyphs, conclude that this area was occupied from about 1000 B.C. to about A.D. 1860.

Mt. Irish Petroglyph Site At A Glance

Best Season: October–May.

Length: Varies.

Difficulty: Easy.

Elevation gain: Minimal.

Trailhead elevation: 5,160 to 5,730.

Warning: Remote gravel road.

Jurisdiction: Basin and Range National Monument.

Directions: Take Interstate 15 north and drive 21 miles, exiting onto U.S. 93 north, the Great Basin Highway. Follow U.S. 93 north for about 85 miles, traveling through Alamo and Ash Springs and go left onto Nevada Route 318. Drive north for about 3.9 miles on Nevada 318 and look for the BLM sign and gate on your left (Old Logan Rd.), then drive in about 6.5 miles to start looking for rock art. Drive about 1.7 miles farther to Paiute Rocks area located on your right. Continue about 0.5 miles farther to the Shaman Knob and Shaman Hill sites found on your left.

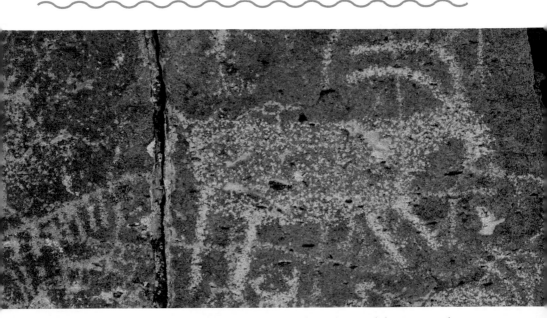

Large for a petroglyph, this depiction of a bighorn sheep is two feet wide. Figure below appears to be anthromorph, bearing horns. Below: Views from Mt. Irish district.

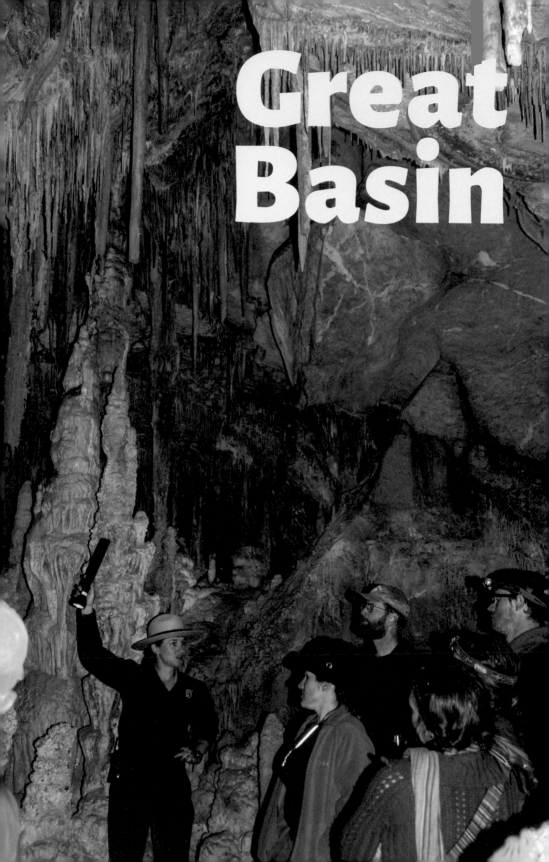

Great
Basin

National Park

Great Basin National Park is one of the least crowded in the nation, because of its remote location near Nevada's border with Utah, in the southern Snake Range. Elevations in the park range from about sixty-two hundred feet up to 13,063 feet at Wheeler Peak, making it ideal for a summer getaway. Nevada's only national park, it was established in 1986 and encompasses 77,100 acres.

That's toward junior-varsity size as national parks go, yet Great Basin offers a surprising variety of things worth doing. The highlights here are to camp, hike, take the Scenic Drive, tour the cavern, and enjoy the night skies, some of the darkest remaining in this increasingly urbanized nation.

Lehman Caves is actually a single cavern of limestone and marble about one quarter-mile long. Park rangers will guide you through the cavern and explain the history of the "Caves" and the formations along the way. The cavern contains stone formations such as stalactites, stalagmites, soda straws, popcorn, columns, draperies and even rare shield formations. Shields are circular plates attached to one another like clam shells, and Lehman has a few hundred of them.

The "caves" were named after a rancher and miner, Absolom Lehman, who discovered the cavern in the 1880s. The story that you might hear on your tour is that Lehman was riding around these hills when his horse, and its rider, accidently fell into the cavern opening. While this sounds likely, the ranger adds that Lehman hung from the opening for days until rescued. This is still possible, but when they

Lehman Caves is actually a limestone cavern and is visited by a ranger-guided tour.

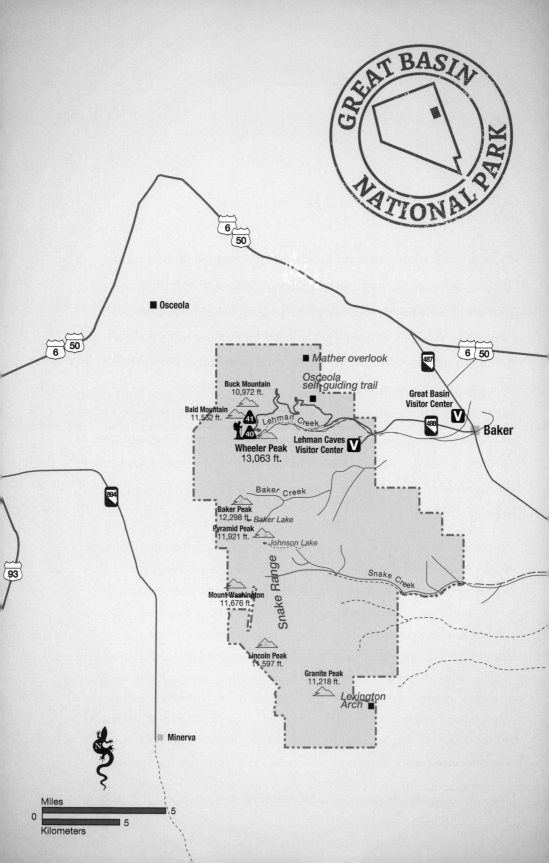

GREAT BASIN NATIONAL PARK

6 50

Osceola

6 50

487

6 50

Mather overlook

Osceola
self-guiding trail

Great Basin
Visitor Center

488

V

Baker

Buck Mountain
10,972 ft.

Bald Mountain
11,562 ft.

41

40

Lehman Creek

Lehman Caves
Visitor Center

V

Wheeler Peak
13,063 ft.

Baker Creek

894

Baker Peak
12,298 ft.

Baker Lake

Pyramid Peak
11,921 ft.

Johnson Lake

93

Snake Creek

Snake Range

Mount Washington
11,676 ft.

Lincoln Peak
11,597 ft.

Granite Peak
11,218 ft.

Lexington
Arch

Minerva

N

Miles
0   5
Kilometers   5

add how the horse was saved as well, you might wonder, because supposedly Lehman clutched his steed between his knees until the rescue. Cavern humor.

Be sure to make reservations for a tour as they sell out fast. Cave tours are either the sixty-minute Lodge Room Tour or the ninety-minute Grand Palace Tour. Tours take place daily year-round except Thanksgiving, Christmas, and New Year's Day. Temperature inside the cavern is always about fifty degrees, so take a light jacket or such even if you're going in summer.

Night skies in the park are glorious with stars, a fact recognized in Great Basin's 2016 designation as an International Dark Sky Park. Besides the obvious requirement — the absence of light pollution — low humidity and high elevation also add to the area's suitability for stargazing. On a clear moonless night, even without a telescope, you may see the Milky Way, Andromeda Galaxy, and five of our solar system's planets.

Visitors to Lehman caves. viewing stalactites. Below: On select days in summer the park offers solar telescope viewing.

The park's "Dark Rangers" will tell you more at frequent astronomy programs. During summer, through Labor Day, these star-themed talks take place on Tuesday, Thursday and Saturday nights. During April, May, September, and October, they're all on Saturday night. Telescopes are provided. For hours and other more information on star parties, and reservations for Lehman Caves tours, please contact the Lehman Caves Visitor Center at (775) 234-7331 or *www.nps.gov/grba*.

Wheeler Peak Scenic Drive is paved, but very steep traveling, gaining some four thousand feet elevation in its twelve miles. The upper portion of the road, past Upper Lehman Creek Campground, is only open from June to October, depending on snow. Not allowed at any time, on this upper portion, are vehicles or combinations exceeding twenty-four feet in length.

The nearby village of Baker has limited services including a gas station, small motels, a café and small grocery store. The park has a café open from late May to mid-October. The park is open year round.

40 Wheeler Peak

ONE OF THE LOFTIEST TRAILS IN NEVADA LEADS TO WHEELER PEAK, 13,063 FEET IN elevation and second-highest peak in the state.

You have two choices where to begin the hike. The official trailhead is about one-half mile from Wheeler Peak Campground, along the Wheeler Peak Scenic Drive. But if you are spending the night at the campground, I would recommend

using the Bristlecone/Alpine Lakes Loop trailhead instead, as it will be less than a five-minute walk from your tent.

Assuming you will use the trailhead closest to the campground, follow the signed trail about two-tenths of a mile and then go right at the signed junction onto the Alpine Lakes Loop Trail. You'll be going counterclockwise on that trail, through a forest of Engelmann spruce and limber pine, and open meadows, and aspen groves. In July you will find many wildflowers at peak bloom, such as Jeffrey's shooting stars, crimson columbine, and mountain bluebells along the trail.

This is a good place to look for butterflies as well. Their heaviest concentrations in the park occur from mid-July through early August. More than a hundred species have been documented, including gossamer-winged, skippers, fritillaries, and swallowtails. Some have come from hundreds of miles away.

From the trailhead it will be about seven-tenths miles until you come to an-

other signed junction. Here you will go left. Follow this for about one-tenth mile and then go right onto the signed Wheeler Peak Trail. The trail initially goes north, then heads west for a short distance, and finally south for the steep ascent to the peak.

The last part of the trail is obvious except in a few places where cairns will help you stay on track. At the peak you will be about two thousand feet above timberline. You will be treated to panoramic views, and on clear days you can see east a hundred miles, well into Utah. To the west is Spring Valley. Thousands of feet below and to the north is the northern Snake Range. Be advised there are steep drop-offs at the summit and it is often extremely

Stella Lake along the Alpine Lakes Loop Trail.

windy. Afternoon thunderstorms are very common and arise quickly, so be sure to hit the trail early in the morning, in order to be safely back in camp "when the lightning walks about."

Since you may be traveling to the park directly from Las Vegas, a good strategy is spending your first day or two hiking easier trails, so you can get acclimated to the high elevation, before tackling the Wheeler Peak hike. One good choice for this purpose is taking the entire Alpine Lakes Loop Trail of two and seven-tenths miles, instead of turning off toward Wheeler Peak.

This Wheeler Peak Trail is a difficult one at high elevation, so be on the lookout for hypothermia, dehydration, and altitude sickness. Hiking buddies should all learn the symptoms and keep a careful watch on one another, as a companion may notice you're having trouble before you figure it out yourself. This is an exposed hike so remember to wear a hat, apply sunscreen often, carry plenty of water, and drink it.

There are five developed campgrounds in the park, including one just for groups. If you come here to hike Wheeler Peak, I recommend the Wheeler Peak Campground, highest in the park at 9,886 feet, and the closest one to the trailhead. The sites have picnic tables, tent pads, and campfire grills, and operate on a first-come, first-served basis. This campground

Wheeler Peak in Great Basin National Park.

is only open June through September, depending on snowfall. In mid-summer at the trailhead area, average daytime highs are in the seventies with nights dropping into the forties.

Wheeler Peak At A Glance

Best season: Mid–June through September, depending on snowfall.

Length: About eight miles roundtrip.

Difficulty: Strenuous.

Elevation gain: 3,075 feet.

Bristlecone Parking Area elevation: 9,988 feet at Bristlecone Parking Area, near the Wheeler Peak Campground entrance.

Elevation gain: 2,903 feet.

Summit Trail Parking Area (official trailhead): 10,160 feet along the Wheeler Peak Scenic Drive.

Warnings: Start early. Wind and risk of afternoon thunderstorms and snow. Watch for signs of altitude sickness.

Jurisdiction: Great Basin National Park.

Directions: From Las Vegas take Interstate 15 north for about 21 miles, exiting to U.S. 93 north, the Great Basin Highway. Follow for about 234 miles and turn right onto U.S. Highway 50. Drive about 30 miles and go right onto Nevada Route 487. Go about 5 miles into Baker and take a right onto Nevada Route 488, the 5-mile access road into Great Basin National Park. Go right onto the 12-mile Wheeler Peak Scenic Drive; at the end of this road are Wheeler Peak Campground and trailhead.

The Alpine Loop Trail takes hikers through a forest of Engelmann spruce and limber pine with perennial streams.

41 Alpine Lakes Loop Trail

THIS IS A GREAT TRAIL FOR ALL AGES, TRAVELING THROUGH MEADOWS, A THICK FOREST and past two alpine lakes, Stella and Teresa. You start the hike at the Bristlecone Parking Area located before the campground. It affords great viewing opportunities for wildlife, wildflowers, and Wheeler Peak.

From the trailhead hike about 0.2 miles and go right at the signed junction onto the Alpine Lakes Loop Trail. The route is easy to follow, and passes through stands of Englemann spruce, aspen and limber pine. The wildflowers in July are usually quite showy. Look for Parry's primrose, Jeffrey's shooting stars, mountain bluebells and crimson columbine. From mid-July to early August you might also be treated to large concentrations of butterflies. Along this trail you might also see mule deer, beaver, and marmots.

Stella and Teresa are subalpine lakes, each occupying a glacial cirque, a particular type of basin named for its shape, suggesting a theater surrounded on three sides by steep banks of spectator seats. They freeze solid in the winter. Never deeper than twenty feet, the majority of the water in these lakes is from snowmelt, so the lakes could be full in late spring, yet disappointingly low by late summer.

Alpine Lakes Loop At a Glance

Best Season: Mid-June through September, depending on snowfall.

Length: 2.7-mile loop.

Difficulty: Moderate.

Elevation gain: Six hundred feet.

Trailhead elevation: Ninety-eight hundred feet at the Bristlecone Parking Area.

Warning: High elevation.

Jurisdiction: Great Basin National Park.

Directions: See Wheeler Peak directions, p. 171.

Ruby

Mountains

The Ruby Mountains contain some of the finest scenery in the state, and their high elevation and northern location make them an ideal place to visit in the summertime. In winter they are covered with snow, usually six to ten feet each year, but in summer the landscape is bejeweled with waterfalls, cascades, creeks, ponds and an abundance of wildflowers.

The Ruby Mountains Ranger District is managed by the forest service and encompasses about 450,000 acres. The district is composed of the East Humboldt Range on the north and the Ruby Mountains Range which lies just a bit southwest. Elevations range from six thousand feet up to 11,387, the latter at Ruby Dome. In July and August you can expect daytime average high temperatures to be in the mid-eighties.

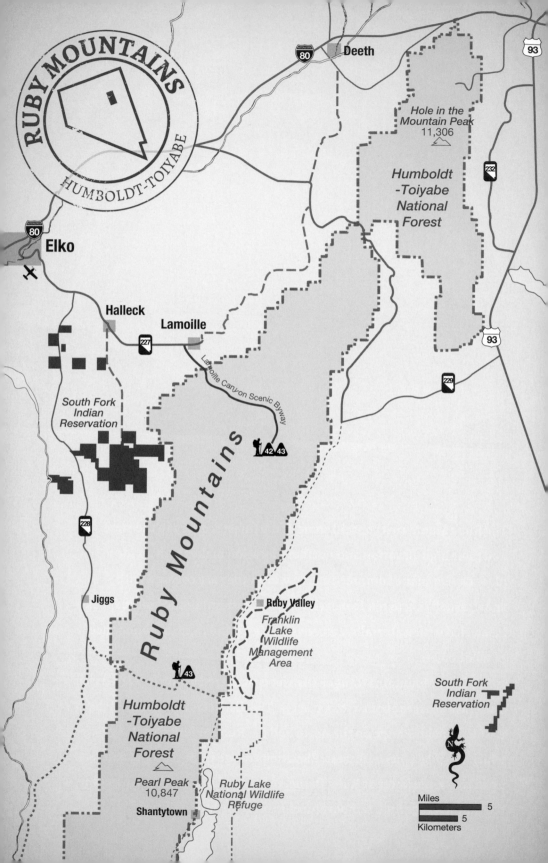

RUBY MOUNTAINS
HUMBOLDT-TOIYABE

Deeth

80

93

Hole in the
Mountain Peak
11,306

232

Humboldt
-Toiyabe
National
Forest

Elko

Halleck

Lamoille

227

Lamoille Canyon Scenic Byway

93

229

South Fork
Indian
Reservation

228

42 43

Ruby Mountains

Jiggs

Ruby Valley

Franklin
Lake
Wildlife
Management
Area

43

South Fork
Indian
Reservation

Humboldt
-Toiyabe
National
Forest

N

Pearl Peak
10,847

Ruby Lake
National Wildlife
Refuge

Shantytown

Miles
5
Kilometers
5

To reach the trail highlights in this chapter you will take the twelve-mile paved Lamoille Canyon National Scenic Byway. This is one of the most stunning drives in Nevada and even if you don't hike, your time will be well spent. The road goes through a U-shaped valley carved by a long-vanished glacier. Many people refer to these mountains as Nevada's Alps or Nevada's Yosemite, and the resemblance here is striking.

It will probably take you more time than you expect to make this drive, as there are so many irresistible overlooks and points of interests to stop you along the way. Besides the viewpoints, there are a couple of worthwhile trails to hike along this road. A one and one-half-mile Nature Trail begins at the Terraces Picnic Area, and at the Thomas Canyon Campground you can begin the Thomas Canyon Trail, a four-mile roundtrip.

Both ranges are full of wildlife, such as Rocky Mountain bighorn sheep, beavers, marmots and pronghorns. If you are hiking the Ruby Crest Trail you might also see Rocky Mountain goats or the Himalayan snowcock, both of which were introduced in the 1960s and 1970s. The snowcock is particularly unusual to see, as it lives in very high elevations.

Neither visitor centers nor services are provided in the Rubies, but Elko is a small city with complete services and interesting attractions including Basque restaurants and good Western museums. For further information on the city, visit *www.exploreelko.com* or (775)738-4091. For the Humboldt-Toiyabe National Forest, it's *www.fs.usda.gov/htnf* or (775) 752-3357.

42 Alpine Lakes

FROM ROAD'S END IN LAMOILLE CANYON THERE ARE NUMEROUS DAY-HIKING opportunities. Keep in mind, though, just driving Lamoille Canyon is an experience full of beauty, so you should allow enough time on your way to stop and gaze on waterfalls and wildflowers. I recommend a couple of hours for this aspect alone.

Several lakes make good day-hike destinations; depending on your group's ages, energy and ability level, you can choose how far you wish to travel. Be aware

that if you have just come from relatively low-lying Las Vegas to a trailhead elevation of about eighty-eight hundred feet, the higher elevation will likely tire you more quickly

To become used to the altitude, if for no other reason, I would recommend your first hike in this country be up to Lamoille Lake, which is only 3.4 miles roundtrip. Along the way it takes you by Dollar Lakes, not as impressive as Lamoille Lake but worth seeing in their own right. You will be using the Ruby Crest Trailhead located at the end of the south end of the loop.

The trail is well-maintained and well-signed, so you can't get lost unless you intentionally leave the trail. No matter what summer month you visit, you might find snow patches and often mud, so pick hiking shoes with good tread, and dress accordingly. If you have some hiking gaiters, wear them, to keep mud from getting in your shoes and on your pants legs.

Once you reach the lake there are lots of places to sit and relax and take in the scenery. The water is beautifully clear, though extremely cold, so be sure to take a swim, as it will be one to put in your memory bank. Even if a few other people are up at the lake, it is big enough, at close to fourteen acres, that you'll feel almost as if you have the shoreline to yourself. This is a place so pleasant and relaxing, you'll wish you were spending the night.

Fishing is allowed if you have a valid license, and the locals tell me the brook trout, raised in fresh, clean, cold mountain water, are the best in the West. In the doubtful event you find trout fishing so good anywhere else, you probably will not find equivalent ambience. I suspect the wonderful setting may be the real reason those trout, pan-fried on the spot, are so tasty.

Left: Cascades and waterfalls can be found throughout the Ruby Mountains in summer.

Alpine Lakes Trail At A Glance

Best Season: June–September.

Length: 3.4 miles roundtrip.

Difficulty: Moderate.

Elevation gain: 990 feet.

Trailhead elevation: Eighty-eight hundred feet.

Warnings: High-elevation hiking. Snow is possible year round.

Jurisdiction: Humboldt-Toiyabe National Forest.

Directions: From Las Vegas take Interstate 15 north about 21 miles, exiting onto U.S. 93, the Great Basin Highway. Drive north 85 miles and turn left onto Nevada 318 North. Drive about 110 miles and turn right onto U.S. 6 East and follow for about 24 miles to Ely. Turn left onto U.S. 93 and drive north about 138 miles. Merge onto Interstate 80 W and drive about 48 miles to Elko. From Elko, drive south on Nevada Route 227 about 18 miles, toward the small town of Lamoille. Go right onto the signed road for the 12-mile Lamoille Canyon Road National Scenic Byway.

43 Ruby Crest Trail

THE RUBY CREST NATIONAL RECREATION TRAIL IS A BACKPACKING ADVENTURE OF ABOUT thirty-four miles, point to point, in one of the most stunning areas to be found in Nevada. It travels from Road's End in Lamoille Canyon south to Harrison Pass, (or vice versa) or, it can be done as an out-and- back, multi-day backpack, traveling as far as you have the energy and time.

For the first few miles you will be sharing the trail with day hikers, those who travel up to the alpine lakes of Dollar, Lamoille and Liberty. After this, you will probably have the trail mostly to yourself, meeting only fellow backpackers from time to time.

Along the way you will find a level of solitude uncommon in other epic hikes around the country. Due to its out-of-the-way location — far from any major city, national park or busy hiking corridor — it is quiet. Yet the views are some of the best in the state. The trail is fairly easy to follow but in some places, especially in July, the wildflowers are so thick they actually cover your path. So who's complaining?

The trail is very undulating and is only recommended for those in good shape, who have experience hiking and camping in high elevations. With the overall elevation gain and length, it is a strenuous hike, so you can't travel very fast. I met someone years ago who told me they did it in one day. I am not sure if that was true or not, but it seemed like a stretch. Bottom line, it shouldn't be a competition or a speed contest. If you are going to hike the trail, the best part is the time you spend looking around and enjoying the views, maybe viewing wildlife or amazing wildflowers, or putting your feet up and taking a well-needed break by a crystal-clear alpine lake. I would suggest a minimum of three nights.

You will be sure to experience déjà vu many times along the way and wonder if you are going in circles, as so many switchbacks and so much elevation gain and loss makes the route seem repetitive. But about the time you think you can handle no more sameness of scenery, your eyes will spy something entirely new — perhaps a more spectacular view, a waterfall, or wildlife — and you will feel renewed and carry on.

If a point-to-point hike is out of the question, a multi-day backpack to some of the highlights, and back, is equally rewarding; except that you won't acquire full bragging rights. If such things don't matter to you, then out-and-back is the best way to do it. While the entire trail is very scenic, the first seven miles or so are the best segment, with the most picturesque scenery and the most lakes. With an out-and-back you can avoid the twelve-mile segment from North Furlong Lake to Overland Lake, which, despite its beauty, has no reliable water sources. Also less enjoyable than the rest of the trail are the last few miles to Harrison Pass, along a gravel road, and also waterless.

From the trailhead it is 1.7 miles to Lamoille Lake, 2.4 to Liberty Pass, and 2.9 miles to Liberty Lake. After seven miles you will reach North Furlong Lake. Soon after, at 7.3 miles from the trailhead, you will reach the highpoint of the trail — Wines Peak, elevation 10,895 feet. Wines Peak is where you have the best chance to see the Himalayan snowcock, and in this vicinity you might see both mountain goats and bighorn sheep. At the actual peak there is a register on a footpath about twenty-five feet off the trail. Seek it and sign it, for you will have earned the right.

After the peak, the trail pretty much follows the crest. At 16.7 miles from the trailhead, there is a junction with Overland Lake Trail; stay right to continue on Ruby Crest Trail and to Harrison Pass.

Currently no fees or permits are required to do this trail, but be sure to get weather updates and other pertinent backpacking information before you set out. I feel that during a multiple-day trip it would be safe to leave a vehicle at Road's End, at the end of Lamoille Canyon, but leaving one at Harrison Pass might be pushing your luck, because it is so remote.

The route is pretty easy to follow, but signs can be knocked down or missing, which could possibly lead one astray, so carrying a good map on this hike is essential. I would suggest getting the map named Humboldt-Toiyabe National Forest-Ruby Mountains Ranger District. You can order it at *www.nationalforest-mapstore.com/*.

Ruby Crest Trail At a Glance

Best Season: July–September.

Length: Thirty-four miles.

Difficulty: Strenuous.

Elevation gain: 8,118 feet.

Trailhead elevation at Road's End: Eighty-eight hundred feet.

Trailhead elevation at Harrison Pass: 7,254 feet.

Warnings: Filter all drinking water. Exposure to the elements and afternoon thundershowers are common. Snow can fall any day of the year. No reliable cell service.

Jurisdiction: Humboldt-Toiyabe National Forest.

Directions to Road's End: Drive south on Lamoille Highway (Nevada Route 227) from Elko. Just before Lamoille, make a right on Lamoille Canyon Road and continue about 12 miles, until you reach the Road's End Trailhead.

Directions to Harrison Pass: To reach the southern end of the Ruby Crest Trail, drive south from Elko on Lamoille Highway (Nevada Route 227) for about 7 miles. Then turn right on Nevada Route 228. Drive about 30 miles, passing through Jiggs, until you reach the junction with Harrison Pass Road (Forest Service Road 113). Turn left (east) on Harrison Pass Road and continue about 10 miles until you reach Harrison Pass. With a high-clearance four-wheel-drive vehicle you can turn left onto FS 107 (signed as "Ruby Crest Trail Jeep Road") and head north for 2.6 miles to the alternate parking area.

Wildflowers carpet the meadows in midsummer.

Death

Valley

National Park

Death Valley National Park sprawls across 3.4 million acres, mostly in Southeastern California with a small triangular section extending into rural Nevada. Death Valley became a national monument in 1933, but it wasn't until 1994 that it gained national park status.

While the park is famous for severe heat and dry weather, you might be pleasantly surprised at the diversity of its landscapes and microclimates. Elevations range from 282 feet below sea level, the lowest place in North America, to 11,049 feet at Telescope Peak. In between you can find spectacular narrow canyons, colorful geologic formations, palm oases, salt pans, and sand dunes, as well as historic sites such as ghost towns and old mining camps.

After a rare heavy rain you might even find shallow water at Badwater.

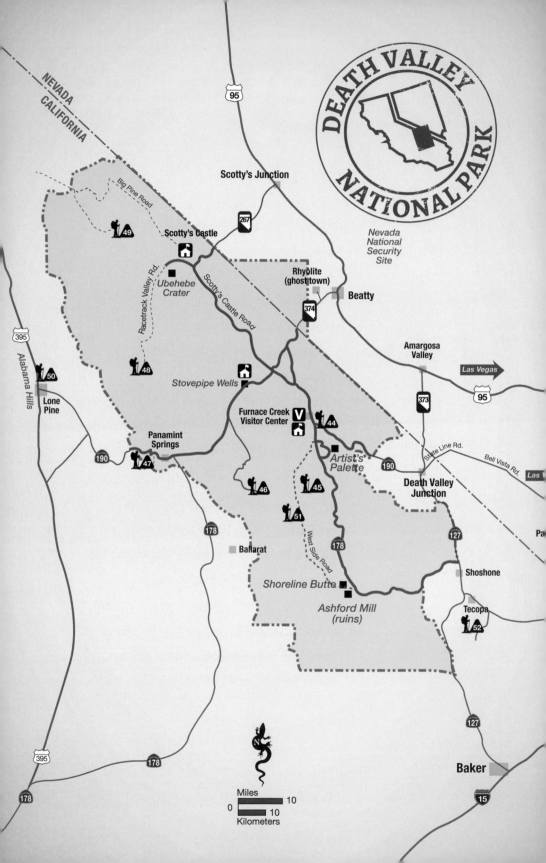

The best place to start a visit is the Furnace Creek area, the hub of the park. Here you will find the park's main visitor center and also Furnace Creek Ranch. The ranch has a concentration of services including two restaurants, a bar, general store with small market, gas pumps, a large motel, golf course, and the Borax Museum.

Just a quarter-mile north of the ranch is the Furnace Creek Visitor Center. Besides a bookstore there is also another museum, featuring great displays of the park's cultural and natural history.

One mile north of the visitor center, just off the main drag, is the site of the Harmony Borax Works, which operated from 1883 to 1889. Just a short walk from the parking area brings you by the ruins of an old refinery and one of the original wagons used to haul borax.

These wagons were enormous, with beds only four feet wide but six feet deep and sixteen long. Rear wheels were seven feet tall. Two such wagons were hitched together, with a tank wagon behind them to water the livestock. It took twenty mules to pull this combination, and two men — a muleskinner and a swamper — to handle so many animals. Twenty days were required to make the 330-mile roundtrip to the railroad at Mojave, but the outfit hauled thirty-six tons of processed borax per trip. The team and wagon became the trademark of the 20-Mule Team Borax brand, indelibly associated with its sponsorship of the TV show *Death Valley Days*, which aired from 1952 to 1975.

The best times to visit most of the park are from fall through spring, but good hiking can be found even in summer on the park's highest mountain, Telescope Peak, or nearby Wildrose Peak. Annual precipitation averages less than two inches per year in lower elevations although high mountain areas often receive more than fifteen inches yearly, and are often snow-covered in winter. Average daily high temperatures, in lower areas in July, run around 115 degrees.

The only gasoline stations are at Furnace Creek Ranch, Stovepipe Wells Village, and Panamint Springs Resort. There are limited medical services in the park. Carry much more water than you expect to need — at the very least, one gallon of water per person, per day, with enough to last several days in case your vehicle breaks down.

Free backcountry permits for backpacking and other camping can be obtained at the visitor center or any ranger station. Dispersed camping is only allowed two miles away from any developed area, paved road or "day use areas" which include some of the gravel back roads such as Wildrose Road and portions of Racetrack Road. Complete camping and backpacking regulations can be obtained at the Furnace Creek Visitor Center, any of the ranger stations or on the park website.

Although heat and exposure claim plenty of victims in Death Valley, the number one cause of death is single-vehicle accidents.

The park is open year-round and round the clock. The Furnace Creek Visitor Center and Museum is generally open daily from 9 a.m. to 5 p.m. with extended morning hours during busy periods. (760) 786-3200 or *nps.gov/deva*.

Directions to visitor center: From Las Vegas, take Interstate 15 south a few miles and exit onto Blue Diamond Road, Nevada Route 160. Drive west about 53 miles to Pahrump. Proceed through Pahrump on Nevada Route 160 another 4.5 miles and turn left (west) on West Bell Vista Avenue (there are brown National Park directional signs). Continue on Bell Vista Road about 20 miles, at the California/Nevada border the road name changes to State Line Road. Follow State Line Road another 6 miles to Death Valley Junction, California. Take California Route 190 west for about 29 miles to the hub of the park, Furnace Creek.

44 Zabriskie Point to Golden Canyon

ZABRISKIE POINT IS LOCATED IN THE BLACK MOUNTAINS, WHICH FLANK DEATH VALLEY proper on the east. This point-to-point hike starts in the Furnace Creek badlands and finishes up near Badwater Road. Of course, if you can't arrange to get picked up at the terminus you can start at either end, travel as far as you feel comfortable, and return the way you came.

When doing this as a through hike it is a moderate 2.5 miles. Although suitable for older children it's not advisable for young ones, as it is a bit long and there are some drop-offs over steep terrain.

It is also an exposed hike, and the badlands terrain holds heat, so be prepared for temperatures even warmer than in nearby areas. Don't forget the hat, sunscreen, and much more water than you expect to need.

The trail starts on the northwest side of the Zabriskie Point parking area.

Before starting on the trail, though, take time to hike up to the point itself. It's less than a five-minute paved walk to the overlook, and here you will be treated to one of the park's most stunning sights. Not only are there far-reaching views of the majestic Panamint Mountains to the west, but also to the vast badlands below, through which you will be hiking. Zabriskie Point is one of the premiere places to take in a Death Valley sunset or sunrise.

The point was named after Christian Brevoort Zabriskie, vice president and general manager of the Pacific Coast Borax Company for thirty-six years, until he retired in 1933.

As you are returning down to the parking area, look for the official trail on your left. It is faint, but it is outlined with small rocks. Immediately the trail heads west and starts descending into the badlands.

Nine million years ago this area was underwater. An ancient lake held water for several million years during which deep sediments collected. These included saline muds, gravel from mountains, and ash from the Black Mountains volcanic field. All this collected debris together is known as the Furnace Creek formation. Building up of the mountains to the west eventually caused the lake to dry up.

Manly Beacon is the prominent point seen in this photo and can be found along the trail from Zabriskie Point to Golden Canyon. Its name honors William Manly, who guided starving Forty-Niners out of Death Valley during the California Gold Rush.

Geological uplift and tilting, followed by erosion, carved out the badlands you see today.

Imagine yourself deep in a maze consisting of thousands of gullies and ravines, and you will have mentally pictured much of this hike's upper end. As you make your way through this labyrinth, it can be very confusing which way to go.

Pay careful attention to the metal signs along the way. Few other trails have so much signage, but on this hike it is essential to avoid getting lost. If you get too far off track in these badlands, it might take a very long time to find your way out.

Altogether you will lose about eight hundred feet in elevation by the time you arrive at the Golden Canyon trailhead, which lies 140 feet below sea level. But the way isn't entirely downhill, and within the first one and one-half miles it undulates quite a bit. This makes more work but will come as a welcome relief for those whose knees suffer during treks that are unrelentingly downhill.

From here the trail ascends steeply and you will arrive on the south side of Manly Beacon. This prominent outcrop was formed because lava cap rock, from eruptions three to five million years ago, protected everything underneath it from erosion. The place was named after William Manly, one of the life-saving men who guided hard-pressed Forty-Niners out of Death Valley during the California Gold Rush.

Continuing on, the trail skirts Manly Beacon to the left and then makes a steep descent into Golden Canyon. From here on you will most likely see many hikers who have traveled the one mile up from the trailhead below. Once in the canyon proper, the official trail goes left but if you have the time and are willing to add another 0.8 miles roundtrip to your outing, go right. This will bring you to an area called Red Cathedral where steep and colorful cliffs dominate the view. Iron oxide creates their reddish tint.

Returning to Golden Canyon, it is about one mile of easy, but sometimes rocky, walking to the trailhead. One of the most interesting things along the way is the evidence of an old road that was once here. In February 1976, a four-day storm dumped more than two inches of rain. A surge of water, mud, and boulders came down these narrows and took most of the road with it.

The moral of the story is, if rain even looks possible, don't take this hike.

Zabriskie Point To Golden Canyon At A Glance

Best season: November–March.

Length: 2.5 miles point to point.

Difficulty: Moderate.

Elevation loss: Eight hundred feet.

Zabriskie Point Trailhead elevation: 660 feet.

Golden Canyon Interpretive Trailhead elevation: *Minus* 140 feet.

Warnings: Exposed hike, route finding. Extreme flash flood danger.

Jurisdiction: Death Valley National Park.

Directions to Zabriskie Point Trailhead: From the Furnace Creek Visitor Center, drive on California Highway 190 east for 4.7 miles and turn right into parking area.

Directions to Golden Canyon Interpretive Trail: Drive east from the visitor center on California Highway 190 for 1.2 miles and go right on Badwater Road. Drive for two miles and go left onto signed access road.

45 Badwater

THE TRIP TO DEATH VALLEY'S MOST FAMOUS LOCATION, BADWATER, IS ONLY A SHORT DRIVE from Furnace Creek, and accesses marvelous scenery. Once you arrive at this salt flat, you will be able to stand on the lowest terrain in North America, 282 feet below sea level. From the parking area look high up on the cliff face across the road, to see a sign marking sea level, and reminding you just how low minus 282 feet is!

Experiencing Badwater can be as simple as strolling the wooden boardwalk, but it's quite enjoyable to walk out on the basin floor itself. It's flatter than the proverbial pancake and you can head out as far as you feel comfortable. Since most others don't venture so far, you can easily leave the crowds behind, kick off your shoes, and walk barefoot on this almost-unique surface. It's like walking in snow yet your feet stay pretty warm and dry. This barefoot experience is for winter only, because summer ground temperature can reach two hundred degrees!

Once out on the salt pan look west to the Panamint Mountain Range and Telescope Peak. Often snow-covered in winter, it is the highest peak in the park, at a lofty 11,048 feet. This is one of very few places you can literally see such a disparity in elevation.

Walking the salt flats at Badwater Basin, at 282 feet below sea level.

Badwater At A Glance

Best season: November–March.

Length: Optional.

Difficulty: Easy.

Elevation gain/loss: Minimal.

Trailhead elevation: *Minus* 282 feet.

Warning: Wear sunglasses.

Jurisdiction: Death Valley National Park.

Directions: From Furnace Creek Visitor Center take California 190 east for about 1.2 miles and go right onto California 178 (Badwater Road). Continue 17 miles to the Badwater parking area located on your right.

46 Telescope Peak

DEATH VALLEY NATIONAL PARK ISN'T TYPICALLY ON ANYONE'S SUMMER HIKING LIST, BUT if you want to climb to the park's highest summit, Telescope Peak, that's the ideal time. While daytime temperatures in Death Valley proper hit 120 degrees in summer, along the Telescope Peak trail you might find high temperatures in the sixties or low seventies.

The trailhead is located at the Mahogany Flat Campground, a rustic place mainly used by those hiking to the peak, because the last one and one-half miles of driving to it are steep, rough and extremely slow going. Make sure you stop and check out the Wildrose Charcoal Kilns along the way. These ten beehive-shaped structures, built in 1876, are some of the best preserved in the West.

You'll start the hike in a pinyon pine woodland, but as you travel higher vegetation will get more sparse. In July cliff rose will be in bloom, as will magnificent lupine. Other wildflowers that might still be showy include red Indian paintbrush, the Panamint and Death Valley penstemons, buckwheats, evening primrose, and Stansbury phlox.

Wildrose Charcoal Kilns, ten beehive-shaped structures, were built in 1876 and are some of the best preserved in the West.

Telescope Peak is the highest in the park.

The first couple of miles are somewhat strenuous as you will gain about fifteen hundred feet in elevation. When you reach Arcane Meadows it levels off, and the incline is minimal for the next one and one-half miles. Common ravens, Steller's jays, pinyon jays, and Clark's nutcrackers are the more commonly seen birds, but keep an eye out for the redtail hawk, mountain chickadee, and the dark-eyed junco, all known to frequent this elevation.

After about four miles the trail descends for about one-half mile and then you begin a steady and strenuous climb for the next couple of miles. Ancient bristlecone pines dot the landscape. Although they appear twisted and tortured by the windy environment, they are really so healthy that many are three thousand years old.

The final ascent involves hiking steep switchbacks and once on top you will be rewarded with one of the most awe-inspiring panoramic views in the nation. To the northwest lies the Sierra Nevada, where you'll see the highest point in the lower forty-eight United States, Mt. Whitney, at a lofty 14,405 feet. Looking down to the east you'll see the Badwater salt flats — the lowest point in the country, at 282 feet below sea level.

Be prepared for any type of weather. Even in summer, freezing temperatures and white-outs from snow storms may occur on the Telescope Peak trail. But there are no potable water sources, so you must bring along all liquid you will possibly need. Camping is allowed on the trail as long as you are at least two miles from the trailhead. You will need to get a backcountry permit from the visitor center in Furnace Creek, but it's free.

Telescope Peak At A Glance

Best season: June–September.

Length: Fourteen miles roundtrip.

Difficulty: Strenuous.

Elevation gain: 2,916 feet.

Trailhead elevation: 8,133 feet at Mahogany Flat Campground.

Warnings: Snow and ice common from November to May. You must have a high-clearance vehicle, preferably four-wheel drive with excellent off-road tires including at least one full-size spare, jack, and lug wrench.

Jurisdiction: Death Valley National Park.

Directions: From Furnace Creek Visitor Center, take California Route 190 west for about 33 miles, go left onto Emigrant Canyon Road for 21 miles and then left on Wildrose Canyon Road. Drive 8.6 miles to Mahogany Flat Campground and trailhead.

47 Darwin Falls

YOU MIGHT NOT EXPECT A STREAM TO FLOW YEAR-ROUND IN DEATH VALLEY NATIONAL Park, but a few do so, and one of them is a great hiking destination. Darwin Creek is a mostly unmodified oasis and a critical sanctuary for wildlife and riparian vegetation. It even boasts romantic pools and waterfalls.

Furthermore, it's readily accessible. Located in the western area of the park, near Panamint Springs, a hike to the lower fall and back is an easy roundtrip of one and six-tenths miles, with minimal elevation gain. Barring the occasional slippery rock, children will relish exploring this canyon, and most will even enjoy getting their feet a little wet in stream crossings.

Driving down the gravel access road off the main highway doesn't give any hint that within a half hour or so you'll be standing at the base of a year-round waterfall in a lushly vegetated box canyon. You will notice a pipeline running along the road; this diverts water from Darwin Creek to the Panamint Springs Resort just down the road.

From the signed trailhead follow the well-worn use trail down an easy-to-navigate embankment, into Darwin Wash. The wash is broad at this point, and you'll probably see a small band of water running down the middle.

At the start, vegetation is pretty sparse, mostly rabbit brush and four-wing salt brush, but as you continue you'll also find Mojave asters and desert globe mallow as well as many healthy colonies of cattails. All the water in the Darwin Falls area is fed by China Garden Spring, located a few miles upstream, just outside the park's boundary.

As the wash narrows and becomes more canyon-like, you'll find a healthy riparian habitat, mostly comprised of Gooding's willows. In the past, invasive, non-native tamarisk was growing throughout, but removal programs have been successful and most of it has been cleared, for the time being.

As you continue you will have to make a few stream crossings but nothing major. Watch where you step, because western and red spotted toads are found throughout the wash.

This area is also a birder's paradise; more than eighty species of birds have been documented. Some of the more interesting ones include the yellow-breasted

Water from a spring upstream creates Darwin Falls, a year-round waterfall in the western area of the park.

chat, yellow warbler, loggerhead shrike, western meadowlark, California quail, Cooper's and red-tailed hawks, and golden eagles.

Near the waterfall the dense vegetation creates a canopy so that even when you first hear the falls, you won't be able to see them. As you follow the path the pool will come into view, and once you skirt it to the north side, you'll see the waterfall that feeds it. At first glance the twenty-foot waterfall appears to be two falls, but it's really one pour-off split by a large boulder before it hits the pool below. Ferns and watercress grow abundantly in this shady refuge.

This lower fall marks the turnaround point for most people. Experienced hikers, if they crave more adventure, can backtrack about thirty yards, then scramble up the southeastern canyon wall. Here you'll find a faint trail that leads you to the valley above. You'll have to seek out the best routes over or around a few more obstacles, but you'll be rewarded with more cascades and waterfalls, including a spectacular one where a ribbon of water free-falls eighty feet down into a deep pool.

Experienced canyoneers rappel down the series of falls from the top, an excellent half-day adventure. Check with the park service for up-to-date regulations and obtain a permit if necessary.

Whether you make this an easy short hike or a more exciting activity, time spent at this oasis, in one of the harshest and hottest regions on earth, is sweet as the center of a chocolate.

Darwin Falls At A Glance

Best season: October–April.

Length: 1.6 miles roundtrip.

Difficulty: Easy.

Elevation gain: 150 feet.

Trailhead elevation: 2,516 feet.

Warning: Wet and slippery terrain within canyon.

Jurisdiction: Death Valley National Park.

Directions: From the Furnace Creek Visitor Center follow California Route 190 west for about 55 miles to Panamint Springs Resort. One mile past the resort, turn left onto Darwin Falls Road. Drive 2.5 miles up the gravel road, bearing right at the fork, to the metal gate that serves as the trailhead.

48 A Racetrack for Rocks

Racetrack Playa. Rocks appear to move on their own, leaving tracks.

DEATH VALLEY NATIONAL PARK OFFERS MORE than one thousand miles of paved and gravel roads, more than any other national park, but half the year, it's too hot and even dangerous to explore many of them.

Especially appropriate, for exploration in cool weather only, is the twenty-seven-mile, unpaved, Racetrack Road. The climax of this drive is the Racetrack, a playa or dry lake bed where rocks seem to move on their own, leaving obvious tracks. But there's plenty of interest even before that point, including the magnificent Ubehebe Crater and whimsical Teakettle Junction.

If you are well prepared, this is a great road trip to one of the most unusual places you might ever visit. The backroad portion of this trip begins at Ubehebe Crater. This crater, known as a maar volcano, was formed about three thousand years ago when molten rock came into contact with groundwater, touching off a huge explosion of steam and gas.

You can hike the trail which circles the crater rim in one and one-half miles, but beware the severe drop-offs. You can even descend to the bottom of the crater, but in that case, consider beforehand the return trip, a steep and severely tiresome trek of about six hundred feet.

From Ubehebe, the road heads south along the valley floor between the Cottonwood and Last Chance ranges. The road surface soon deteriorates into tooth-rattling washboard, but twenty miles of it will bring you to Teakettle Junction. For many years, the wooden sign marking this intersection has been festooned with several old teakettles, and tradition suggests you should bring one of your own to leave hanging there. Most are hand-decorated and marked with names, places and dates. You won't find any old dates as the kettles are removed from time to time, I assume by the park service. I have heard speculation how this custom originated, but if anyone knows for sure, I'd like to hear the story.

At Teakettle Junction you stay to your right and continue for about seven more miles to the north end of Racetrack Playa. The first parking area you come to serves the Grandstand, a large pile of boulders of quartz monzonite. It's worth walking to the Grandstand, for it is a good vantage point to see the whole playa, three miles long and two wide.

The playa is usually dry but when it rains it becomes mud. Don't walk on this mud when it's even a little wet, for footprints can stay there for years, ruining the landscape's natural beauty. And never drive on it, even if it's dry.

Visitors often leave a teakettle at this junction on their way to the Racetrack. Origin of tradition is uncertain, but the place is now called Teakettle Junction.

After enjoying the views here, head farther south about two miles to the second parking area. If the lake bed is dry, walk out about one-half mile, toward the southeast part of the playa, and the rocks which look out of place on the otherwise-smooth lakebed.

These rocks are various sizes from just a few pounds to some that must weigh more than a hundred. Each has a trail extending some distance from it, often in a graceful arc, but sometimes changing direction sharply. Some rocks have moved as far as fifteen hundred feet. Many theories were proposed over the years to explain the mysterious movements, but a research group claims to have found at least a partial answer in January 2014, using time-lapse photography. They discovered that on rare occasions when the playa is covered with water, and it's just cold enough to create a thin sheet of ice on the water surface, the ice can break up and, propelled by the wind, push the rocks around. Thicker ice doesn't seem to have the same effect.

Remember, this trip should only be undertaken in winter and should always be preceded by a stop at the Furnace Creek Visitor Center or other ranger station to check on road conditions, for they can change daily. If they tell you the lake is wet, consider postponing the visit to some time it's dry, when you can ethically walk on the playa. Since signs can be missing along the route, be sure to bring a map.

Even under good conditions, allow an entire day for your trip. To give you an idea what the road can be like, a Death Valley park ranger once told me he wouldn't even drive on it unless he had at least *two* spare tires.

Racetrack At A Glance

Best season: November–March.

Length: At Playa, walk as far as you feel comfortable.

Difficulty: Easy.

Elevation gain/loss: Minimal.

Trailhead elevation: 3,718 feet at parking area.

Warnings: This is isolated territory so preparation is essential for this trip. You must have a high-clearance vehicle, preferably four-wheel-drive, excellent off-road tires including at least one full-size spare, a jack, and a lug wrench. Cell phones mostly don't work in this area and sometimes many days pass before another person will come along to help you or summon rescuers. So your life may depend on having with you plenty of water, warm clothing, and matches. Food would be nice, too.

Jurisdiction: Death Valley National Park.

Directions: From the Furnace Creek Visitor Center drive north on California Route 190 for about 17 miles and go right onto Scotty's Castle Road. Follow for about 33 miles, go left onto Ubehebe Crater Road and drive 5.7 miles to crater. Continue south on the gravel Racetrack Road for about 27 miles to Racetrack Playa.

49 Eureka Dunes

IT TAKES DRIVING MANY MILES ON REMOTE GRAVEL ROADS TO REACH THE REMOTE EUREKA Dunes, but once you get there, you will find some of the tallest sand dunes in North America. The dunes are located in Eureka Valley, in the extreme northern end of the park. They have a base elevation of about three thousand feet and rise up nearly seven hundred feet more.

These dunes are approximately ten thousand years old and considered very stable. They are a National Natural Landmark, designated by the Department of the Interior in 1984. Unlike so many dunes in the Southwest, these are closed to off-highway vehicles, horseback riders and sandboarders, making a visit there more serene.

If you are up to the task, the greatest thing to do is hike up to the highest peak. Because of the soft sand this is a grueling hike, but it will reward your effort. There is no trail but the best way to hike it is heading up in the northwest corner by the

Eureka Dunes are some of the tallest in North America.

camping area, where the route has a more gradual climb to the first peak. Once you arrive on the first peak you can follow the rolling ridgeline to the southeast and the summit. "Eureka!"

The Eureka Dunes are known to "sing" or "boom," a phenomenon only heard in thirty-five desert locations around the world. When the sand is very dry, interesting sounds occur when sand avalanches down the steep sections. The sound supposedly results from sand grains sliding against each other. People say the sound resembles that of an airplane in the distance while others compare it to a deep note on an organ.

Other singing dunes include Panamint Dunes here in the park and Kelso Dunes in Mojave National Preserve, California. In Nevada there are Big Dune in Amargosa Valley, Sand Mountain near Fallon, and Crescent Dunes north of Tonopah.

While the sand is what people come to see, some interesting flora and fauna are found here. There are five endemic species of beetles and three endemic plants — Eureka dunegrass, Eureka Dunes evening primrose, and shining milkvetch. The most commonly seen animals include coyotes, black-tailed jackrabbits, and of course, rattlesnakes.

From the park's central visitor center at Furnace Creek, it is about ninety-seven miles to Eureka Dunes. The Big Pine/Death Valley Road travels north and then heads west over to Eureka Valley and is gravel except for the final four-mile section to the Eureka Dune Access Road turn-off. This access route is ten miles of fairly rough gravel, but most high-clearance vehicles can handle it, unless it rains. There is an alternate route to the dunes coming in from Big Pine, California.

Eureka Dunes At a Glance

Best Season: October–April.

Length: Varies.

Difficulty: Moderate-strenuous.

Elevation gain: Seven hundred feet.

Trailhead elevation: Three thousand feet.

Warning: Extremely remote gravel roads.

Jurisdiction: Death Valley National Park.

Directions: From the Furnace Creek area of the park drive north on California 190 about 17 miles and go right onto Scotty's Castle Road. Follow for about 33 miles and go left onto Ubehebe Crater Road. Follow for about 2.7 miles and go right onto Big Pine Road. Drive for about 34 miles, then go left onto the Eureka Dunes Access Road. Follow 10 miles to sand dunes.

~~~~~~

50 Lone Pine/Alabama Hills

LONE PINE IS LOCATED IN THE OWENS VALLEY ON THE EASTERN SLOPE OF THE LOFTY SIERRA Nevada mountain range. This small town, of about two thousand people, serves as a jumping-off place for visiting the thirty-thousand-acre Alabama Hills Recreation Area, as well as the Whitney Portal Road. This road takes you to the trailhead for Mt. Whitney, at 14,494 feet, the highest peak in the contiguous forty-eight states.

The Alabama Hills are characterized by granite boulders of all shapes and sizes, some of which might look very familiar to you. For more than ninety years Hollywood has used the hills as scenery for movies and TV shows. Two classic films shot here were 1948's *Yellow Sky*, with Gregory Peck and Anne Baxter, and 1936's *Charge of the Light Brigade*, with Errol Flynn and Olivia de Havilland. Other popular and more recent films include 1990's *Tremors*, starring Kevin Bacon and Fred Ward; 2000's *Gladiator*, starring Russell Crowe; and 2008's *Iron Man*, starring Robert Downey Jr.

To visit the Alabama Hills, first pick up a map and the "Visitor's Guide to Inyo County" at the Chamber of Commerce. Also pick up the Movie Road self-guided tour booklet. There is a network of gravel roads in the park and both booklet and map come in very handy if you want to access some of your favorite movie sites or just explore the hills on foot.

From Main Street in Lone Pine, take Whitney Portal Road 2.7 miles. Go right on

Right: While you are in the area drive the paved, 13-mile Whitney Portal Road. At the terminus of the road, at an elevation of 8,300 feet, you will find a fishing pond, streams and wonderful refreshing cascades surrounded by forest.

Movie Road and head out on the well-maintained gravel road. There are hundreds of great places to stop, explore and hike around.

The name Alabama Hills might be confusing to some. The story is, it was named during the Civil War by Southern sympathizers who were mining in this area. They adopted the name to honor the CSS Alabama, a Confederate warship then famous for its successful raids on Union shipping.

One of my favorite hikes along this road is The Alabama Hills Nature Trail, which features a couple of natural arches. One of them, Mobius Arch, forms a perfect picture frame around a view of Lone Pine Peak and Mt. Whitney. From

the corner of Whitney Portal Road and Movie Road drive 1.5 miles northwest on Movie Road. At the obvious fork in the road go right and you will find the parking area immediately on your left. This easy loop trail leaves on either the west or east side of the parking area. The trail undulates but it is only about fifteen to twenty minutes roundtrip to see the arches. The trailhead is located at about 4,666 feet, and the elevation gain is pretty minimal, about forty feet over the 0.8 mile loop.

While you are here be sure to drive up the entire paved, thirteen-mile Whitney Portal Road. At the terminus of the road you will find an elevation of about eighty-three hundred feet. You will also find a fishing pond, streams, and wonderful refreshing cascades surrounded by a heavily forested area. This road is closed once the snow hits each winter.

This is also where the trailhead is located for one of the main trails up to Mt. Whitney. This route is a strenuous hike of 10.7 miles one

It is a short hike to this arch that frames Lone Pine Peak, to the left, and Mt. Whitney. Below: The Alabama Hills are characterized by granite boulders of all shapes and sizes.

way, with an elevation gain of more than six thousand feet. If you complete this one, you're allowed some bragging rights. Unfortunately, it is so well known and so popular you must have a permit to hike it, even for a day hike. Most permits are distributed by lottery, and you need to apply well in advance at *www.recreation.gov*. Sometimes you can get a permit by applying in person at the Eastern Sierra Interagency Visitor Center in Lone Pine, starting at 2 p.m. the day before you hope to hike.

If you are especially interested in the films that were shot in the area, be sure to stop by the Museum of Western Film History, and enjoy its large collection of memorabilia. The museum stands at 701 S. Main Street, Lone Pine. For hours, museum events, and other information contact (760) 876-9909, *www.lonepinefilm-historymuseum.org*. Every Columbus Day weekend, the town hosts the Lone Pine Film Festival, which honors the heroes and heroines of the silver screen.

For more information on the Lone Pine area, be sure to visit the Eastern Sierra Interagency Visitor Center on your way into town. It's two miles south of Lone Pine, at the intersection of U.S. 395 and California Route 136. It is open daily, except major holidays, 9 a.m. –5 p.m., yet opens at 8 a.m. May 1–Nov. 1. Contact *www.sierranevadageotourism.org* or (760) 876-6200. You might want to also visit the Lone Pine Chamber of Commerce, 120 S. Main St. It's open Monday through Friday, except major holidays, 8:30 a.m.–4:30 p.m. (760) 876-4444 or *lonepinechamber.org*.

Lone Pine At A Glance

Best Season: May–October.

Lone Pine elevation: 3,727 feet.

Services: Lone Pine has a variety of lodging, restaurants, and gas stations, plus a small market and a hardware store.

Directions: From Las Vegas take Interstate 15 south to Blue Diamond Road, Nevada Route 160. Drive west for about 56 miles, traveling through Pahrump, and go left on Bell Vista Avenue. Drive west about 20.5 miles to Death Valley Junction, California. Go right onto California Route 127 for 0.2 miles and go left onto California Route 190. Drive about 133 miles (the road turns into California Route 136 just before Keeler) to U.S. 395. Turn right and drive less than two miles to Lone Pine.

51 West Side Road

THE FORTY-MILE, GRAVEL WEST SIDE ROAD SKIRTS BADWATER BASIN'S WESTERN "SHORE," hugging the foot of the Panamint Mountain Range. There are lots of historic sites to visit, hiking opportunities, and places to find good wildflowers in season. More often than not, you'll have the countryside to yourself.

About nine miles from the start of the road, on your left you will find the grave markers of James Dayton, a caretaker for the Pacific Borax Company in Furnace Creek, and of Frank "Shorty" Harris, one of the region's most famous prospectors. James Dayton died in July 1898, followed by Harris in 1934. Shorty had requested to be buried next to his friend Jim. In part the plaque on the grave reads "Here lies Shorty Harris, a single blanket jackass prospector, 1856–1934."

Behind the grave is a good starting point to walk across the entire Badwater Basin itself as long as you have someone to pick you up on the other side. It is a straight shot across and although it may look easy, it is moderately difficult traverse of about six miles. If you do the trek you will be surprised how varied the walking terrain is. The easy part is the hard salt pan but there are muddy areas, and you might also find small streams of water, as this is the final destination of the mostly underground Amargosa River, which starts outside of Beatty, Nevada. About a mile or two out from the Badwater parking lot, there is an area of hard salt buildup shaped like honeycomb. This is quite hazardous to walk in, and if you take a fall, it will not only be painful but will certainly cut you up. Never attempt to hike this if it has rained or rain threatens.

Just after Hanaupah Canyon Road, and about twelve miles from where you entered from Badwater Road, you can take a left turn to see the ruins of the Eagle Borax Works, listed on the U.S. National Register of Historic Places. It was the first borax refinery in Death Valley, yet short-lived, operating only from 1882 to 1884. The site at one time contained a storage tank, open tanks for crystallizing

Depending on Mother Nature, wildflowers can carpet the valley.

the borax, and a small house for workers. The present ruins are a boiler fire box and a mound where the house once stood.

Just after this is the sign for the California Historical Landmark of Bennett-Arcane Long Camp. This splinter group of the Death Valley Forty-Niners, emigrants from the Midwest, were stranded near this spot for weeks and almost starved to death. They were eventually rescued by William Lewis Manly and John Rogers, two members of the party who trekked more than three hundred miles to Mission San Fernando, fetching back supplies for the others.

When Manly and Rogers returned they found one man had already perished and many in their party had already moved on. Only two families remained, and they were led to safety. It is said as they headed west out of the valley, one of them said "Goodbye Death Valley," thus naming the area.

If you are looking for excellent remote hiking, just drive up the side canyons of the West Side Road, into the lower reaches of the eastern Panamint Mountain Range, and head out on foot. Only one road, Warm Springs, can be traveled all the way over the range. Three of the best hiking areas are Hanaupah, Johnson, and Warm Springs canyons. Before going there, ask at the visitor center about road conditions. To drive these canyons, be sure to have a high-clearance, four-wheel-drive vehicle, plenty of supplies, and *two* spare tires, for the roads are extremely rough and sidewall punctures are common. Warm Springs is usually in the best shape of any of them, yet I actually had two flat tires there, within a couple of miles of each other, years ago.

The best wildflower bloom is often found by driving up some of these side canyons, as there is more vegetation there than in the lower elevations along West Side Road. Peak wildflower bloom varies year to year, but is often in February. In this area look for desert gold, desert five-spot, brown-eyed evening primrose, and purple caltha-leaved phacelia. The park has a wildflower report on its website, telling where in the park bloom is likely to be best during the time you visit.

West Side Road At a Glance

Best Season: November–March.

Length: Forty-mile drive, point-to-point, plus optional side canyons.

Difficulty: Rocky and sandy roads.

Trailhead elevation: Below sea level.

Warnings: Never attempt to hike or drive this road from April to October, and when you go, be

West Side Road is little used, so self-reliant travelers can often have the vast landscape to themselves.

equipped to survive an unexpected and long stay. It could be days or weeks before another vehicle comes along in this area, and cell phones do not get a signal. Stay away if rain threatens.

Jurisdiction: Death Valley National Park.

Directions: Starting at the Death Valley Visitor Center in Furnace Creek, take California Route 190 about 1.2 miles east to the Badwater Road (California Route 178). Go south for about 6.2 miles and turn right onto the signed West Side Road.

52 China Ranch

CHINA RANCH DATE FARM, AN agricultural operation with a hospitable and playful streak, is one of the most unusual family attractions the region affords. It lies on one route to Death Valley, just a couple of miles outside Tecopa, California, about thirty-five miles west of Pahrump, Nevada.

Photo taken from the Mesa Trail, looking down over China Ranch Date Farm.

Although details are sketchy, China Ranch is so named because a Chinese man farmed and raised livestock in this lush canyon to provide food for local mining camps. In 1900, he apparently was run off at gunpoint by a white man who wanted the place for himself. Various owners followed, but things finally settled down in 1970, when it was bought by the Brown family that still owns and runs it.

Six trails start at the ranch, including easy ones for children. No matter what other hikes you choose, it's fun to begin with the two-hundred-yard Creek Trail, which starts behind the main building on the east side of the parking area, and makes an alternative and enchanting way to get to the date palm grove. Follow the trail as it takes you under a canopy of riparian vegetation along the narrow, yet free-flowing, China Ranch Creek.

Along this trail you will find a variety of water-loving vegetation including screwbean mesquite, seep willow, Gooding willow, and Fremont cottonwood. In the stream are crayfish and a native fish called the Nevada speckled dace. At the end of the trail you will come out along the gravel road near the edge of the date palm groves.

With different varieties of dates and ripening times, harvesting starts in the fall and usually continues through December. When ripening, date bunches are draped in cloth to protect them from rain, wind, and birds. The ranch reuses old clothing for this purpose. On a windy day, shirts and dresses flapping in the breeze suggest multi-colored ghosts playing in the palms.

One good hike is the Crack Trail, which leaves from the south edge of the parking area and heads down the west side of the canyon. The trail is about four miles roundtrip with about a 350-foot elevation change. This trail and some others travel off the private property into the jurisdiction of the Bureau of Land Management and other government agencies. Crack Trail has lots of diversity, including access to the Amargosa River about one mile from the start. There are also an old railroad bed, evidence of mining, and a slot canyon. This slot turns into a box canyon with a couple of ten-foot-high dry falls, which block most people from going farther.

The ranch and surrounding area provide homes for a variety of wildlife including gray foxes, kit foxes, bobcats, coyotes, jackrabbits, and cottontails. Birders enjoy China Ranch because migratory fowl can be found here, as well as year-round resident species. More than two hundred species of birds have been logged here.

Mesa Trail is about two and one-half miles roundtrip with an elevation gain of about five hundred feet. It begins across from the front door of the gift shop and

heads steeply up to the ridge where you will find elevated views of the ranch and down the canyon. Children will need to be watched carefully as there are steep drop-offs along the trail. For much of the year you can see the dark green ribbon of riparian vegetation and date trees, and appreciate what a spectacular oasis is tucked into this canyon.

The more challenging Cliffs Trail, about two miles long, requires rock scrambling and walking on scree. Ranch View Trail is two miles roundtrip with high drop-offs and steep areas, but as the name suggests, has wonderful views of the ranch. Bad-

In fall, ripening dates are draped with old clothing to protect them from rain, wind, and birds.

lands Trail is a good one for children, about one and one-half miles roundtrip. The gift shop has a trail guide with more details on the hikes.

The gift shop is open from 9 a.m. to 5 p.m. daily, closed Christmas. If you arrive prior to its opening, you are still allowed to hike. But once you've enjoyed the trails, I recommend you do not leave the premises without partaking of pleasure in that shop.

They give free tastes of different date varieties, so you'll know better which to buy. If you still can't make up your mind, they sell a variety pack. Tasty as they are, dates are fairly healthy, averaging only twenty-three calories each, free of sodium, fat, and cholesterol, yet a good source of fiber.

Often, they also offer warm date nut bread and date cookies. And they're always ready to whip up a date milkshake, which for many people constitutes the highlight of a visit to China Ranch. (760) 852-4120, *www.chinaranch.com*.

China Ranch At A Glance

Best season: October–April.

Length: Six trails vary in length from two hundred yards to more than four miles roundtrip.

Difficulty: Easy to strenuous.

Trailhead elevation: 1,237 feet.

Jurisdiction: Private and Bureau of Land Management.

Map: Trail map available at ranch.

Directions: From Las Vegas take Highway 160 west about 25 miles towards Pahrump. Before you get to Pahrump look on your left for the sign to Tecopa. Go left onto Tecopa Road (Old Spanish Trail Highway) and follow for about 31 miles. Go left onto Furnace Creek Road and drive about 1.4 miles. Go right onto China Ranch Road and drive 2.0 miles to the gift shop and parking area.

Mojave

National Preserve

Mojave National Preserve, as the name accurately implies, preserves for the nation a substantial slice of the unique landscape and habitat of the Mojave Desert. Located in southeastern California, south of Interstate 15 and north of Interstate 40, it's only a couple of hours south of Las Vegas.

Yet it doesn't get the level of use seen in other parts of the National Park system, so the quintessential desert experience — solitude — is still readily available here.

Its 1.6 million acres offer enough geologic and biological diversity to keep one occupied for weeks. Elevations in this park range from about eight hundred feet near Baker, to 7,929 at Clark Mountain's summit in the northern section. Highlights include sand dunes, lava beds, Joshua tree forests, seeps, springs, and historic landmarks. There are hundreds of miles of gravel roads to explore, including the historic Mojave Road.

If you have never before visited the preserve, the best place to start is Kelso Depot. The former Union Pacific train station, built in Mission Revival style in 1924, is worth the trip by itself. After the preserve was established in 1994 as part of the Desert Protection Act, the depot building was restored and now serves as the preserve's main visitor center and museum. Highlights include historic displays on the Chemehuevi and Mojave Indian tribes, railroad history, and early ranching and mining. Although trains no longer stop at the depot you can watch them up close, yet safely, from behind a fence as they speed by, about once an hour.

One of the best things you can do at Kelso Depot is pick up a map of the preserve, which will be a traditional, folding-paper version big enough to depict the sprawling preserve in detail. But since you will be traveling some distance into the park before reaching the visitor center, it's a good idea, before embarking, to download and print one from a desktop computer. Gasoline and other services

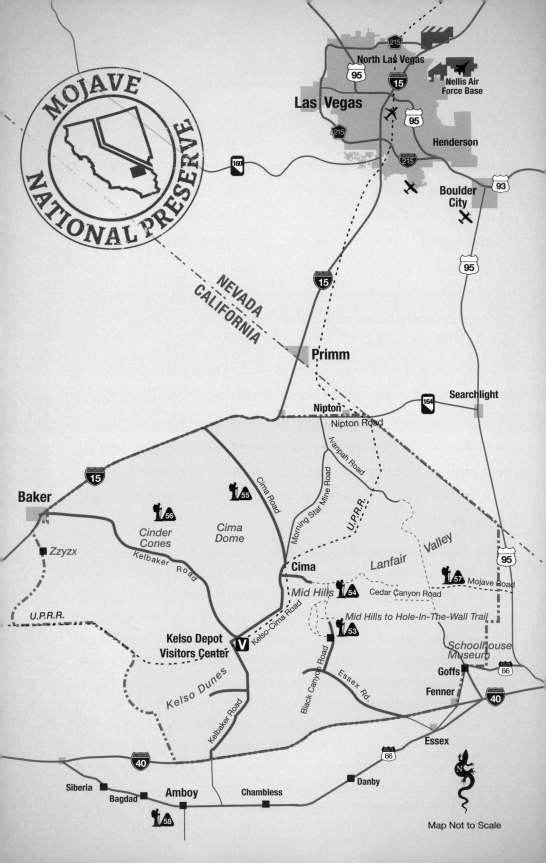

are unavailable in the park, so be sure to fill your gas tank before entering. Two of the closest places you can fill up are Baker, California and Primm, Nevada.

Lower elevations of the park are too warm to hike from May to September, except in early mornings. In July, daytime high temperatures average 109 degrees.

Hunting is allowed in some areas of the park. Peak seasons for very popular species, such as deer and doves — in September and October — are among the few times campgrounds are likely to become crowded, so plan accordingly. California and national park hunting and firearms laws are both linked to the preserve website.

The preserve is open year round, twenty-four hours a day. The Kelso Depot Visitor Center is generally open Thursdays through Mondays, except Christmas, from 10 a.m. to 5 p.m. However, days and hours seem to change often so always call first, to (760) 252-6108. The preserve's website is *www.nps.gov/moja.*

Directions: From Las Vegas take Interstate 15 south some 50 miles. Exit onto Nipton Road and go east 4 miles. Turn right onto Ivanpah Road for 3.1 miles. Go right onto Morning Star Mine Road and travel about 15 miles to Cima. Here, at the railroad tracks, the road becomes Kelso/Cima Road. Continue about 19 more miles to Kelso Depot.

53 The Rings Trail

THE RINGS TRAIL IS A SHORT HIKE BUT FULL OF FUN, DESCENDING THE DRAMATICALLY named Banshee Canyon and through a steep, tight slot. It's not a hike you will soon forget, for you'll make your way through this steepest part using metal rings and pins bolted into the rock.

From the parking area, the official trail is an obvious one that begins just behind two interpretive signs. But before you even start on that route, it is interesting to go left and follow a short spur trail to a fenced overlook, down into another canyon below. This is a hanging canyon — that is, a canyon whose mouth emerges on a cliff, so you can't simply walk into it. Once you descend the Rings Trail you will be able to head left and see the dry fall that formed at the little canyon's mouth, as water drained out over the centuries.

A hiker climbs the Rings Trail.

Returning to the official trail, just follow the path and in less than a minute Banshee Canyon starts its descent and narrows considerably. Head on down, picking the easiest route around the rocks and small boulders. The canyon then takes a sharp left turn and you will be standing at the top of the initial drop-off and first set of ringbolts. Here there are four. The ring system was installed by the Bureau of Land Management in the 1970s.

I estimate the first descent to be only about eight feet, but it's a tricky one to get started. The safest way to do this is to first turn around so you will be facing the wall as you go down. Position yourself so you can grab the first ring firmly with your hand, and then lower one of your feet and place it firmly on one of the bolts. Then grab the next ring beneath and so on, repeating this ladder-like pattern as you climb down to terra firma.

After this there will be a very short section where you will be able to walk normally, and then you reach the second drop-off and another set of rings. This segment has six rings and is a longer drop, but the rings seem to be placed better, so it will seem easier.

Since the rings were put in place with adults in mind, children will have to reach farther to grasp them, and the pins can be slippery to stand on. But with a strong adult below and another above to help, it's safe enough for children, yet so unusual they seem to particularly love this hike.

Once down at the bottom of the slot area, head out to where the canyon widens substantially. Banshee Canyon can be an eerie place, and not just because of the sinister name and unusual formations. When the wind blows it often causes a peculiar sound, suggesting the mourning call of the banshee in Irish legends.

This area was formed about eighteen million years ago when massive volcanic eruptions occurred here. Gas was trapped in the ash and formed the thousands of holes, windows, and odd shapes. Over time, rain and wind have enlarged these holes. Fossils from plants and animals can sometimes be found in the rock.

As for the hanging canyon I mentioned earlier, once you head out of the slot area head to the left and you will find the dry fall. It is perhaps twenty feet high with small hand- and footholds that have been chipped into the rock. In the Southwest these are often referred to as Moki steps. Years ago there used to be a climber's rope here and people would head up using the steps and rope together. The rope is no longer there, and I advise against attempting this climb.

Hole-in-the-Wall was named by Bob Holliman, a local small rancher and reputed gunfighter. The canyon reminded him of a Wyoming place of the same name, infamous as a refuge for outlaws.

After exploring return the way you came. The climb is a lot easier going up.

Rings Trail At A Glance

Best season: September–May.

Length: Three hundred yards with optional opportunity to extend eight more miles one-way to Mid Hills.

Difficulty: Moderate.

Elevation loss: Sixty-six feet. (1,200 feet elevation gain if extended to Mid Hills for point-to-point hike.)

Trailhead elevation: 4,288 feet.

Warnings: Tricky maneuvering on climb down slot canyon, using rings bolted to rock. Pants of canvas, heavy denim, or other rugged material are highly recommended. The slot is very narrow, so rubbing against the rock wall is unavoidable, and the rock can easily tear lightweight fabrics.

Jurisdiction: Mojave National Preserve.

Directions: From Kelso Depot drive north on Kelso-Cima Road 14 miles. Go right onto Cedar Canyon Road and follow for 6 miles. (After about 2 miles the paved road becomes gravel, but is well maintained and suitable for all vehicles except during or after heavy rain.) Go right onto Black Canyon Road and follow 10 miles, then turn right to Hole-in-the-Wall Visitor Center and Rings Trailhead parking area.

54 Rock Spring Loop

A RELIABLE WATER SOURCE IN THE MOJAVE DESERT DREW PREHISTORIC INDIANS, MINERS, cattlemen, and travelers to Rock Spring. You can follow the footsteps of centuries on the Rock Spring Loop Trail.

This hike is easy for all ages, only a mile long with a mere hundred feet of change in elevation. Yet it includes a historic stone house, a canyon with year-round water, the ruins of an old ore mill, the site of a nineteenth-century Army post, and dozens of petroglyphs.

From the trailhead enter the hiker's gate, and it's only a few minutes' walk to the Rock House. It was built in 1929 by homesteader Bert G. Smith, who reportedly came to the desert to prolong his life after poison gas damaged his lungs in World War I. It worked; he lived there twenty-five years. In the early 1980s, artist Carl Faber dwelt and painted in it. Nobody lives there today, but you're allowed to peek in the windows.

The loop trail starts at the west end of the Rock House and heads south, but soon swings east. On your left you will see foundations remaining from a mill that operated in the 1930s.

After the trail passes through another hiker's gate, continue down the right side of a short, narrow canyon. Then the terrain opens onto a natural bench above a wide sandy wash. Here you will see a sign giving a brief history of this site.

Camp Rock Springs stood here from late 1866 through early 1868. It was one of many U.S. Army posts established to assure safe passage of U.S. Mail and supply wagons along the remote Mojave Road between California and Arizona Territory. Conditions at the camp were harsh; fresh food and other supplies were difficult to obtain, so many men fell ill. Of seventy-three stationed here during the post's fifteen-month existence, more than twenty deserted!

Once the trail drops into the wash, turn right and head upstream. Look at the granite walls for petroglyphs — drawings etched into the rock by prehistoric American Indians. Never touch petroglyphs, as the oil from your hands can destroy them. Also, avoid climbing on rocks to get a closer look, for rocks can tumble, endangering not only the petroglyphs but also your life. Bring binoculars for a safer and less strenuous peek.

On the south side of the canyon is another interesting rock inscription which reads "Stua, 4th Inf. May 16." This was apparently written in either 1863 or 1864 by Charles Stuart, a musician in Company "B," Fourth California Infantry Regiment, California Volunteers.

A dozen yards or so upstream you will find a small flow of water. How much varies with season and precipitation, but even in the driest times there will be some. Sometimes it ices over, for the low sun of winter doesn't reach deep into the canyon.

When you are done visiting, return down the main wash and pick up the main trail as it continues east. Here you will find another interpretive sign, then the trail heads northwest to a ridge with fine views of the New York and Hackberry Mountains. The northern part of the loop is faint in many places, so be sure to look for the metal trail markers that will guide you around the rest of the loop, which ends between the Rock House and the parking area.

Rock Spring Loop At A Glance

Best season: September–May.

Length: One-mile loop.

Difficulty: Easy.

Elevation gain/loss: One hundred feet.

Trailhead elevation: 4,898 feet.

Jurisdiction: Mojave National Preserve.

Inscription on canyon wall, carved by soldier in 1863 or 1864. Later, U.S. Army established Camp Rock Springs here.

Directions: From Kelso Depot drive north on Kelso-Cima Road 14 miles. Go right onto Cedar Canyon Road. (After about 2 miles the paved road becomes gravel, but it's well maintained and suitable for all vehicles, except during or after heavy rain.) Follow 10.7 miles and go right 0.2 miles to parking area and trailhead.

55 Teutonia Peak Trail

Joshua trees, signature plants of the Mojave Desert, are especially dense near Teutonia Peak Trail.

THIS TRAIL TO TEUTONIA PEAK TRAVELS through the world's largest concentration of Joshua trees. Then it leads up and onto a rocky granite outcropping, where you will be treated to far-reaching, panoramic views of the Mojave Preserve's mountain ranges, sand dunes, cinder cones, lava beds and more.

Since there aren't any obstacles or drop-offs on the first section of the trail, that part would be suitable for children. But the last mile is a moderately strenuous ascent over rocky terrain, with uneven footing, so I can't recommend doing the entire hike with younger children.

From the signed trailhead just head southwest, up the obvious double track gravel road, toward the large granite outcropping which is your destination.

Here you will find a dense concentration of Joshua trees, one of the signature plants of the Mojave Desert. With long, twisting branches bearing palm-like leaves only at the tip, they suggest, to modern Americans, trees that might have been drawn for a children's book by Dr. Seuss. To early pioneers, they suggested the Biblical leader, Joshua, waving the Children of Israel forward to conquer the Land of Canaan. They're actually members of the lily family, and in spring bear basketball-sized bunches of white, edible flowers. Joshuas grow at elevations between two thousand and seven thousand feet, and thrive in a deep sandy soil along fairly flat or rolling terrain. There are some sizable ones along this trail, one towering more than twenty feet high.

Interspersed with the Joshua trees you will also find yucca, cholla, blackbrush, and Mormon tea. Keep an eye out through the vegetation for some interesting granite-like formations of a mineral called white monzonite. Some of this rock lies as flat as a pancake, almost appearing like a manmade slab, while other examples occur in shapes and forms that appear unworldly.

About one mile from the trailhead you will find evidence of an old silver mine: some timbers and tailings. Although at first glance they don't appear dangerous, it's safer to stay away from any mining area.

From here just continue on the trail as it heads west to the base of the outcropping. Head up this fairly steep section on the noticeable trail until you reach the ridge. Here you will get your first look to the west. Go left and travel along the faint route to higher ground and continue as far as you feel comfortable. The actual peak is too difficult to reach, unless you possess proficient climbing skills.

From up here there are sweeping views of the east Mojave. To the west lie cinder cones and lava beds and beyond that, you can even make out the world's largest thermometer, about thirty miles away in Baker, California.

Still farther to the west you can see the San Bernardino and San Jacinto mountains. To the south you can see the Kelso Sand Dunes at Devil's Playground, and the Providence Mountains. To the north you can see Clark Mountain, the highest peak in the park with an elevation of 7,929 feet. Clark is about fifteen miles away in the one isolated section of the preserve, north of Interstate 15 near Mountain Pass.

Teutonia Peak Trail At A Glance

Best season: September–May.

Length: Four-mile roundtrip.

Difficulty: Moderate.

Elevation gain: About five hundred feet, depending upon how far up the peak you travel.

Trailhead Elevation: 5,027 feet.

Jurisdiction: Mojave National Preserve.

Directions: From Kelso Depot drive north on Kelso-Cima Road for 19 miles and go left onto Cima Road. Drive 6 miles to parking area and trailhead on left.

56 Lava Tube

ONE OF THE MOST INTRIGUING ADVENTURE OPPORTUNITIES IN THE MOJAVE PRESERVE IS exploring an underground lava tube. This is a self-guided expedition, so your safety is in your own hands. But for the reasonably prepared, it's neither risky nor difficult.

A lava tube looks like a cave, but instead of being hollowed out by water, it was formed when flowing lava cooled and hardened on top, while the lava beneath ran out, leaving a tunnel of rock.

This lava tube is part of Cinder Cone National Natural Landmark, designated in 1973, an area that includes more than thirty conical mounds and hardened lava flows spread over fifty-seven square miles. The first eruptions occurred nearly eight million years ago, while others were as recent as ten thousand years. Still remaining are cinder cones about 150 to five hundred feet high, and thirteen hundred to three thousand feet wide.

The parking area is fairly large, but circular, so when you park, pull over completely to the side so other visitors can circle around and out. From here just walk north on the rocky jeep road for about three hundred yards. Look for a ten-foot-long section of rocks placed by human hands along the right side of the road, as well as some four-foot metal poles. This is where to look for the well-worn spur path that heads uphill toward a small cinder cone. There isn't much vegetation in this area except some creosote and yucca.

It only takes a minute or so to walk this side trail to the main entrance, but go slow and look on your left, just a couple of yards off the trail, for some small openings that lead into the tube. If you miss them don't worry, as on your return you will know where to find them. Just

Natural light filters in from a small hole, a natural opening, in the roof of the lava tube.

after these you will see your entry point, a segment of the tube that collapsed at some point.

When I first visited the lava tube years ago, there was an unsecured and flimsy ladder to aid you in getting down inside. Now there are some sturdy metal stairs. The staircase reduces one's sense of adventure but also minimizes actual peril, which those with children will appreciate.

Once down the stairs, head left and carefully climb down the rocky, uneven slope. At first it will look like you can only go about twenty feet, but once you turn on your headlamp and look closely, you will see the passage continues. You will have to bend down for a few yards and duck-walk to get through the narrow opening; if you're especially tall, you may even have to crawl. But once you're through this area the tube becomes less confining, with a fairly flat floor about as big as small bedroom's, but ceilings fifteen or twenty feet high. And it's sunlit, thanks to a natural skylight in the roof.

Lava Tube At A Glance

Best season: October–April.

Length: Three hundred yards roundtrip.

Difficulty: Easy.

Elevation gain: Forty feet.

Trailhead elevation: 3,560 feet.

Warnings: The lava tube is accessed by a metal ladder. Bring a headlamp or flashlight and wear long pants to crawl into tube. The access road is suitable for regular passenger vehicles except after a rain.

Jurisdiction: Mojave National Preserve.

Directions: From the southwest side of Kelso Depot, go northwest on Kelbaker Road. Drive about 15 miles looking for the large sandy parking area on your right, which marks the beginning of the unsigned Aiken Mine Road. Follow the gravel road about 4.1 miles, staying left at the signed fork near the second corral, to the circular parking area which serves as the trailhead.

57 Fort Piute

In the 1860s the major travel route between Arizona and California was the Mojave Road. The U.S. Army built Fort Piute to ensure safe passage of travelers, supply wagons, and the U.S. Mail, and to protect local water sources.

LOCATED IN THE EXTREME EASTERN region of the park, Fort Piute makes an ideal half-day excursion away from the city. It is in an isolated area of the park and involves driving on a remote gravel road to reach it, but once there, you will find the remains of an old military outpost, American Indian petroglyphs, and a small perennial stream.

In the 1860s the major travel route between Arizona and California was the Mojave Road. To ensure safe passage of travelers, supply wagons, and the U.S. Mail, and to protect local water sources, the U.S. Army built military outposts along the route, at remote places where perennial water was found. Fort Piute was built at the base of the Piute range at the mouth of the canyon from which Piute Creek flowed. The creek runs mostly underground except in this area.

Built on volcanic rock on a small rise above the creek, the miniature fort could protect teams and drivers at their most vulnerable, when they were watering after a long haul. It is thought the garrison was never more than eighteen men. There were two structures, one for the soldiers and one for horses. You can still see the footprint of these buildings outlined by the remains of walls of local rock. The original walls contained loopholes for firing rifles or muskets, and the entrance to the soldiers' dwelling had a screening wall built inside so that some attacker could not easily shoot through the doorway and hit an occupant.

This fort was only occupied for a few months, as the portion of the Mojave Road that traveled through here was abandoned and relocated a little farther south.

A rifle shot south of the fort you can see Piute Creek, which supports a healthy growth of cottonwood trees, willow, baccharis, and mesquite. On surrounding hillsides you will also find Mojave yucca, buckhorn cholla, barrel cactus, and beavertail cactus. With this reliable water available, many birds frequent the area, including red-tailed hawks, golden eagles, phainopeplas, and Gambel's quail. Red-spotted toads live by the stream.

In between the fort and the creek, look for the foot path that heads west by some boulders covered with desert varnish. Here you will find American Indian petroglyphs. This area was used by the Paiute, Mojave, and Chemehuevi people, and the last farmed here in the 1850s. Much of the rock art is abstract but there are some bighorn sheep and a great sun petroglyph.

It was once possible to see tracks in the bedrock, created by iron-tired wheels as wagons made their way up or down Piute Gorge, but the last time I was there they were hidden by vegetation. Hike up into Piute Gorge itself as far as you feel comfortable, on the visible trail on the north side of the creek.

Fort Piute At a Glance

Best Season: October–April

Length: Varies.

Difficulty: Easy.

Elevation gain: Minimal.

Trailhead elevation: 2,773 feet.

Warnings: Driving here requires a high-clearance vehicle with good off-road tires.

Petroglyphs can be seen at Fort Piute.

Jurisdiction: Mojave National Preserve.

Directions: From Las Vegas take U.S. 95/93 south for about 23 miles. At Railroad

Pass go right onto U.S. 95 south for about 55 miles. Drive on past the Route 163/ Laughlin turnoff and you will cross into California. Drive about 6.5 miles past the state line (to mile marker 75) and go right onto gravel road. Follow this for 7.1 miles and go right onto the power line road. Drive 1.3 miles and go left onto gravel spur road, and follow for about 1.7 miles to parking area.

58 Amboy Crater

VOLCANOES INTEREST ALMOST EVERYBODY, SO UNLESS THEY ARE SPEWING MOLTEN ROCK and poison gas, they are great to visit and especially fun to hike. Amboy Crater has been dormant for about ten thousand years, but it was once very active. It is surrounded by a forty-three-square-mile lava field, so rugged it was used to test the Mars Rover.

The crater was created by at least four eruptions, as they formed a collection of four coaxially nested cones, meaning the cones all had the same center.

From the trailhead follow the obvious trail toward the crater. The hike will bring you to the north of the crater and then to its west side, where you enter it from a breach in the crater wall. From here you can head up to the rim, which is about three hundred feet above.

The crater is about fifteen hundred feet in diameter and even though it isn't very tall, there are fine views from the rim. To the north are the Old Dad and Granite Mountains in the Mojave National Preserve, and to the east you can see the Old Woman Mountains. Directly west is the Twentynine Palms Marine Corp Base, so be sure not to travel in the lava field west of the crater.

In the mid-twentieth century, when U.S. Route 66 was the favored highway for travelers bound to and from Southern California, and others rode in comfort aboard passenger cars on the nearby railroad, Amboy Crater was a celebrated landmark on the journey. Everybody got to say they had seen a "real volcano." The custom declined due to the migration of auto traffic north to Interstate 40, and dwindling numbers of train passengers.

But looking in the other direction, from rim to tracks, train watching remains an excellent pastime today. It seems as if a train passes every few minutes on the Burlington Northern Santa Fe.

Back in 1883 the Southern Pacific laid tracks from Needles and Barstow, California, building water stations and depots along the way. They named them in alphabetical order starting in Amboy and going east. Most are mere ghost towns now, but are still signed: Amboy, Bolo, Cadiz, Danby, Essex, Fenner, Goffs, and so on.

The crater played a role in a wonderful story that happened back in the first decade of the twentieth century. A group of railroad workers, from the nearby town of Bagdad, brought to the top of the crater a lot of dried vegetation and anything else flammable they could find. When a passenger train was coming through Amboy, they lit it up and fooled the travelers into fearing the volcano was about to erupt.

After I had written that story in an article, I immediately received an e-mail from a fellow Southern Nevadan, who admitted he and his buddies pulled a similar prank in the 1970s. They worked for days to bring as many tires as they could up to the rim. Then they set up a timer to light them on fire, after they had left the scene, in hopes of establishing alibis based on being elsewhere. After a plume of smoke went up above the crater, tourists, and locals all went into panic mode and started to evacuate the area. Local lawmen caught on, though. The perpetrators weren't arrested but got a memorable tongue-lashing.

Amboy Crater At A Glance

Best Season: November–March.

Length: Three miles roundtrip.

Difficulty: Moderate.

Elevation gain: 260 feet.

Trailhead elevation: 670 feet.

Warning: Very rocky and uneven terrain when hiking in the crater.

Jurisdiction: Bureau of Land Management.

Directions: From Las Vegas, take Interstate 15 south some 50 miles, then take the Nipton Road exit, going east. Drive three miles and turn right onto Ivanpah Road for 3 miles, then turn right onto Morningstar Mine Road. Drive about 15 miles to Cima and stay left onto the Kelso-Cima road. Continue about 14 more miles to the Kelso Depot. Turn left onto Kelbaker Road. Continue south for 32 miles (crossing under Interstate 40) and turn right on Historic Route 66. Drive 7.7 miles and go left into the Amboy Crater access road. Drive one-half mile to parking area and trailhead.

Amboy Crater has been dormant for about 10,000 years, but it was once very active.

Zion *National Park*

Zion National Park, in southeastern Utah, offers some of the most stunning scenery in a spectacular state. The park encompasses 147,551 acres with elevations ranging from 3,666 feet in the southwestern area of the park, up to 8,726 feet in the northwestern section.

One of the premiere destinations in the park is the Zion Canyon Scenic Drive, which follows the North Fork of the Virgin River for about six miles upstream. Within this canyon are some of the finest of the giant sandstone monoliths for which the park is famous, some rising more than two thousand feet above the canyon floor.

One of the premier destinations in the park is Zion Canyon, where high sandstone walls and monoliths add drama to the scenic drive.

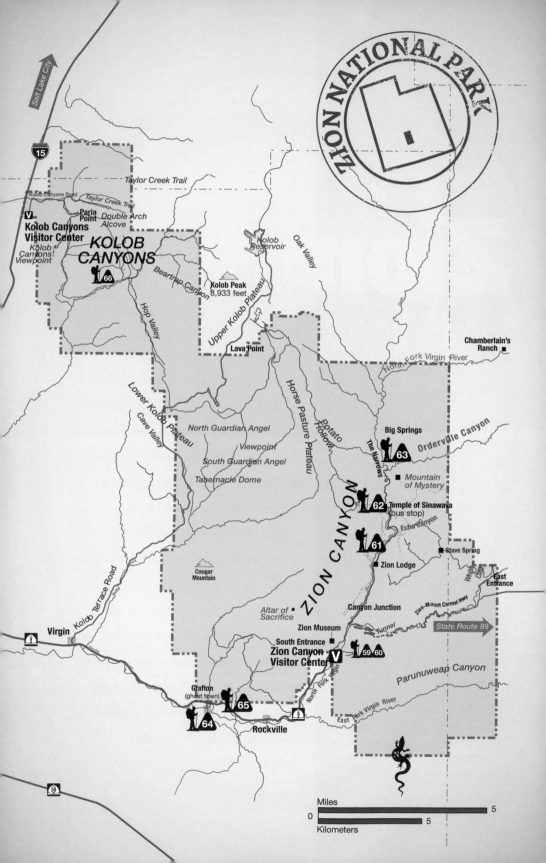

ZION NATIONAL PARK

Salt Lake City

Taylor Creek Trail

Kolob Canyons Road
Taylor Creek Trail

Paria Point
Double Arch Alcove

V Kolob Canyons Visitor Center

Kolob Canyons Viewpoint

KOLOB CANYONS

66

Beartrap Canyon

Kolob Reservoir

Oak Valley

Kolob Peak 8,933 feet

Upper Kolob Plateau

Lava Point

Hop Valley

Lower Kolob Plateau

Cave Valley

North Guardian Angel

Viewpoint

South Guardian Angel

Tabernacle Dome

Horse Pasture Plateau

Potato Hollow

North Fork Virgin River

Chamberlain's Ranch

Big Springs

The Narrows

Orderville Canyon

63

Mountain of Mystery

62 Temple of Sinawava (bus stop)

Echo Canyon

ZION CANYON

61

Zion Lodge

Stave Spring

Cougar Mountain

Altar of Sacrifice

Canyon Junction

Zion-Mount Carmel Hwy

Parunuweap Canyon

White Cliffs

East Entrance

Virgin

Kolob Terrace Road

Zion Museum

South Entrance
Zion Canyon Visitor Center

Tunnel

State Route 89

59 60

V

North Fork Virgin

Grafton (ghost town)

65

64

Rockville

East Fork Virgin River

North Fork Virgin River

N

Miles
0 5

Kilometers
5

Even if you came just to hit the trails, be sure to stop in at the Zion Lodge, the only accommodation within the park. The lodge has a gift shop, an excellent restaurant, and a large lobby. There is a superb collection of historic photographs on display both downstairs and upstairs in the lodge's restaurant. Outdoors, the front lawn area is the best place to see mule deer in the early evenings, and it is also frequented by wild turkeys.

While in the park, be sure to drive up to its east side. The road is still Utah Route 9 but is also called the Zion-Mt. Carmel Highway. Steep switchbacks take drivers up more than one thousand feet; then the road goes through the mile-long, dark and narrow Zion-Mt. Carmel Tunnel. This engineering feat took three years to build and was completed in 1930.

Spring and fall are the best times to visit although winter offers more solitude. Summers are hot and can easily reach one hundred degrees in July, so you will need to hike in the early mornings. In July and August thunderstorms are common which can cause flash floods in the canyons. Be sure to check at the visitor center and get a weather forecast before hitting the trails. Winters in the main area of the park are usually mild, but they do see an occasional heavy snow.

Free Shuttle Services: Zion Canyon Scenic Drive can be accessed only by shuttle in the busy season, generally from mid-March through October and weekends in November. Shuttles run from early morning to late evening, and during the busy seasons, as often as every seven minutes. Buses are fully accessible. Shuttle buses are also available throughout the town of Springdale.

Services: Springdale offers gas stations, a grocery store, restaurants, lodging, and specialty stores. Limited medical services are available in Springdale and Hurricane, and a regional hospital in nearby St. George.

The park is open year round, twenty-four hours a day. Zion Canyon Visitor Center is just inside the park's entrance station near Springdale. It is open daily except Christmas, from 8 a.m. to 5 p.m., with extended afternoon hours in summer and fall. The Kolob Canyon Visitor Center is open daily except Christmas, usually from 8 a.m. to 4:30 p.m. (435) 772-3256, *www.nps.gov/zion*.

Directions: From Las Vegas, take Interstate 15 north 125 miles to Utah Route 9 (Exit 16-Hurricane/Zion National Park). Follow Route 9 east for 19 miles to the main entrance of Zion National Park.

Directions to Kolob Canyons Visitor Center: From Las Vegas take Interstate

15 north about 150 miles to exit 40. Go right a short distance to the Kolob Canyons Visitor Center.

59 Pa'rus Trail

IT'S THE CLASSIC DILEMMA OF THE HIKING FAMILY: WHERE CAN WE FIND ADVENTURE satisfactory to adults and children, the robust and the rotund, bonded by blood or affection but varying in physical ability? The Pa'rus Trail in Zion National Park, Utah, is the best answer I've ever found. It is suitable for baby strollers, wheelchair accessible, and the only trail in the park that allows bicycles. You can even bring the family pet if it's on a leash.

The trail not only has stunning views of the park's signature red sandstone monoliths but also flanks the North Fork of The Virgin River. Here you will find a lush riparian ecosystem dominated by Fremont cottonwoods, and including mature single-leaf ash and box elder trees as well. Because of the mature vegetation and the year-round water supply, this is a great spot for birding and wildlife viewing.

It is an exposed hike, so slather on the sunscreen, wear a hat, and bring plenty of water.

The Pa'rus Trail is one of the easiest trails to hike in the park, because it is practically flat the entire way and paved, except one thirty-yard section. That short stretch shouldn't be an issue; I have been on it after heavy rains and it remained easy to negotiate.

The hike is less than two miles one-way, and runs from near the Zion Canyon Visitor Center, at South Campground to Zion Canyon Junction, located at the start of the Zion Canyon Scenic Drive. Pa'rus comes from the Paiute language, meaning "tumbling waters." By park standards it is a new trail, only constructed in 1995. Some of the park's other popular routes, such as West Rim Trail, date back to the 1920s.

The trail lies between the campsites at South Campground and the river. In this area there are plenty of short spur trails worth taking, to bring you down to river's edge.

You will be walking within the campground area for about one-third of a mile, and then it becomes more remote. The trail crosses a park service road and then over the first of five foot bridges. This one crosses Oak Creek, a drainage that is usually dry except after rain.

While you are traveling along the south side of the river, look at the wide-open meadow on your right. Mormon pioneers used this area to grow crops and fruit trees. With close inspection you can still see piles of reddish rocks that were moved aside to clear the field, and even some slight indentations still visible from the crop rows.

The towering monolith to the south, or right, is Bridge Mountain, 6,814 feet high. With some luck you will spot Crawford Arch. It is visible to the naked eye but much easier to find with binoculars. It bows out in vertical position below the left side of the peak, to the right of the saddle. The arch is about 150 feet long yet only maybe three to four feet across. It is named for pioneer William Crawford, who homesteaded in the Oak Creek area.

The paved Pa'rus Trail is great for hiking and biking along the North Fork of the Virgin River.

The most commonly seen animals in this area are mule deer. Although they might appear gentle, remember they are wild. Never approach them, feed them, or wander from the trail to get a closer look. Some visitors seeing a fawn by itself leap to the conclusion it has been abandoned. But in the majority of cases this is a mistaken conclusion, for a doe will often leave her fawn alone much of the day, returning when it's time for the little one to nurse. The mule deer's chief predator is the mountain lion. Lions are rarely seen here but their tracks are often found.

At the third bridge look upriver and you will see a diversion dam. The Flanigan Ditch dam was built to shunt part of the river's flow into Springdale for irrigation. The fifth bridge takes you over the river's confluence with Pine Creek, which drains down from Zion's east side, and flows through a narrow slot canyon. The trail continues under a bridge on Utah Highway 9, then up the short, yet steep grade to reach Zion Canyon Junction. Here you can return the way you came or hop on the free shuttle to return to the visitor center. All the shuttles can carry two bikes and accommodate strollers, and are wheelchair-accessible. With the exception of guide dogs, pets aren't allowed on the shuttle.

Pa'rus Trail At A Glance

Best season: Year round.

Length: 3.5 miles round trip.

Difficulty: Easy, paved. Handicap accessible.

Elevation gain: Fifty feet.

Trailhead elevation: 3,915 feet.

Warnings: Fully exposed to sun, hot in summer.

Jurisdiction: Zion National Park.

Directions: From the Zion Canyon Visitor Center walk across the main access road and across the bridge to the north, then go right for junction with South Campground.

Crawford Arch is 150 feet long yet only three or four feet across; with sharp eye or binoculars can be seen from Pa'rus Trail. It's located on the right side of the saddle, to left side of Bridge Mountain.

60 The Watchman Trail

THE WATCHMAN TRAIL IS ONE OF THE BETTER PLACES TO WARM UP BEFORE TACKLING ONE of the Zion National Park's more strenuous trails. Despite its name, this trail won't take you to The Watchman's 6,545-foot summit, but to a wide, flat natural bench below the spire of that name. This bench, however, offers a picturesque bird's-eye view of the town of Springdale and one of the best views in the park of prominent cliffs called The Towers of the Virgin.

The trailhead lies directly across from Zion Canyon Visitor Center. Since most visitors hop on the shuttle here and head to more famous trails along Zion Canyon Scenic Drive, this hike is often overlooked. You might have the trail to yourself and almost certainly will enjoy an uncrowded encounter with nature.

Children who can handle the trail's distance will enjoy the hike but there are a couple of drop-offs and lots of prickly pear cactus, so you will have to keep an eye on little ones. Rocky stretches with uneven footing might require a helping hand. There's little shade, so wear a hat and lots of sunscreen, and carry more water than you think you will need.

From the Zion Canyon Visitor Center, walk out to the access road, go left and directly before the bridge take a right at the signed trailhead. The obvious gravel trail first follows the east side of the North Fork of the Virgin River. In this section it is fairly flat as it travels through a riparian habitat made up primarily of Fremont cottonwood trees. The trail then veers away from the river, through a meadow and across a little-used park service road. There is a painted crosswalk here — which seems funny, as more wild animals cross this road than do humans — but it does serve as a signpost telling you where to pick up the trail on the other side.

Constructed in 1934, this trail is one of only two in the park that were made by the Civilian Conservation Corps, the public-works program responsible for many of the park's historic buildings and signposts. The majority of Zion's trails are either improved versions of those used by early settlers, or built by the National Park Service, some as early as the 1920s.

Watchman Trail begins next to visitor center.

Once you cross the service road you will head up the steep bank along wooden steps. If there has been rain recently this area becomes very muddy and slippery.

Here you are traveling through woods of pinyon pine and juniper, one of Zion's most common habitats. But at the top of the stairs, the trail starts up into a wide unnamed sandstone canyon. There are plenty of animal trails throughout this section, mostly worn down by mule deer, so be sure you're still following the wider and more obvious maintained trail.

Along the way you will probably see lots of lizards. These will most likely be plateau and western whiptails, the most common in Zion. If you are on the trail at dawn or dusk you might even glimpse a ring-tailed cat. I have never been fortunate enough see an entire ring-tail but have had a couple of quick looks at their bushy, black-and-white-banded tails as they scurried into hiding places in rocky cliffs.

As the trail continues on it makes a moderate yet steady ascent via switchbacks along the canyon's left bank. When you reach the trail's deepest point into the cliffs, you will find a little spring-fed stream amid the overhanging rocks. The waters support a small hanging garden of maidenhair ferns and other moisture-loving plants. From here the trail heads out of the depths of the canyon and up to the bench and overlook at the base of The Watchman.

Here you can rest, nibble sandwiches, and fairly feast on the visual treats spread around you. Far below you can see the community of Springdale, the main campgrounds, and the visitor center complex. You're also in the best place to fully appreciate the Towers of the Virgin, Oak Creek area, and the Three Patriarchs. And to top off a satisfying day among the pleasures of Zion, this is also one of the most easily accessed places to watch the park's legendary sunset.

Watchman Trail At A Glance

Best season: March–November.

Length: 2.7 miles round trip.

Difficulty: Moderate.

Elevation gain/loss: 368 feet.

Trailhead elevation: 3,906 feet.

Directions: Located across access road from Zion Canyon Visitor Center.

Warning: Muddy after rain.

Jurisdiction: Zion National Park.

61 Angels Landing

ANGELS LANDING IS KNOWN TO HIKING CONNOISSEURS THE WORLD OVER. THE TRAIL offers spectacular views and just enough actual danger to make it a genuine adventure.

The last half-mile of this hike makes it legendary. Hikers cling to heavy chains bolted into the rock while they walk a narrow ridge between dizzying drop-offs. The hike is no place for children or those scared of heights, but for the seasoned and surefooted, it's quite a thrill.

The trailhead is just off Zion Canyon Scenic Drive on the west side of the North Fork of the Virgin River, and is accessed by a wooden footbridge. The signed West Rim Trail serves as the lower part of the Angels Landing trail. From here looking north, Angels Landing is the giant red sandstone monolith.

The paved trail starts in riparian woodland of Fremont cottonwoods and velvet ash, then enters a rocky landscape of pinyon pine and juniper. Along the way you will also find scrub oak, serviceberry, manzanita, and ponderosa pine. If you head out at dawn you might see the ring-tailed cat, skunks, or even a gray fox in search of a meal. If you don't catch a glimpse of these elusive creatures you will probably see their droppings along the trail, often appearing purple — evidence they have been dining on the resident prickly pear cactus. Birds to look for include the spotted towhee, pinyon jay, canyon wren, raven, and peregrine falcon.

The trail heads north, gaining elevation steadily, and then west to the steep canyon wall. Here in the mid-1920s a series of steep switchbacks were cut into the rock wall to access the hanging canyon above. This passageway, called Refrigerator Canyon, is home to big-tooth maple and white fir, rare at this elevation of about

Hikers head towards Angel's Landing, the towering monolith seen here.

five thousand feet. On the right, the sandstone walls have naturally eroded into fascinating shapes, overhangs, and cave-like formations.

About a half-mile farther along, the trail takes a major turn to the right, bringing you to the base of Walter's Wiggles. This engineering feat is a series of twenty-one short switchbacks that climb more than three hundred feet, the brainchild of Walter Reusch, first acting superintendent of Zion.

The Wiggles lead you up to a large saddle called Scout Lookout, where the paved trail ends and there is a large sandy and flat area to rest. From here, those continuing on the West Rim trail head northwest for twelve more miles to Lava Point, located in the Kolob Terrace area.

But if you're heading for Angels Landing, you have only another half-mile to go. However, it is a half-mile you'll never forget. At some places the ridge is so narrow only one person can pass at a time, and in one section the drop-offs on each side are twelve hundred feet! I have seen few folks too proud to clutch the safety chains and bolts. In fact, on those dizzying stretches, I have seen people who weren't too proud to crawl!

On top it is fairly flat and there is plenty of room to move around, but there are no guardrails or any other safety measures. Windblown pinyon pines, twisted and stunted by weather, grow from breaks in the sandstone.

Panoramic views from here are among the park's finest. Allow at least four hours, to include enough viewing time. If you have fair warning of thunderstorms, ice, or mere rain, leave the trip for another day.

But do come back, for if you're ever in some other part of the world and someone mentions the famous hike to Angels Landing, you'll enjoy seeing the jaw-dropping envy when you quietly say, "I've been there."

Angels Landing At A Glance

Best Season: March–November.

Length: About five miles round trip.

Difficulty: Moderate to strenuous.

Elevation gain: 1,488 feet.

Trailhead elevation: 4,270 feet.

Warning: Cliff exposure with steep drop-offs. Not for anyone fearful of heights.

Jurisdiction: Zion National Park.

Directions: From the Zion Canyon Visitor Center take the free shuttle to the Grotto Picnic Area. Walk across Zion Canyon Scenic Road and across footbridge over the North Fork of the Virgin River and go right for West Rim/Angels Landing.

62 Riverside Walk

IF YOU WERE SHORT ON TIME IN ZION, AND COULD ONLY HIKE ONE TRAIL THAT WOULD BE good for all ages and abilities, then the Riverside Walk would be a good choice. In just a two-mile roundtrip your walk will follow the North Fork of the Virgin River, within a lush riparian environment, surrounded by Zion's signature red and orange sandstone walls. The trail is slightly undulating but overall the elevation gain is only sixty feet. It is quite common to see a lot of wildlife here, and it is an especially lovely trail to do in the fall when the leaves are at their most colorful, usually in early November.

The paved trail starts at the Temple of Sinawava Shuttle stop. The entire route takes you along the east side of the river. In the first quarter mile or so you will find yourself surrounded primarily by cottonwood trees, with a few bigtooth maples, velvet ash, and box elder. In this area of the trail it is also common to see deer, wild turkeys, and rock squirrels.

As you head upstream, be sure to stop and see the many places where water seeps down the canyon walls. There you will find maidenhair ferns, columbine, and shooting stars growing out of the cliff face. You will also see a couple of desert swamps thriving with many water-loving plants such as horsetails, cattails, and scouring rush.

There are many unpaved spur trails that take you down to water's edge, and they make this a great place to have a picnic, get your feet wet, or just rest while listening to the sounds of the water.

About one mile from the trailhead, the trail ends and you will be standing at the Gateway to the Narrows. This is the beginning of the world-famous hike where you drop into the river and head upstream, using the river as your trail. Conditions always vary here, and it takes planning to do even a day hike upstream, because of

The paved Riverside Walk travels one mile along the North Fork of the Virgin River. Its end is the place to begin an upstream day hike into the Zion Narrows. Below: In spring waterfalls are commonly seen on the trail.

the severe danger of flash flooding, especially possible in the late summer months. Outfitting yourself properly is also important. If you are interested in hiking it, see how in the next chapter, Zion Narrows.

Riverside Walk At A Glance

Best Season: Year round.

Length: Two miles roundtrip.

Difficulty: Easy.

Elevation gain: Sixty feet.

Trailhead elevation: Forty-four hundred feet.

Warnings: Ice and snow possible in winter. Flash flood danger.

Jurisdiction: Zion National Park.

Directions: From the Zion Canyon Visitor Center take the free shuttle (or in off-season, you may drive) up the 6-mile Zion Canyon Scenic Drive to Temple of Sinawava and Riverside Walk.

63 Zion Narrows

THE ZION NARROWS IS ONE OF THE MOST FAMOUS HIKES ON EARTH, AND FOR GOOD REASON. Imagine hiking up a riverbed through a canyon where red Navajo sandstone cliffs tower more than fifteen hundred feet above you, yet these walls stand only ten or fifteen feet to your left and right. Furthermore, along the way you will encounter lush hanging gardens, intimate alcoves, and spring-fed cascades falling from the canyon walls into the river.

The North Fork of the Virgin River serves as your trail. Over millions of years the river has carved a stairway through heaven for those willing and able to hike it. Often, it becomes a life-changing experience, inspiring hikers to reevaluate whether they're investing their short time on earth in the things that truly matter.

Depending on what type of adventure you are looking for, the Narrows can be done in a variety of ways. For most people a day trip upstream is satisfying enough, and it's a good choice if you haven't ever before hiked a canyon with your feet underwater.

This upriver route makes it practical to turn around and come back whenever you feel satisfied or tired. One good destination is the river's confluence with Orderville Canyon, less than two miles from the end of Riverside Walk. This is the

North Fork of the Virgin River serves as your trail for hike upstream to the Zion Narrows.

spot to assess your group and decide if you want to continue another two miles upstream to Big Springs. Those who meet the challenge will feast their eyes on deep pools, ferns, hanging gardens, and cascading waterfalls. And this next leg of the hike includes the narrowest, most romantic part of the canyon.

Hiking upstream past Big Springs requires a permit.

The definitive Zion Narrows experience is a through hike, which also requires a permit, and can be done either as a long day hike or an overnight. The latter requires reserving one of the designated campsites. It's a sixteen-mile trip, point-to-point, and coming downstream, so you'll have to arrange private transportation to the Chamberlain's Ranch trailhead.

With slippery rocks, hundreds of river crossings and unavoidable dips in cold water, even those in tip-top shape will find the journey demanding. Through hikes usually take about ten to twelve hours, depending on your group and rest stops. Carry a headlamp in case you need to finish your trip after dark.

Whether you're taking the short day trip upstream or daring the longer through hike, it is a must to wear hiking boots with good ankle supports, and take a sturdy walking stick to serve as a third leg on the river crossings. (Depending on your height and weight, a heavy-duty wooden dowel from a home improvement store, about an inch to inch and one-half thick and about five and one-half feet long, is about right.) Always outfit yourself in synthetic fabrics. Never wear cotton on any outdoor adventure, for it loses all insulating value when wet.

Line your backpack with a heavy garbage bag to waterproof it for the inevitable slip and fall into the chilly waters. With water so cold, strong currents, slippery rocks, and deep pools, this is obviously no hike for small children.

Even the experienced should not underestimate it. It is a lovely excursion well worth calculated risks, but those risks are real.

Flash flooding is the biggest concern and many people have died in this canyon, as there are no escape routes during much of the hike. It can be sunny and clear in Zion even while storms miles away flood the canyon in seconds. So it's imperative to check in at the Back Country Desk, the day of your trip or no more than one day ahead of it, about weather upstream. The desk can give you a weather forecast and also estimate flash flood potential and water flow. Measured in cubic feet per second (CFS), the flow is the most important indicator of what your trip will be like. A CFS of seventy or lower usually makes a trip into the Narrows a pleasant one.

A canyoneer makes his way downstream
in the world-famous Zion Narrows.

Permits for the through hike, and for camping, are available either by advance reservation at the park website, or on a walk-in basis the day before your planned hike. But the number issued is limited, and they go fast.

By late fall or winter you will need a drysuit and other special equipment to do it safely. May, June, September and October are usually the best times.

Zion Narrows At A Glance

OUT-AND-BACK HIKE

Best season: May–September, but avoid late July and August due to high flash-flood potential. Year-round if prepared with drysuit and other winter canyoneering clothing and footwear.

Length: Travel upstream as far as you feel comfortable or to Big Springs.

Difficulty: Difficulty depends on water flow in the Virgin River, which serves as your trail. Under seventy cubic feet per second (CFS) will make a moderate hike upstream, but deep holes always lurk.

Trailhead elevation: Forty-four hundred feet at Riverside Walk entry.

Warning: Small children should not hike the Zion Narrows.

Flash flooding: All narrow canyons are potentially dangerous and conditions change daily. Mid-summer and early fall are prone to flash floods. Always check forecast of weather and flash flood potential at the Zion Canyon Visitor Center.

Permit: Not needed for day hike upstream as far as Big Springs.

Equipment: Walking stick, hiking boots with ankle support, dry suit in winter.

Directions to Riverside Walk Trailhead: From Zion Canyon Visitor Center take the free Zion shuttle to Temple of Siniwava shuttle stop. Walk the 1-mile paved Riverside Walk, drop into the North Fork of the Virgin River and head upstream.

POINT-TO-POINT HIKE

Best season: May–September, except late July and August, which have high flash flood potential.

Length: Sixteen miles to Riverside Walk.

Difficulty: Strenuous.

Elevation loss: Thirteen hundred feet.

Trailhead elevation: 5,700 feet at Chamberlain's Ranch.

Permits: Mandatory for through hikes and for camping in the canyon. Many dates, especially weekends, are filled quickly. Permits will not be issued if water flow is more than 120 CFS.

Warnings: Hypothermia danger. Dress in layers of synthetic fabrics such as fleece, no cotton. Wear Neoprene booties. Waterproof all belongings. Bring a sturdy walking staff. All canyon water requires purification before drinking.

Shuttle to Chamberlain's Ranch trailhead: Private vehicle or reservation through Zion Adventure Company, Springdale, Utah.

Directions to Chamberlain Ranch: From Zion's east entrance on Utah Route 9 (Mount Carmel Highway) drive 2.4 miles, go left on North Fork Road and drive 18 miles. Turn left at small bridge and drive .25 mile to the Chamberlain's Ranch gate.

64 Grafton

WHEN VISITING ZION NATIONAL PARK BE SURE TO MAKE A SIDE TRIP TO THE GHOST TOWN of Grafton. It is about a twenty-minute drive from the park's entrance and if you are coming from Las Vegas, it will be only a ten-minute drive out of your way.

On the National Register of Historic Places, Grafton is better preserved than most pioneer towns, so it is worth walking around here for half an hour or so. Here you will find a bucolic setting of meadows and fruit orchards, all with a Zion backdrop.

This will be a self-guided tour, but they have a map and guide available on site that gives you information on the historic buildings and cemetery. Don't be surprised if you are the only visitors there, as most people are unaware of Grafton's existence.

The town was first settled in 1861, on the banks of the Virgin River about one mile downstream from its current location. A powerful flash flood in 1862 destroyed the town but the townsfolk relocated and started over. Flooding remained a problem, as it still does today along the Virgin River banks. And when the hot summer weather came in dry years, sometimes there wasn't enough water for their crops.

The restored Grafton Schoolhouse/church was built in 1886 and is a two-story building made with adobe on top of lava rocks used as a foundation. The school was closed after the 1918–1919 school year, when only nine students answered the roll call. By 1906, the majority of the residents had moved down to the settlement now called Hurricane, Utah. The townsfolk there had built the Hurricane Canal which diverted some of the Virgin River's water to be used to water crops. In 1945, no one was living in Grafton.

If Grafton looks familiar to you, it may be because it was one of the locations in the popular movie *Butch Cassidy and the Sundance Kid*. A famous scene shot here depicted Butch Cassidy (Paul Newman) and Sundance's girlfriend Etta Place (Katharine Ross) riding around on a bicycle and also Cassidy showing off his

The historic schoolhouse in Grafton. Right: Visitors can even take a swing here.

solo bike tricks. It is a classic scene and the background song from it, "Raindrops Keep Falling on My Head," remains well known.

After walking around the town, make sure to visit the small Grafton Cemetery, located about one-third of a mile from the main townsite. The cemetery was used from 1862 to 1924, and supposedly holds between seventy-four and eighty-four graves, although many headstones are missing.

A visit here will make you realize how tough life was for these early settlers. In 1866 alone they buried six victims of diphtheria, two of scarlet fever, two from a freak accident, one of unknown cause, and three killed by Navajo raiders.

The Townsite is under the watchful eye of the Grafton Heritage Partnership Project. The partnership has raised more than one million dollars and has bought and restored the Grafton schoolhouse and the Russell Home. It also has been responsible for keeping the fencing in place and installing interpretive signs. (435) 635-2133, *graftonheritage.org*.

Grafton At A Glance

Best Season: Year round.

Difficulty: Easy.

Trailhead elevation: 3,678 feet.

Warnings: The road to Grafton can be muddy and impassable after or during rain or snow.

Directions: From Las Vegas take Interstate 15 north 125 miles to Utah Route 9 (Exit 16- Hurricane/Zion National Park). Follow Utah 9 east for about 16 miles to Rockville. Go right at Bridge Street. Cross over the Virgin River using the one-lane bridge, then follow the road for about 3.5 miles, staying right when in doubt, until it dead ends. The route is paved at the beginning then becomes a well-maintained gravel road, suitable for most passenger vehicles except after or during rain or snow.

65 Huber Wash

WHILE ZION USUALLY ENJOYS FAIRLY MILD WINTERS, HEAVY SNOW SOMETIMES WILL FALL IN the park, severely limiting the trails you can safely do. If you are visiting when snow (or severe cold) arrives, it is best to head down to the park's desert lowland area. It is located in the little-visited southwestern corner of the park, near Rockville, and offers a few quality trails, all having the virtue of a high level of solitude.

Huber Wash trail is 4.6 miles roundtrip and is located near the base of Mt. Kinesava. The Trail itself is primarily in a sandy wash with a few rocky areas, and it ends in a box canyon with a petrified log jam. Just enough water seeps out here to support hanging gardens of water-loving plants. These are fairly rare in the desert but found throughout Zion on many trails. There is some minimal rock scrambling in a few areas of the wash, but most children, or even adults with bad knees, if able to hike that distance, should be able to handle the scrambling.

From the parking pullout, pass through the gate, leaving it opened or closed as you found it. You will start walking north on a gravel road and then drop down to your left into the obvious wash on one of the many spur paths, and head right, away from the highway. The trail enters the park boundary about 0.4 miles from where you parked.

As you hike, look for animal tracks in the sandy wash. You might see evidence of a gray fox, mule deer, bobcat. mountain lion, or other animal. Other things to look for are small pieces of petrified wood. Please admire it but don't be tempted to keep even a small sample. It is illegal and in every town around this area there

A pleasant stroll along Huber Wash.

junction for Kolob Arch. The La Verkin Trail continues but you will go left on a half-mile spur trail. Assess the weather before heading up, as it is subject to flash flooding. You will have to do some rock scrambling along this segment. If you have been here before, you'll notice there has been a rock fall fairly recently, but the route is still accessible.

Measuring an arch is not as easy as it sounds and at one time Kolob Arch was thought to be the largest free-standing natural arch in the world. After measuring the arch in 1996, the Natural Arch and Bridge Society now considers it to be the second longest, with a span of 287.4 feet (plus or minus two feet). This is not much shorter than the 290.1-foot (plus or minus eight-tenths of a foot) span of Landscape Arch, also in Utah at Arches National Park.

Camping is allowed only in designated sites. Camping permits can be obtained in person at the Kolob Canyon Visitor Center, or you can make reservations online for some of the campsites. This is a popular backpack, so be sure to make those reservations well in advance, or else be the first person at the visitor center in the morning to secure a permit. Always have an alternate hiking and camping plan in case the campsites are full.

Day hikers do not need a permit but should check at the visitor center for updated trail conditions before heading out. The weather in this area of the park can be unpredictable. I once attempted this hike in early October but was turned back when Kolob Canyon Road was closed by heavy snow. On the other hand, I once did the hike on Dec. 24, and the entire trail was snow-free.

Kolob Arch At A Glance

Best season: March–November.

Length: Fourteen miles roundtrip.

Difficulty: Strenuous.

Elevation loss: Seven hundred feet.

Trailhead elevation: 6,074 feet.

Permits: Needed for camping, not for day trip.

Warning: Flash flood danger.

Jurisdiction: Zion National Park's Kolob Canyons.

Directions: From Kolob Canyon Visitor Center, drive east on Kolob Canyon Road for about 3.5 miles to Lee Pass parking area and the signed La Verkin Creek trailhead.

Kolob Canyons section of Zion in the northwestern section of the park.

Cedar

Breaks

National Monument

Located on the west-facing side of the ten-thousand-foot-high Markagunt Plateau, Cedar Breaks National Monument is the highest unit operated by the National Park Service. Summer average high temperatures are between sixty and seventy Fahrenheit with overnight lows thirty to forty, but snow can fall any time of the year. Although it's open year round, deep snows usually cover the monument from late October through mid-May, and access then requires snowshoes, cross-country skis, or a snowmobile.

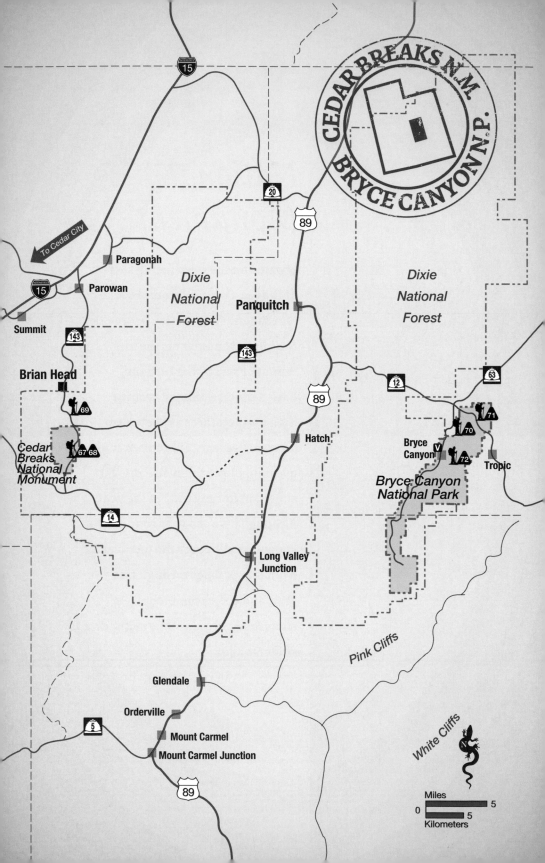

CEDAR BREAKS N.M.
BRYCE CANYON N.P.

To Cedar City

15 INTERSTATE

Paragonah

15 INTERSTATE
Parowan

Summit

143

Brian Head

69

Cedar Breaks National Monument

67 **68**

14

Dixie National Forest

20

89 US

Panquitch

143

89 US

Hatch

Dixie National Forest

12

63

71

70

Bryce Canyon

V

72

Tropic

Bryce Canyon National Park

Long Valley Junction

Pink Cliffs

Glendale

Orderville

5

Mount Carmel

Mount Carmel Junction

89 US

White Cliffs

N

Miles
0   5
Kilometers
                    5

The principal feature of Cedar Breaks is a giant amphitheater that is three miles wide and two thousand feet deep. Some Indians called this "The Circle of Painted Cliffs," for reds, oranges, pinks and even purples paint the landscape, and the palette varies even more in the changing light throughout the day. In the amphitheater are many unusual geological formations, some called "fins" that look like free-standing walls; some arches; and some upright columns called "hoodoos" because some people think they look as if grotesque living beings had been somehow turned to stone.

They're actually a product of weather, not witchcraft. It rains and snows a good deal here, so water trickles down through cracks in the cliffs, eating away the limestone. Water in the cracks repeatedly freezes and thaws, expanding the cracks, which eventually become gullies. A portion of cliff between gullies is left standing like a narrow wall, extending from the cliff face. This wall or "fin" is protected from erosion above by a capstone of harder rock. But erosion continues on each exposed side of the fin, until the fin is worn through, creating an arch. Eventually, the unsupported capstone over the open arch may collapse, leaving a freestanding column, or hoodoo.

The process produces a confused landscape of little use for farming or grazing, so settlers called places like this "badlands" or in this case "breaks," which means the same. And they added "cedar" to the name because many juniper trees, which were incorrectly but commonly called cedars, grew there.

Though not of practical use, its aesthetic beauty was always appreciated, and the

Views into the natural amphitheater filled with hoodoos.

The historic visitor center was built in 1937 by the CCC, directly on rim of natural amphitheater.

area was named a national monument in 1933. Four years later the Civilian Conservation Corps built the historic log cabin visitor center along the amphitheater rim. Just a short walk from the parking area, it is generally open from late May through mid-October from 8 a.m. to 6 p.m. (435) 586-0787, *www.nps.gov/cebr*.

There are no gasoline stations or restaurants in the park. but Brian Head, just a few miles down the road, has these services. Full services are available in Cedar City.

Directions: From Las Vegas, take Interstate 15 north 162 miles to exit 57, Cedar City, Utah. Go north on Utah Route 14, taking a right after 2 miles, which continues Route 14. Drive 15.4 miles farther and go left onto Scenic Byway 148. Drive about 3 miles to Cedar Breaks National Monument main entrance.

37 Alpine Pond Trail

THERE IS NO BETTER TIME THAN THE END OF JULY, WHEN WILDFLOWERS ARE AT THEIR PEAK, to hike the Alpine Pond Trail. And while flowers also grow elsewhere, this trail has attributes superior to others nearby, so it's a better choice. You will be treated to spectacular views into a natural rock amphitheater two thousand feet deep, and pass by a serene alpine pond. You'll never have to retrace your steps, because the hike can be done as a loop or a figure eight.

Because the monument lies at such a high elevation, you will also enjoy wonderfully cool temperatures. Summer daytime temperatures average in the seventies with nighttime in the forties.

If you take the complete figure-eight hike, you will travel about two miles. If you choose to just go to the pond and loop back to the trailhead, it will be about one mile. This is a great trail for a family, as the elevation gain is less than two hundred feet and therefore not too strenuous even for little ones. If you do have children along, keep a close eye when walking near the rim, as there are several areas with high drop-offs but without guardrails. The rest of the trail is fairly safe except for some uneven footing, mostly from tree roots.

From the Chessman Overlook, pick up the obvious path and follow it into the woods toward the rim. Right from the start you will be in a sub-alpine forest surrounded by bristlecone pines, fir, and Engelmann spruce. The spruce trees won't be hard to identify anywhere on the plateau, as they are now mere standing skeletons, victims of the bark-beetle epidemic of the 1990s.

Wildflowers peak in late July, but you can usually find a good show of flowers through mid-August. Along the trail you will find dense concentrations of lupine and Colorado columbine. You might see a few hummingbirds, but most likely you will be looking at white-lined sphinx moths. They look and act like hummingbirds but are smaller and seem to favor these flowers. It isn't uncommon to see dozens at once taking their fill of nectar from inside the blooms.

Wildflowers thrive on the plateau because of fertile sedimentary soil and monsoon moisture. The latter is a product of the plateau's high elevation. Moist air from the Pacific comes this way in summer. Because hot air holds more moisture, these currents remain moist as they cross the Mojave Desert. But upon hitting the colder plateau, the air cools, and releases its moisture as monsoon rain.

Try to get on the trail early because these rains generally hit from 10 a.m. to 11 a.m. daily. Also be prepared for thunderstorms in the afternoons. They can come on fast and furious.

The alpine pond is located where the figure-eight loop meets in the middle, and because of special conditions there are additional types of wildflowers to be seen. Some worth noting are Canada violet, wild strawberry, Parry primrose, heartleaf bittercress, and bog violet.

I have never seen anyone fishing in this pond, but if you are a licensed Utah angler you could try catching some exotic brook trout. This pond was stocked with them for about sixty years, until 1975, and some of their descendants still live there. Even

Alpine Pond Trail in late July boasts wildflowers such as lupine, seen here.

though the pond freezes in winter, the source springs continue to pour unfrozen water under the ice, so the trout survive.

If you are here in the early mornings or evenings, you might get a glimpse of an elk or deer; for this is a popular waterhole.

From the pond you can go right and loop your way back to the trailhead or continue along the rim to follow the complete figure-eight trail. This will take you to the northernmost end of the figure-eight loop and near an alternate starting point, called Alpine Pond Trailhead.

Alpine Pond Trail At A Glance

Best season: July–September.

Length: 2.1 miles double-loop.

Difficulty: Moderate.

Elevation gain: 180 feet.

Trailhead elevation: 10,462 feet at south trailhead.

Warnings: High elevation, cliff exposure, thunderstorm potential. Roads are usually closed from fall through late spring because of heavy snowfall.

Jurisdiction: Cedar Breaks National Monument.

Directions: From the Cedar Breaks National Monument main entrance drive 1.6 miles north on Highway 146 and go left into the Chessman Overlook parking area, which serves as the south trailhead. Another trailhead is one mile north.

68 Winter Yurt

MOST PEOPLE DON'T THINK ABOUT VISITING CEDAR BREAKS IN WINTER. AFTER ALL, ITS elevation is more than ten thousand feet, annual snowfall averages about fifteen feet, and the park's main roads are therefore closed. If you love to hike, though, think about briefly trading your hiking boots for a pair of snowshoes or cross-country skis, to see the park at perhaps its most glorious.

The amphitheater is a sight to behold in winter, when the contrast with the white snow covering much of the landscape makes the colorful limestone formations seem to glow like embers.

Once a heavy snow hits the plateau, usually in November, the main road through the park, Utah 148, remains closed to automobiles, often through May. But it serves as an ideal trail for skiers or snowshoe users to visit some of the many overlooks into the amphitheater.

It is only about one mile to the park's yurt, yet on the way you can conveniently access the fine views from some of those overlooks. The yurt is an American model

Cross-country skiers head out on the snow-covered road to visit the rim's viewpoints.

of the circular all-weather tents designed and used by Mongolian nomads. It is staffed on an irregular schedule, but if you call ahead they can tell you what time it will be open during your visit. If it is open, head inside and warm up by the wood-stove, have a cup of hot chocolate or other warming beverage and relax. This is a fine place to assess yourself and your group, and decide if you want to go farther.

The easiest way to access the trailhead is by driving south from Brian Head Resort, three miles on Highway 143. Park your vehicle at the junction in the snow-plowed parking area and head up the snow bank and onto the wide trail. The park service tries to keep the trail groomed, as best they can dependent on weather, so most of the time it is very easy to snowshoe or ski on it.

Keep in mind that snowshoeing or cross-country skiing, even on the same trail that you might ordinarily hike without snow, is a much more strenuous activity. Don't plan on going as far as you might go on foot, and pack energy bars and plenty of fluids.

Be dressed and prepared for the frigid cold, and other uncomfortable weather conditions, before you set out for this trip. For instance, if you go in February, average high temperatures are thirty-two degrees, with average lows at eleven degrees, but it isn't abnormal for temperatures to be below zero. Furthermore, average snowfall here is five feet in February alone. Don't head out if there is heavy snow forecast, as the visibility into the amphitheater will be limited, and if there are speedy snowmobiles on the trail, their riders might not see you.

If you don't have your own snowshoes or cross-country equipment, they can be rented easily from Georg's Ski Shop in Brian Head. They even rent jackets and ski pants, and offer shuttle services as well as guided tours. (435) 677-2033, *www. georgsskishop.com.*

Cedar Breaks National Monument offers Cedar Breaks Family Ski/Snowshoe hikes outings in winter. For information on winter activities and the yurt, call the park at (435) 586-9451.

Winter Yurt At a Glance

Best Season: Late November to early April, dependent on snow level.

Length: Two miles or longer roundtrip.

Difficulty: Moderate.

Elevation gain: Minimal.

Trailhead elevation: 10,590 feet.

Warnings: High-elevation winter excursion. Never get too close to the rim as there are severe drop-offs at overlooks.

Jurisdiction: Cedar Breaks National Monument.

Directions: From Brian Head Resort drive south on Highway 143 about three miles to the junction with Utah Highway 148 (Cedar Breaks Scenic Drive). Here you will find a plowed parking area and trailhead.

69 Bunker Creek Trail

THIS ROUTE IS GOOD FOR PUTTING MILES ON HIKING BOOTS OR KNOBBY BIKE TIRES, WHILE enjoying spectacular summer scenery or one of the earliest foliage seasons in our region.

Located on Dixie National Forest land near Cedar Breaks National Monument and the town of Brian Head, the lofty Bunker Creek trail starts at about eleven thousand feet and descends twelve miles, one-way, through conifer forests, aspen groves, and open meadows. It's downhill practically the entire way, with only a few strenuous uphill sections. Overall, it loses about twenty-six hundred feet in elevation.

At this altitude, fall foliage season starts early. Aspens will begin to change in late August and often reach their most golden glory by late September.

Whether hiking or biking, the trail is best done as a point-to-point excursion, so you will need to arrange for a pick-up at trail's end or in nearby Panguitch Lake. If you don't have a friend to pick you up, Brian Head Resort offers a trailhead shuttle service, by reservation, in season.

The trail starts from the gravel road to Brian Head Peak. As you drive up toward the trailhead look off to the right in an area known as "Little Ireland." You might see a flock of grazing sheep or glimpse a few yellow-bellied marmots making their way through the meadows. Before you even stop at the trailhead, drive past it a short way to Brian Head Peak itself. At 11,307 feet you can take in one of the premiere panoramas from the plateau. On clear days you will be able to see into Nevada and Arizona.

Heading back the way you came to the large signed parking area marked Sidney Peaks Trail, park and then walk across the road. Head up a short but steep hill and you will be ready to go. A couple of other trails leave from this same trailhead so be sure to bring a good map, just in case one of the trail signs, intended to tell you which path you should follow, has gone missing. Without that map, it would be easy to head in the wrong direction and end up many miles from where you wanted to go.

The first few miles are fairly easy; then you will reach a strenuous uphill section through a meadow. After this you will descend to a stunning overlook with great views down into Parowan Canyon. The trail continues along the ridgeline, back

The Bunker Creek Trail is an ideal summer hike, with a starting elevation about 11,000 feet.

through the trees and after about four miles from the trailhead, you will arrive at Sidney Valley Road.

Cross to the east side of the road and you will see signed trailheads for the left and right forks of Bunker Creek Trail. The choice is yours. If you are traveling on foot either fork is suitable, as you won't notice too much difference in the terrain. But if you are relying on pedal power, you will find the left fork more technical. Since forks are customarily named from the bottom of the drainage looking upstream, and you'll be looking down, the right fork will be on your left and left fork on your right. Got that?

Whichever fork you choose will certainly be the highlight of the entire trail. After about three miles they join back up, becoming the Bunker Creek Trail once again.

Both forks are highly vegetated; dense conifers are interspersed with stands of aspen and tall grasses. If you are biking be aware these single-track trails have lots of twists and turns, occasional drop-offs, and many rocky areas. Because the plateau receives afternoon thunderstorms some times of year, be prepared to travel through very muddy areas.

About seven miles from the original trailhead both the narrow single-track forks meet, and your path widens into an old jeep trail. Don't be surprised if you come across free-roaming cattle in this area.

The remainder of the route is self-explanatory except for one unmarked fork in the road where you will stay left. The jeep trail gets easier to travel the farther you go, and eventually turns into a maintained gravel road. Follow this out through a wide-open meadow called Blue Spring Valley to the junction with Utah Highway 143.

If you have a friend picking you up, this intersection makes a good meeting spot. But if you have arranged for the Brian Head shuttle, go left onto the main road and travel about one mile to the Panguitch Lake General Store to meet your arranged transport back to the resort.

Since the whole trail lies at a high elevation, the air is thinner and your outing might seem more exhausting than at lower levels. By September, temperatures will be cool. Be prepared for daytime highs in the fifties or even below, with a realistic possibility of freezing temperatures at night.

Bunker Creek At A Glance

Best season: July–September.

Length: Twelve miles point to point.

Difficulty: Strenuous.

Elevation loss: 2,670 if traveling to Panguitch General Store, or 2,580 at junction of 143 and gravel road.

Trailhead elevation: Eleven thousand feet at Sydney Peak Trailhead.

Warning: Trail is shared with mountain bikes.

Jurisdiction: Dixie National Forest.

Map: Trail map available at Brian Head Resort and other local businesses.

Directions: From Las Vegas, take Interstate 15 north about 180 miles to Exit 75, at Parowan, Utah. Take Utah Highway 143 for 15 miles to Brian Head Resort. For the Bunker Creek Trailhead continue south on Highway 143 and go left onto Brian Head Peak Road. Drive for 1.7 miles and park in the large trailhead parking area on the left. Trailhead is directly across road.

Bryce Canyon National Park

Bryce Canyon National Park boasts one of the earth's most extraordinary landscapes. Its natural amphitheaters, along the eastern rim of the Paunsaugunt Plateau, are filled with tall pillars, pinnacles, and spires that suggest an audience of supernatural beings. No wonder pioneers decided to call them "hoodoos," and the name stuck. The area became a national park in 1928, now encompasses 35,835 acres, and is open year round.

The rim, with its elevations varying from about eight thousand to ninety-one hundred feet, offers not only views of the hoodoos but vistas a hundred miles deep on clear days. And the park contains a multitude of trails, ranging from an easy stroll along the rim to extended backpacking adventures below. It's a pleasant place to hike even in summer. During July, the park's warmest month, you can expect normal daily high temperatures around eighty-three degrees with night-time lows around forty-seven.

Although it is called Bryce Canyon, singular, it really consists of about a dozen deep amphitheaters which formed in the chromatic limestone off the eastern escarpment of the plateau. The thousands of colorful hoodoos, pinnacles, and spires of rock within these amphitheaters were created by a special sort of erosion that takes place mostly during the two hundred days a year when temperatures fluctuate greatly. Fissures in the rock fill with melted snow water, which then freezes and expands, causing the rock to split and flake. This process is called frost wedging, and over time it creates new hoodoos in this ever-changing landscape.

Walking among the hoodoos feels like visiting another planet. Let your imagination run wild and the same hoodoo that looked like a witch on a broomstick, for instance, as you approached, might resemble a big puppy once you've passed to the far side. Even their colors seem to change.

Left: Bryce Canyon National Park is a land of deep amphitheaters filled with colorful formations called hoodoos.

Most trails in the main area of the park start at the rim and descend into the amphitheaters, so you'll be hiking uphill on your return, when you are already tired. And you will be more tired, at this altitude, than on a similar trail in the lowlands, making it especially important to build plenty of extra time into your plan for the hike.

Although hiking the trails of Bryce makes a fine daytime adventure, there's still another uncommon pleasure after sundown. In the absence of artificial light, night skies here are some of the nation's darkest, and on a moonless night it is possible to see about seventy-five hundred stars. The park offers astronomy programs during the summer.

You will probably see some kind of wildlife during your visit. In the amphitheaters, keep an eye out for gray foxes, ringtail cats, and peregrine falcons. Elk, Clark's nutcrackers, and Steller's jays frequent the forests. In sagebrush areas, you might see pronghorns, jackrabbits, cottontails, or golden eagles, and in open meadows, prairie dogs or wild turkeys. Mule deer and coyotes can show up in any of the habitats.

During the busy summers, the visitor center is generally open from 8 a.m. to 8 p.m., with shorter hours other seasons. (435) 834-5322, *www.nps.gov/brca*.

Directions: From Las Vegas, take Interstate 15 north 125 miles and take Exit 16 (Hurricane/Zion National Park and Utah Route 9). Follow Route 9 for 57 miles through Zion and turn left at Mount Carmel Junction onto U.S. 89. Go north 43 miles and turn right onto Utah Route 12. After 14 miles, turn right on Utah Route 63, for 3 miles, to Bryce Canyon National Park entrance station. Take a right to visitor center parking.

70 Fairyland Loop Trail

PEOPLE FROM ALL OVER THE WORLD COME TO BRYCE CANYON NATIONAL PARK TO HIKE among hundreds of hoodoos, multi-colored limestone formations so-called because an imaginative person can see in them the shapes of humans, or perhaps not-quite-humans.

If you have at least a half-day to spend walking, a great hoodoo hike is the eight-mile Fairyland Loop. Fairyland doesn't have the heavy foot traffic found on some other trails because it's still relatively unknown. The access road is located before the park's main entrance and visitor center, and is unsigned as you enter the park.

From the trailhead, pick up the obvious trail. Over the next one and one-half miles you will be descending into Fairyland Canyon. Overall the trail has an elevation change of about twenty-three hundred feet, crossing undulating terrain including some steep grades. When you factor elevation gain and loss into the mileage, you'll realize this hike is somewhat strenuous for most adults and too strenuous for most children.

As you make your way around the loop it's easy to spot lifelike forms in the rock, limited only by the amount of whimsy in your imagination. Some forms resemble dogs, cats, or wildlife; others broccoli, cauliflower, or asparagus.

At first look you might think this area is all about stone, but there is a variety of plant life along the trail. You will see Douglas firs, limber and ponderosa pines,

Bryce Canyon National Park hoodoos are multi-colored formations of limestone and fill the natural amphitheaters.

and even some bristlecones. In season you will find blooming pockets of summer wildflowers, such as Wyoming paintbrush and Southwestern stoneseed.

Once you have hiked about five miles you will have looped back to the rim, and here you will head north, or right. This will take you about three miles farther to return to the Fairyland trailhead. This is the most northern segment of the Rim Trail, a moderate hike that runs five and one-half miles from Fairyland Point to Bryce Point along the eastern escarpment. It's a good place to see golden-mantled ground squirrels and Uinta chipmunks.

Thunderstorms are common in the park during July and August. Always get a weather report at the visitor center before heading out. On all hikes, but this one especially, be prepared to look after yourself; cell phones are unreliable in Bryce Canyon. Hike early in the day, because this is an exposed trail with very little shade, and can get hot despite the elevation. Furthermore, an elevation of 8,152 feet at the trailhead increases the risk of both dehydration and sunburn. Wear a hat and sunscreen, and bring plenty of water. Bring plenty of food, too, if only because all those hoodoos shaped like vegetables will make you hungry.

Fairyland Loop At A Glance

Best season: May–October.

Length: Eight miles.

Difficulty: Moderate to strenuous.

Elevation gain/loss: 2,309 feet.

Trailhead elevation: 7,775 feet.

Warnings: No shade, slippery terrain when wet.

Jurisdiction: Bryce Canyon National Park.

Directions: From the Bryce Canyon Visitor Center drive out of the parking area and go left. Drive north, as if leaving the park, on Utah Route 63 for 0.9 miles. Go right and drive one mile to trailhead.

71 Mossy Cave Trail

IF YOU ARE SHORT ON TIME, OR WANT TO AVOID THE CONGESTION OF BRYCE'S MAIN AREA, the little-known Mossy Cave Trail may be your answer.

While most of the park's official trails are accessed from the eighteen-mile scenic drive, the Mossy Cave Trail lies in the more remote, northeastern area of the park along Scenic Byway 12. Besides hiking among Bryce's signature hoodoos, you'll also get to visit a spring-fed cave and a waterfall.

From the signed trailhead walk up the worn trail, through a pinyon-juniper woodland with a scattering of ponderosa pines. The trail goes up the south bank of Water Canyon and crosses a bridge to the north side. Continue upstream, where you will cross the drainage once more.

Throughout the hike you will see hundreds of hoodoos. Hoodoos change their shapes constantly, sculpted by two hundred cycles per year of alternately soaking with snowmelt and freezing overnight.

Even when weather isn't freezing, rainwater also contributes to the work. Runoff creates small creeks and gullies leaving tall, narrow "fins" of rock between. Eventually erosion wears right through a fin, leaving a hole or "window" below a bridge of rock that still connects the fin to the mother cliff. And when the part of the fin above the window collapses, a free-standing column or hoodoo remains.

After the second bridge the trail will fork, with both ways worth exploring. To the left is the short, yet steep spur trail that dead ends at Mossy Cave. Merely standing at the entrance, you will feel cooler air, and for most of the year the cave has large ice deposits. During summer you will most likely find only dripping water and small forests of moss. This grotto is created by an underground spring. Standing at the overhang's entrance you'll almost wish it were hotter outside, to enjoy the cave's cool contrast all the more.

Returning to the fork and taking its other branch, head north and you will find yourself at the top of a fifteen-foot waterfall, usually flowing from May to October.

When the Mormon pioneers first arrived in this area they realized they had no reliable year-round water supply to farm the valley below Bryce Canyon. From 1890 to 1892, using only picks and shovels, they dug the ten-mile Tropic Ditch. This

canal starts at the East Fork of the Sevier River on the Paunsaugunt Plateau, flows down the plateau's eastern edge and feeds water through natural drainages such as this one. Then the water flows into more man-made drainages, and eventually reaches the communities of Tropic and Cannonville.

Mossy Cave At A Glance

Best season: May–October.

Length: 0.9 miles roundtrip.

Difficulty: Easy.

Elevation gain: Three hundred feet.

Trailhead elevation: 6,805 feet.

Warnings: Severe erosion on trail to waterfall, so stay well back from the edge. Drop-offs in upper reaches.

Jurisdiction: Bryce Canyon National Park.

Directions: From Bryce Canyon National Park's main entrance, take Utah Route 63 north about 3 miles to Scenic Byway 12. Go right and follow for about 4 miles to parking area on the right.

Left: This waterfall is often flowing from May to October, and is found on the Mossy Cave Trail.

72 Bryce Canyon in the Winter

VISITING BRYCE CANYON IN WINTER IS A SPECIAL TREAT. THERE ARE NO CROWDS, ROOM rates are at their lowest, and there is a plethora of outdoor activities to keep you busy for days. With the right equipment, and dressed for the cold, you can snowshoe, ski cross country, take a horseback or sleigh ride, ice skate, check out the overlooks, take in a ranger program or even hike some of the trails.

Of course some of these activities are dependent on snow levels, but for three months in the winter there is usually enough snowpack to enjoy the park to your heart's content. The best months for snow activities are January and February, when average snowfall is about seventeen inches per month. March is nearly as good with about 15.7 inches.

In the park itself there is the Bryce Canyon Snowshoe Program, great for most

ages, except small children. They even lend out snowshoes and poles for free. A ranger will take the group on a guided two-hour tour. You will learn correct snowshoe techniques and at the same time learn about the geology and wildlife in the park. You must have snow boots or waterproof hiking boots to participate. They also offer ranger-guided full-moon hikes, as long as there is at least a foot of snow. Make a reservation at the Bryce Canyon Visitor Center or call at (435) 834-4747.

If you have your own equipment you are all set, but you can easily rent it at Ruby's Inn, located just before the park entrance. Within the park itself, the best places to ski cross country are the Rim Trail between Fairyland Point and Bryce Point, the Bristlecone Loop, and the unplowed Fairyland and Paria Point Roads.

Winter hiking can be fun as well but for safety, you will need to have traction devices under your boots. They are available at outdoor stores such as REI and also at the visitor center and at Ruby's Inn store. Popular brands are Yaktrax,

STABILicers and Kahtoola. Along the rim, the best place to hike is the one-mile roundtrip walkway between Sunset and Sunrise Points. Depending on ice and snow, hiking is possible below the rim, but conditions vary. Just check in at the visitor center, and they can tell you which trails are the best for when you are visiting.

If you are short on time, just drive into the park and take in some of the overlooks. In winter the best ones are Bryce, Inspiration, Sunset, and Sunrise.

The nearby lodge, Ruby's Inn, has its own Winter Adventure Center. They rent snowshoes, cross country skis, and ice skates. They also have an ice skating rink and offer horseback adventures such as trail rides and sleigh rides. From the Inn you can directly access more than thirty kilometers of groomed trails and even ski or snowshoe into the park from there. They offer lodging, a general store, and restaurants. (866) 866-6616, *www.rubysinn.com.*

With snow, the rim and the surrounding forest are great places for snowshoeing or cross-country skiing.

Grand Staircase-

Escalante
National Monument

This 1.9 million-acre monument takes some time to reach, but its hiking opportunities are well worth the extra effort. The Grand Staircase is a long-standing geologists' term for a sequence of sedimentary rock layers that stretch from Bryce Canyon south to Grand Canyon. The expansive park named for that formation lies to the east and south of Bryce Canyon, north of the Arizona Strip, south of Capital Reef National Park, and extends eastward to Glen Canyon National Recreation Area.

GSENM is well known for its backpacking and slot canyons within and around the canyons of the Escalante River. To reach the majority of the trailheads you will be taking remote gravel roads, of which the park has nearly one thousand miles.

Evidence suggests that the first inhabitants of the area were the Basketmaker people and Ancestral Puebloans, starting around A.D. 500. It was briefly occupied by the Fremont, Hopi and Paiute people as well.

The Escalante River area was the last place in the United States to be mapped, and it didn't happen until the 1940s. In 1996, by executive order of President Clinton, it was declared a national monument, the first to be managed by the Bureau of Land Management instead of the National Park Service.

The best maps to use for traveling and hiking in this chapter are *National Geographic Trails Illustrated Maps: Canyons of the Escalante* and *Glen Canyon*. They identify the trailheads, gravel roads and waterways clearly. They are available

Left: The creek serves as the trail in Hackberry Canyon.

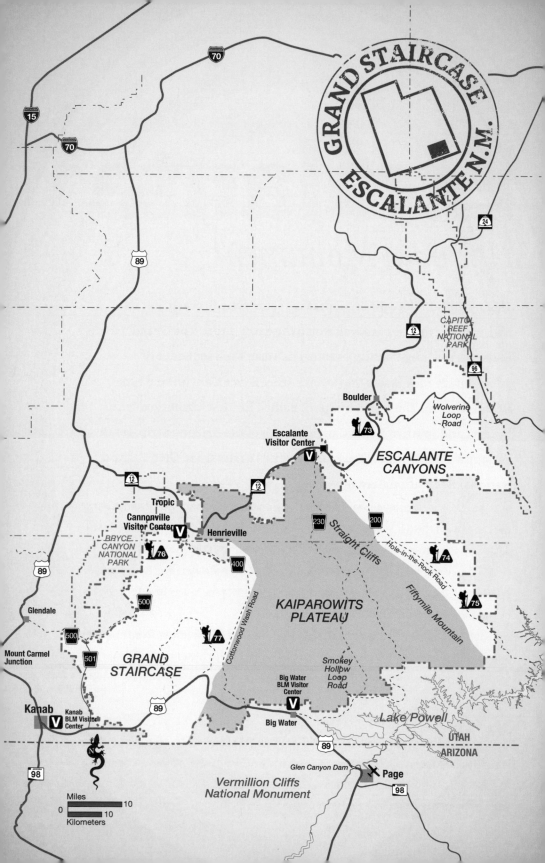

GRAND STAIRCASE ESCALANTE N.M.

70

15

70

89

70

24

CAPITOL REEF NATIONAL PARK

12

96

Boulder

73

Wolverine Loop Road

Escalante Visitor Center

V

12

ESCALANTE CANYONS

Tropic

Cannonville Visitor Center

V

12

Henrieville

230

200

Straight Cliffs

Hole-in-the-Rock Road

BRYCE CANYON NATIONAL PARK

76

400

74

89

Glendale

500

KAIPAROWITS PLATEAU

Fiftymile Mountain

75

500

77

Cottonwood Wash Road

501

Mount Carmel Junction

GRAND STAIRCASE

Smokey Hollow Loop Road

Kanab

V

Kanab BLM Visitor Center

89

Big Water BLM Visitor Center

V

Lake Powell

UTAH

ARIZONA

Big Water

89

N

98

Glen Canyon Dam

✕ Page

98

Vermillion Cliffs National Monument

Miles
0   10

Kilometers
0   10

through Amazon.com or at the visitor centers. Be sure to also get the free visitor information guide and map published by the park, as this has an overall map of the park. Services are few and far between in this area. Gas, groceries, lodging and camping are available in both Cannonville and Escalante, but there is no reliable cell service. Kanab has cell service and most everything else the aforesaid villages do not.

You can get information about the entire park from two sources, Grand Staircase-Escalante National Monument, *www.ut.blm.gov/monument*, and Glen Canyon National Recreation Area, *nps.gov/glca*. But since the monument is so spread out, there are four main visitor centers. Hours change for each center depending on the season, so always call ahead to the visitor center you wish to visit.

Escalante Interagency Visitor Center, 755 W. Main Street, Escalante, Utah. (435) 826-5499.

Cannonville Visitor Center, 10 Center Street, Cannonville, Utah. (435) 826-5640.

Kanab Visitor Center, 745 E. Highway 89, Kanab, Utah. (435) 644-1300.

Big Water Visitor Center, 100 Upper Revolution Way, Big Water, Utah. (435) 675-3200.

Directions to trailheads in this chapter are given from the visitor center most conveniently located to the hike, so directions to those three centers follow.

Directions to Cannonville Visitor Center: From Las Vegas take Interstate 15 north 125 miles into Utah and take the Hurricane/Zion National Park exit. Follow Route 9 for 57 miles through Zion National Park and turn left onto U.S. 89 north. Take Utah Route 89 for 44 miles to a right onto Utah Route 12. Drive about 26 miles and go right onto N. Main Street. Drive 0.1 miles and go right into visitor center parking area.

Directions to Escalante Interagency Visitor Center: From Las Vegas take Interstate 15 north 125 miles into Utah and take the Hurricane/Zion National Park exit. Follow Route 9 for 57 miles through Zion National Park and turn left onto U.S. 89 north. Drive 44 miles to a right onto Utah Route 12. Follow for 59 miles and go right into visitor center parking area.

Directions to Kanab Visitor Center: From Las Vegas take Interstate 15 north 125 miles into Utah and take the Hurricane/Zion National Park exit. Drive nine miles and go right onto Utah Route 59 east. Follow Utah 59 for about 23 miles; there it becomes Arizona Route 389 at the state line. Continue an additional 33 miles on Arizona 389, until it ends in Fredonia, Ariz. Go left onto U.S. Route 89A north. Drive about 6.5 miles, entering Utah once again and turn right onto U.S. 89 south (as if going to Lake Powell.) Drive for .75 miles and go left into visitor center parking area.

73 Calf Creek

WHILE THE MAIN REASON PEOPLE COME TO LOWER CALF CREEK FALLS IS THE WATERFALL itself, the entire trail is a fine one. The route travels within a wide red-and-orange Navajo sandstone canyon with high cliff walls. There are also a few archaeological sites to see along the way and you will have a good chance to see plenty of wildlife, especially if you are on the trail first thing in the morning. This is a good trail for older children as long as they can handle the distance. The trail is relatively flat except for many areas where you will have to climb up and down the natural sandstone, which serves as steps.

You will find the trailhead in the back and north side of the Calf Creek Recreation Area's campground. The well-worn trail is easy to follow, but at the trailhead, be sure to pick up a brochure which will help you find the points of interest along the way. Bring binoculars to get a close-up look at the two granaries along the route, and to view the large pictograph panel that depicts warriors.

The trail more or less follows Calf Creek until near the end, where it begins to hug the stream bank until you reach the falls. Look for a few beaver dams along the way.

Streamside vegetation becomes thick and canopies trail before you reach Calf Creek Falls. Right: It is about six miles roundtrip to visit 126-foot Calf Creek Falls.

In the last half-mile or so the vegetation becomes quite dense, and you will notice mature deciduous trees. You will even experience a big drop in temperatures once you are in the shady canyon. Look for wildlife here, or tracks in the sand, as lots of animals visit the pool in early mornings.

You will be able to hear the waterfall before you see it. Once in the box canyon you will be at the base of the falls and at the edge of its pool. This is refreshingly cool and clear water, perfect for a soak or a shallow swim. Or you can just sit on the beach and breathe in the cooling mist from the falls. Because of the moisture in the canyon and the seeps on the walls, you will find all sorts of water-loving plants such as alcove columbines, scarlet monkey flowers and maidenhair ferns.

Calf Creek At A Glance

Best Season: April to mid-June and mid-Sept. to November.

Length: Six miles roundtrip.

Difficulty: Moderate.

Elevation gain: 190 feet.

Trailhead elevation: 5,346 feet.

Warning: Popular trail that becomes crowded by late morning. Start early to enjoy solitude.

Jurisdiction: Grand Staircase-Escalante National Monument.

Directions: From the Escalante Interagency Visitor Center drive east on Utah Route 12 for 16 miles and go left into the BLM Calf Creek Recreation Area and parking area.

74 Peek-a-boo and Spooky Slot Canyons

PEEK-A-BOO AND SPOOKY SLOT CANYONS ARE USUALLY DONE TOGETHER ON A ONE-HALF-day trip.

These two slots are really fun to explore and photograph, but keep in mind Peek-a-boo involves some rock scrambling, while Spooky is dark and gets extremely narrow, and is therefore not good for claustrophobics.

Children will especially like these slots as long as they have a strong adult with them to help get them get up and into Peek-a-boo. The trail begins at the parking area and involves a one mile, fairly steep descent over slick rock, marked by cairns. The hike then drops you down into the sandy Dry Fork Wash.

Once in the wash, walk directly across it, and you will see the opening to Peek-a-boo Canyon. This canyon has been cut by water flowing through the red, orange, and pink Navajo sandstone. Sometimes you might see a log placed to help you up and into it, but most of the time you need to climb up about twelve feet on the natural sandstone steps, often referred to as Moki steps.

After you make it inside, you walk, crawl, and duck your way up through the corkscrew canyon. If there has been rain recently, expect some of the sand-

The trail involves a one-mile, fairly steep descent over slick rock, marked by cairns, to reach Peek-a-boo and Spooky.

stone's natural bowls to contain puddles of water, especially the first such natural *tinaja* after entering the canyon.

One of the delights of this canyon is a double natural bridge inside.

This canyon is almost a tunnel in places, but about two-thirds of a mile from the entrance, it widens enough to see much sky. Return the way you came.

Once out of Peek-a-boo Canyon, head downstream to reach Spooky. You will need to walk about one-half mile and look closely on your left for the cairns, directly before a large sandstone outcropping, that mark the route. It is about a five minute walk to bring you behind the outcropping and to the entrance of Spooky Canyon. I have seen a rattlesnake on two different visits to Spooky, so be careful when entering. It is dark, and a rattler might have slithered into the canyon's entrance for shade. A headlamp comes in handy in this slot.

You will need to remove your backpack for this canyon. Basically you just walk in and go as far as you feel comfortable. It gets so narrow in places that even those who don't suffer from claustrophobia will be sure to feel slightly uncomfortable, once it tightens so much they have to walk sideways.

Spooky is dark and gets extremely narrow, therefore not good for claustrophobics.

For both these slots be sure to wear clothing that won't tear easily. Long rugged pants are best for crawling, and be advised they might get permanently stained by the wet sandstone.

Peek-A-Boo and Spooky At A Glance

Best Season: April through mid-June and mid-Sept. through November

Length: 3.5 miles roundtrip.

Difficulty: Moderate.

Elevation gain: 285 feet.

In some places in Peek-a-boo you can stand straight up. In most parts you will be scrambling over rocks.

Trailhead elevation: 4,950 feet.

Warnings: Hole-in-the-Rock Road is impassable after or during rain. Flash flood danger. Rock scrambling.

Jurisdiction: Grand Staircase Escalante National Monument.

Directions: From the Escalante Interagency Visitor Center drive east on Utah Route 12 for six miles, then turn right onto the well-marked Hole-in-the-Rock Road. Follow this gravel road for about 26 miles and go left on Dry Fork Road, staying left at the fork, and follow about 1 ½ miles to trailhead.

75 Coyote Gulch

SOME OF THE MOST STUNNING SCENERY I HAVE EVER SEEN IS LOCATED BY TAKING MULTI-day and longer backpacks in the remote canyons in and around the Escalante River. Most of them involve technical climbing skills but a few are just moderately difficult backpack adventures.

Coyote Gulch is one such hike and a good one to start familiarizing yourself with backpacking in this canyon region. You will hike in a riparian setting, with cascades and many pools of refreshing water to soak in. You will see a natural bridge, several arches, and pass numerous archaeological sites. The hike travels about twenty-five miles roundtrip, or can be done as a fourteen-mile point-to-point if you have parked a vehicle at the alternate Fortymile Ridge trailhead, or if you have a pickup person. The hike starts in GSENM and travels into Glen Canyon National Monument about three miles down Hurricane Wash. To enjoy all the sights, I would recommend at least two nights in the canyon.

The first five miles of the hike involve a pretty unexciting trek through Hurricane Wash. It is totally exposed to the sun and has sandy conditions underfoot. But once you reach the confluence of Coyote Gulch, turning right or downstream, the going immediately becomes cooler, and remains pleasant the rest of the way in the gulch. There will be some rock scrambling all along the way but for the most part it will be walking in the cooling creek, with a stable sandy streambed, or on paths along the bank.

Only two miles from where you entered the gulch you will be looking up at Jacob Hamblin Arch. Cut through a natural fin of Navajo sandstone, this arch spans about one hundred feet. Once you reach the other side of the arch, be sure to look on your left, about eye level within the canyon wall's vegetation, for the natural spring where you can fill your water bottles.

The next highlight, Coyote Natural Bridge, is about two miles farther. You will walk right under it. Another two miles will bring you to Cliff Arch, an arch shaped like a jug handle. There are some tricky river crossings after this, and you might have to backtrack here and there, but it is fairly obvious what you need to do.

After about twelve miles the canyon narrows. You will need to skirt some dry falls and waterfalls to continue downstream just a third of a mile to the Escalante River, but it is a very dangerous undertaking unless you are an experienced climber or canyoneer. So this is where you must decide: Continue to the Escalante over dangerous terrain, turn around, and retrace your hike, or head out to the Fortymile Ridge Trailhead via the aptly named Crack-in-the-Wall. The Crack-in-the-Wall/

An arch seen along the Coyote Gulch hike.

Fortymile Trailhead exit route will be on your right looking downstream, just before you reach the dangerous part on the way to the Escalante River.

For Fortymile Ridge Trailhead, hike up the steep and very sandy slog on the obvious path to Crack-in-the-Wall. It is worth a side trip to Crack-in-the-Wall, even if you aren't planning on heading out that way. You will get a superb view of Stephens Arch, one of the largest arches in this area. It spans 230 feet and is located about six hundred feet above the Escalante River streambed. A fellow hiker, whom I happened to meet on this route, told me he saw a small airplane fly through the arch many years ago.

If you are continuing to Fortymile Ridge Trailhead, be aware that Crack-in-the-Wall itself is fifty feet long and only eighteen inches wide in places, so you won't be able to fit through wearing your backpack. One member of your party must carry a rope up through the crack and then lower it off the cliff to another hiker, who will tie on the packs to be hoisted to the top. You *did* bring a long rope, didn't you?

Once up above the crack, travel cross country, following the cairns, to the parking area. Just this section, from where you leave Coyote Gulch to Fortymile Ridge, is more than two miles and has an elevation gain of nearly nine hundred feet.

Always check in at the Escalante Interagency Visitor Center before embarking on this trip. You can pick up maps, get weather and road conditions and find out about the risks of flash flooding during your visit. Camping is allowed in the canyon. Be sure to obtain a free Backcountry Use Permit at the visitor center or self-permit at the trailhead (located 0.2 miles down Hurricane Wash). Camp at least one hundred feet (two hundred feet if possible) from any water source. No campfires are allowed, but you may use a camp stove.

Coyote Gulch At A Glance

Best Season: April to mid-June and mid-September to November.

Length: Twenty-five miles roundtrip or fourteen miles point-to-point from Hurricane Wash Trailhead to Fortymile Ridge Trailhead.

Difficulty: Mostly moderate with a few strenuous sections.

Hurricane Wash trailhead elevation: 4,570 feet.

Fortymile Ridge trailhead elevation: 4,630 feet.

Warnings: Very popular trail. Hole-in-the-Rock Road is gravel, rough in places, and impassable during or after a rain. Deadly flash flooding can occur in canyon. Treat or filter water before drinking. To use the Fortymile Ridge trailhead, backpackers will need a fifty-foot rope to retrieve their backpacks when traveling through Crack-in-the-Wall. The Fortymile Ridge Trailhead access road is extremely sandy in areas and usually not passable by vehicles other than four-wheel-drive with high clearance. If you don't own such a vehicle, though, you can avoid the part that requires one by parking at the water tank at mile five and walking the remaining two miles to the trailhead.

Jurisdiction: Grand Staircase-Escalante National Monument and Glen Canyon National Recreation Area.

Directions to Hurricane Wash Trailhead: From the Escalante Interagency Visitor Center drive east on Utah Route 12 for six miles, then turn right onto the well-marked Hole-in-the-Rock Road. Drive 33 miles to Hurricane Wash Trailhead on left (parking area is on right.)

Directions to Fortymile Ridge Trailhead: From Hurricane Wash Trailhead drive south on Hole-in-the-Rock Road three miles farther. Go left and drive seven miles to Fortymile Ridge parking area and trailhead.

76 Willis Creek and Bull Valley Gorge

WILLIS CREEK NARROWS AND BULL VALLEY GORGE ARE CANYONS LESS THAN TWO MILES from each other in the White Cliff area of the park. They are often seen together. Willis is suitable for children but Bull Gorge is not, as it has very severe drop-offs.

If you are coming from Cannonville the logical place to begin is Willis Creek. From the parking area you can just cross Skutumpah Road and pick up the obvious trail on the north/left side of the canyon. You will be in a pinyon pine and juniper plant community, and after just a few minutes walking you will drop into the canyon itself.

Willis Creek is a perennial stream that drains down from the limestone

Bull Gorge is a narrow slot canyon. Remains of truck that went off the road decades ago can be seen buried among boulders, above the slot canyon.

pink cliffs of Bryce Canyon to the northwest. Once in the creek you will usually find only one or two inches of water at your feet, but some pools can be deeper.

The best narrow sections will be to your left but it is worth going right first, traveling upstream a couple of minutes to see a cascade or seasonal waterfall. While it isn't very big, perhaps six feet or so, it is a great place to cool off on a warm day.

Once you have seen the waterfall, head back down the canyon, past where you first entered, to reach its narrows. This canyon isn't as skinny as a true slot canyon, but it is an appealing one. In some areas it is about five to six feet wide, but its Navajo sandstone walls rise up nearly one hundred feet, blocking out much of the sky.

After about one-half mile from where you entered, you will find the canyon opens up. Here it is usually dry beneath your feet, and this is where you might turn around.

While you are in this area be sure to go take a look at, or even hike along, Bull Valley Gorge. It is about one hundred feet deep and a true slot canyon. Even people with the slightest fear of heights should avoid the trail as it is a scary one, where one wrong move could send you into the abyss.

In 1954 three men were driving the narrow Skutumpah Road when their truck went over the edge of the small bridge, into the ravine. Their bodies were recovered, but the truck was left where it came to rest. A new bridge was built on top of it by

A small waterfall
along Willis Creek.

placing boulders and rocks for stabilization. If you walk down the trail a bit and look back under the bridge, you can still see exposed parts of the truck.

You can access the gorge by walking along the path about one-half mile and easily drop in. If you go left you can head deeper into the canyon but you will need very good climbing skills to get back out, over the very steep dry fall sections at the beginning of the slot. Don't try it without those skills, plus experience.

When traveling along Skutumpah Road take it slow, as cattle roam freely about, and once I even came upon two bison standing in the middle of the road. If it has been raining or rain threatens, do not attempt to drive the road, for it becomes impassable, with mud and deep pools of water.

Willis Creek and Bull Valley Gorge At A Glance

Best Season: May–October.

Length: Two miles roundtrip.

Difficulty: Easy.

Elevation gain: Minimal.

Trailhead elevation: Six thousand feet.

Warnings: Flash flooding possible in both canyons, and severe drop-offs along trail to Bull Gorge. Skutumpah Road is gravel and you will need a high clearance vehicle with good off-road tires.

Jurisdiction: Grand Staircase-Escalante National Monument.

Directions: From the Cannonville Visitor Center drive south 2.9 miles on Cottonwood Road (BLM 400). Turn right onto Skutumpah Road (BLM 500). Drive about 6 miles west to the Willis Creek parking area located on your right. For Bull Valley Gorge continue another 1.8 miles on Skutumpah Road to trailhead parking located on your right.

Alternate Directions: From the Kanab Visitor Center head east on U.S. 89 for about 6.5 miles, then go left on Johnson Canyon Road. Follow for 16 miles and go right onto Skutumpah Road. Drive about 24.7 miles to Bull Valley Gorge or 26.5

miles to Willis Creek Trailhead and large parking area, each located on the left side of the road.

77 Hackberry Canyon

THIS IS AN ENCHANTING DAY HIKE IN A LOVELY CANYON THAT IS OFF THE BEATEN PATH AND usually not crowded. For most of the way, the creek serves as your trail, and it is pretty easy walking in the streambed if you only travel up a couple of miles and return. The most dramatic part of the canyon is within the first two miles. Hackberry Canyon is also ideal for a multi-day backpack trip, exploring the various side canyons upstream.

From the parking area and trailhead, follow the path down about twenty yards into Cottonwood Wash, cross the wash, then immediately go northwest away from the trailhead and into the mouth of Hackberry Canyon. For the first quarter-mile the canyon will be dry, but then you will start to see a trickle of water. You can avoid getting your feet wet at first, but why bother? Within minutes you will be walking in water. The water is usually only a couple of inches deep and it is pleasant walking in the sandy streambed.

Visually the most stunning part of this canyon is at the beginning, within two miles from the trailhead. Here you will find a riparian setting with Navajo and Kayenta sandstone walls only twenty feet apart in some places, yet the cliff walls rise up about one hundred feet.

If you want to continue, a good day destination is Sam Pollach Arch, located in a side canyon on your left about 2.75 miles from the trailhead. The best way to reach the arch is to follow the canyon upstream about one-half mile, where further progress is blocked by a dryfall. Just backtrack about one hundred yards and head up on the north side of the canyon, bypassing this obstacle and returning to the canyon bottom. From here it will be about one mile to the arch.

No permit is needed for a day hike but if you plan on backpacking you will need one. Pick one up at any visitor center in the park or self-permit at the trailhead.

Hackberry Canyon At A Glance

Best Season: April to mid-June and September to mid-November.

Length: Four miles or longer roundtrip for day hike.

Difficulty: Easy to strenuous, depending on length of travel.

Elevation gain: About 150 feet for two-mile day hike.

Trailhead elevation: 4,775 feet.

Warnings: Flash flooding. Cottonwood Road becomes impassable after or during rain. No water available in upper reaches of canyon.

Jurisdiction: Grand Staircase-Escalante National Monument.

Directions: From the Kanab Visitor Center take U.S. 89 east (toward Lake Powell) for about 36.5 miles and go left onto Cottonwood Road (BLM 400). Follow the gravel road north about 14.5 miles to the signed parking area and trailhead located on your left.

Alternate Directions: From the Cannonville Visitor Center drive south for 8 miles on Cottonwood Road (BLM 400) to the Kodachrome State Park sign. At this point the road becomes gravel, but continue straight ahead about 23 miles and go right to the Hackberry Canyon parking area and trailhead.

The lower portion of Hackberry Canyon beckons with riparian beauty.

Other

The Gifford Homestead
Barn is found along the
Scenic Drive in Fruita.

Utah

National Parks

Capitol Reef National Park

Capitol Reef National Park became a national park in 1971. It encompasses 243,921 acres and is best known for the park's most obvious geologic landform, the Waterpocket Fold, a wrinkle in the earth that extends almost one hundred miles. The park has 140 miles of roads and more than 150 miles of trails and backcountry routes. Places to explore include arches, natural bridges, waterfalls and slot canyons. Elevations in the park range from thirty-eight hundred to eighty-two hundred feet.

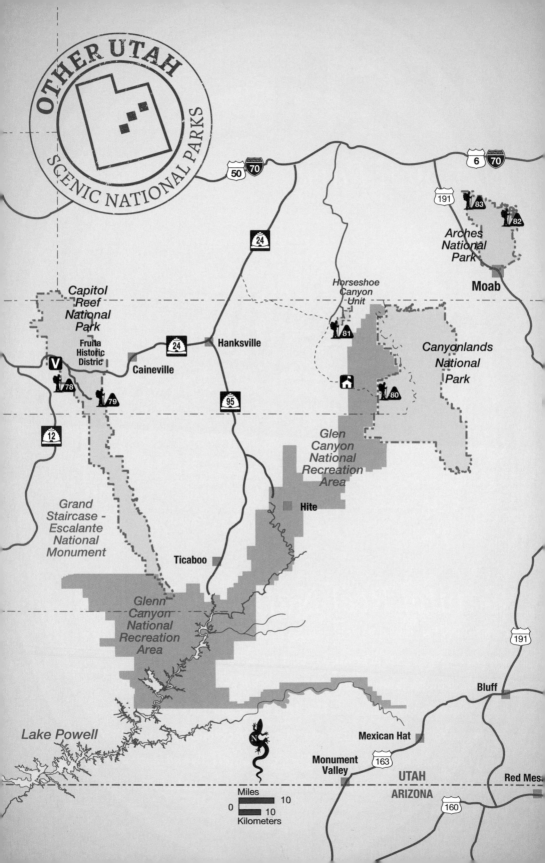

OTHER UTAH
SCENIC NATIONAL PARKS

50 70

6 70

191 83

24

82

Arches National Park

Moab

Horseshoe Canyon Unit

Capitol Reef National Park

81

Canyonlands National Park

Fruita Historic Distric

V 78

Hanksville

Caineville

79

80

12

24

95

Glen Canyon National Recreation Area

Grand Staircase - Escalante National Monument

Hite

Ticaboo

Glenn Canyon National Recreation Area

191

Lake Powell

Bluff

N

Mexican Hat

Monument Valley

163

UTAH

Red Mesa

ARIZONA

Miles
0   10
10
Kilometers

160

Capitol Reef boasts the largest historic collection of orchards in our park system. Because the area did not become a national monument until 1937, or upgraded to a national park until 1971, some of the lands had already been developed for agriculture. We owe these orchards to the Mormon pioneers who settled the town of Fruita in the early 1880s. They tapped the Fremont River with irrigation ditches and planted fruit trees not only for subsistence but also for a cash and bartering crop.

Today, the park service maintains the orchards, which contain thirty-one hundred trees, primarily apple, apricot, peach, pear and cherry. But there are also nut trees including almond, pecan and walnut. In season you can pick the ripe fruit. The park even provides ladders, bags, and hand-held pickers, devices with small baskets at the end of long poles. Scales are provided, and there is a small charge per pound. You use self-pay stations, on the honor system. There is a bonus; while in the orchard you can eat as much fruit as you want, for free. You can access any orchard as long as it has unlocked gates and is signed as open for picking.

Of course, different fruits ripen in different months, and those harvest times vary slightly from year to year. But people typically pick cherries from mid-June to early July, apricots from late June to mid-July, peaches and pears from early August to early September, and apples from early September to mid-October.

The visitor center is open daily, except major holidays, from 8 a.m.to 4:30 p.m., with extended hours in summer. For more information on the park, including driving tours, hiking trails, camping and the historic fruit orchards, contact Capitol Reef National Park at (435) 425-3791 or *www.nps.gov/care*. While there are no services in the park, the town of Torrey, only eleven miles away, offers restaurants, cafes, a market, gas stations, and a wide variety of lodging. Check it out at *www.torreyutah.com/*.

Directions: From Las Vegas, take Interstate 15 north for 162 miles to exit 57, Cedar City, Utah. Go north on Utah Route 14 for about 2 miles to historic Main Street. Go right to continue on Utah 14 and drive about 40 miles. Go left onto U.S. 89 for about 20 miles and go right onto Scenic Byway 12. Follow for 124 miles to Torrey, then go right on Utah Route 24 and drive 11 miles to visitor center.

78 Fremont River Trail

THIS TRAIL IS LOCATED IN THE FRUITA HISTORIC DISTRICT OF THE PARK. YOU WILL PARK your car in Loop B or Loop C of the Fruita Campground and follow a footpath to the amphitheater, where you will see the trail. From either parking area you will be walking by a couple of the Fruita orchards. If the fruit is in season, be sure to grab a ripe apple, peach or pear to bring on your hike.

The Fremont River in this section flows through a riparian environment of willow and cottonwood trees. There are often Bullock's orioles flitting around here in summer. Check out the nearby trees for their hanging, pouch-shaped nests. You might also see a covey of chukars, exotic partridges easily recognizable with their bright red beaks and legs, and vibrant stripes along their sides. Deer and wild turkeys are frequently seen, foraging for fallen fruit in the orchards.

The trail is hard-packed gravel and easy to walk. After about 0.4 miles you will pass through a fence. Only hikers are allowed to continue after this, and people on bicycles, or accompanied by pets, must turn around.

Once past the fence you will leave the streamside, and the riparian vegetation along the trail will gradually be replaced by a plant community primarily of sage brush. The trail starts gaining elevation as you head up the slope on the east side of the river. Along this segment you will enjoy fine views of the Fremont River Gorge below, with the ribbon of green surrounding the river.

Once on top you will be in a sparsely vegetated pinyon/juniper

With about 3,100 fruit and nut trees, the park is home to the largest historic collection of orchards in our park system. Visitors can pick the fruit when it is ripe.

area. There are several places to get excellent sweeping views. An especially dramatic one looks down upon the lush greenery of Fruita, surrounded by the rugged and barren sandstone cliffs and monoliths in the park. Another, to the east, offers a good view of the Waterpocket Fold.

Fremont River Trail At a Glance

Best Season: April–October.

Length: About 2.6 miles.

Difficulty: Easy to moderate.

Elevation gain: 480 feet.

Trailhead elevation: 5,450 feet.

Warning: Drop-offs in upper reaches.

Jurisdiction: Capitol Reef National Park

79 Capitol Gorge

THIS IS A WONDERFUL OUTING FOR ALMOST ALL AGES. THE ROUTE FOLLOWS AN ABANDONED road, through a narrow sandstone canyon that contains American Indian petroglyphs, other inscriptions left by pioneers, and some natural tanks or waterpockets.

With the settlement of Fruita , and the other pioneer towns to the east, a better road was badly needed. The original route to and from Fruita was a rough one for travelers and often involved danger in crossings of the Fremont River. In 1884, a local man, Elijah Behunin, and a small crew, cleared boulders and vegetation in this gorge to make a new wagon road. Even though the road was subject to severe flash flooding, it was used as the main east-west road until 1962, when the current State Highway 24 was opened.

From the trailhead, just head up the well-worn trail. You could drop down into the wash itself here but if you did that, you might miss the petroglyphs. After walking about 0.4 miles you will find some panels on the north, or left, cliff wall. These petroglyphs were made by the Fremont Culture Indians and are seven hundred to one thousand years old. The Fremonts were hunter-gatherers, but supplemented their diet by farming corn, beans and squash. They lived in pit houses dug into the ground, which they covered with brush.

Soon after the rock art, extremely high on the south cliff wall, you will see the names of six men who were surveyors here in 1911. There are still more inscriptions besides these. About 0.6 miles from the trailhead, look on the sandstone walls, on the north side, for the Pioneer Register. The Register contains dozens of names etched into the soft sandstone by miners, settlers and other travelers. One signed J.E. Smith, from 1871, predated the road. Further additions are illegal, and you will be fined if caught adding one.

Around 0.2 miles farther there is a spur trail on the north side of the wash, which takes you on a fairly steep climb up about 0.3 miles to the "tanks." Formed by erosion of the sandstone, these depressions are locally called "waterpockets," giving their name to the geological structure in which they occur. Especially picturesque when full of rainwater, they vary from a few gallons capacity to the size of a small swimming pool. These serve as precious water sources for the wildlife in the area.

Capitol Gorge At A Glance

Best Season: March–October.

Length: Two miles roundtrip.

Difficulty: Easy.

Elevation gain: One hundred feet.

Trailhead elevation: 5,437 feet.

Warning: Flash flooding.

Jurisdiction: Capitol Reef National Park.

Directions: From the visitor center drive south 7.9 miles on the paved Scenic Drive. Go left onto the well-maintained gravel Capitol Gorge Road. Drive 2.7 miles to parking area and trailhead.

Capitol Gorge used to be the main road to and from Fruita and was used up until 1962. Now it serves as a trail to see petroglyphs, pioneer inscriptions, and natural water tanks.

Canyonlands National Park

Canyonlands National Park, Utah, encompasses 337,570 acres around the junction where the Green River, flowing from the northwest, joins the Colorado, flowing from the northeast. Elevations range from thirty-nine hundred feet on the Colorado River, south of Cataract Canyon, to 7,180 feet in the Needles District's Big Pocket.

This park was established in 1964, one of four national parks founded during the administration of Secretary of the Interior Stewart Udall, a lifelong conservationist from Arizona. However, the park's true father is considered to be Bates Wilson, the first superintendent of what is now Arches National Park, who lobbied more than a decade for the region's protection. The law creating it was introduced by Sen. Frank Rose, a Utah Democrat. Other interests had hoped to create a major dam there, instead of a natural preserve.

Canyonlands has several geographic districts. The Island in the Sky District is a triangle of sweeping canyon lands between the rivers, and this area is the most visited, as it is conveniently located near Moab. The Needles District, to the south, lies east of the Colorado River.

The most remote section, the Maze District, is west of both the rivers. Still farther west is Horseshoe Canyon District, a detached unit of the park, created in 1971, which is managed by the Maze District. The rivers within the park are managed as their own unit.

The following routes are in the most remote areas of the park and will require plenty of preparations for a safe and enjoyable visit. Good maps are essential when traveling in this region, especially the *National Geographic Trails Illustrated Map* named "Maze District, Canyonlands National Park," as well as a very detailed Utah road map for the drive there.

For more information contact Canyonlands National Park at (435) 719-2313, www.*nps.gov/cany/*.

Left: *The Holy Ghost panel in the Great Gallery.*

80 The Maze

THIS IS A TRIP FOR UTTERLY SELF-SUFFICIENT BACKCOUNTRY ADVENTURERS WITH EXCELLENT, proven skills in both route finding and off-road driving. To understand how remote this area is, consider that only a couple of thousand people a year come here, compared to more than a quarter-million who visit Island in the Sky District in the same national park. The hikes are primitive, and most likely you and your group will be the only ones on the trail. If you get into trouble, there will be no timely rescue.

Yet, if you are one of those people I described above, and you make the extensive preparations required, it will be possibly the favorite trip of your life!

If you are that seasoned hiker and backroad tripper, you will probably have everything needed for a trip here, but if you are new at this game, you will need to gather some gear. The trip requires a high-clearance vehicle which has low-range four-wheel drive. Popular crossover SUVs (i.e., those built on auto bodies) may have only high-range, so make sure what your vehicle has, before you decide to take this trip. Have true off-road tires on it, plus at least one *full-sized* spare. (I

recommend two.) I strongly suggest bringing a shovel and heavy gloves for moving small boulders to get your vehicle up hills after washouts. You will also need to bring all your own water, extra gas, and a high-lift jack. Also, if you come between October and April, you should have tire chains because of possible weather.

Permits are required for all overnight trips and for many

Left: The Chocolate Drops, among the most famous formations in Canyonlands National Park, seen from the Maze Overlook. Right: The Maze is located in one of the most remote areas in the nation.

day-use excursions in this area, so you absolutely should arrange them in advance to avoid making such a long drive in vain. After all, just driving to the Hans Ranger Station from Las Vegas will take about seven or eight hours, before you even set out on the backroad adventure into The Maze. For visiting anywhere in The Maze, the absolute minimum stay in this district would be two nights, but that would be pushing it. Three to four nights is ideal.

If you could go to only one area of The Maze my personal choice would be the Maze Overlook, but only if you can procure a campsite permit for that area.

You will need to go to the Hans Ranger Station first to pick up your pre-arranged permit. Backcountry regulations must be followed to a tee, and at the ranger station they will check your vehicle and equipment before letting you set out. No fires, except charcoal in a fire pan. No pets. It is also required that you have a cleanable, reusable toilet.

To get to the Maze Overlook will require a three- to four-hour drive from Hans Ranger Station on unbelievably rough roads. So it might be best to disperse camp on BLM land on the outskirts of the park the night before you enter, so you can get an early start into the district itself. Alternatively, if you already arranged for

a permit, and arrived to check in at the ranger station before it closed, you could camp at one of the campsites on the way to Maze Overlook: North Point, Flint Seep, or Happy Canyon.

Don't set out here unless you have the *National Geographic Trails Illustrated Map* named "Maze District, Canyonlands National Park," as well as a very detailed Utah road map for the way there. Study and mark your route before you leave from home, so you don't waste time once in the district. Always show the ranger the park map, with your expected route marked on it. This area really is a maze!

The Flint Trail (the main driving route to the Maze Overlook, down from the plateau from Hans) can be quite an adventure, and I have found it to be extremely intense to drive in a few spots. Being clay, the road can be treacherous when wet, but it is the only logical choice, and the quickest, except hiking, to get down through the Orange Cliffs from the ranger station. If you make it to the overlook to camp, rejoice, and enjoy either sunrise, sunset, or both at this remote setting.

The panoramic view is one of the finest in the park, with deep canyons, mesas, buttes, and hoodoos in every direction. The most famous formation is the Chocolate Drops, four vertical columns of reddish-brown sandstone that rise close to two hundred feet above the ridgeline in the landscape known as Land of Standing Rocks.

When you are ready to leave The Maze, I would recommend taking the southern route that will bring you out near Hite, Arizona. Taking this road to Hite is usually easier than returning back up the steep Flint Trail, but that depends on the time of year. Check at the ranger station for advice and weather conditions.

The Maze At a Glance

Best Season: April–May and September–October.

Hans Ranger Station Elevation: 6,585 feet.

Maze Overlook elevation: 5,160 feet.

Warnings: Reservations are needed for a permit through the Hans Ranger Station for most backcountry travel and campsites in The Maze. Be aware of flash flooding danger in all canyons and roads. People do get lost in here and directional signs may be missing, so be sure to have updated maps and to use them

Jurisdiction: Canyonlands National Park.

Directions to Hans Ranger Station: From Las Vegas take Interstate 15 north 242 miles to Interstate 70. Go east, drive about 149 miles and go right to Utah Route 24 west. Follow about 24 miles and go left onto a gravel road, between mile posts 135 and 136, just one-half mile south of Goblin Valley State Park. Drive about 46 miles, staying right at the obvious signed fork (at about 24 miles) for the Hans Ranger Station.

81 Horseshoe Canyon

IF YOU ARE INTERESTED IN PICTOGRAPHS, THE RARER FORM OF PREHISTORIC DESERT ROCK art, you will be in awe visiting Horseshoe Canyon. Famous for its best-known panel, The Great Gallery, Horseshoe Canyon is one of the most significant rock art sites in North America.

Lying in a detached unit of Canyonlands National Park, the canyon is otherwise unremarkable, with sheer sandstone walls and a riparian plant environment.

The Great Gallery is the best known pictograph panel in Horseshoe Canyon.

But the art is unique. The Great Gallery's highlights are the reddish-brown pictographs that feature anthropomorphic figures painted in the Barrier Canyon Style. Some of them have an ethereal appearance, suggesting people were painting a personal depiction of something they saw. It has been suggested that what those ancient artists saw were aliens. Depending on one's interpretation, the paintings are life-size or larger than life; some are more than seven feet tall.

Some pictographs at the Great Gallery are almost seven feet tall.

On the 6.5-mile roundtrip hike to Great Gallery you can easily visit the other rock art sites named High Gallery, Horseshoe Shelter, and Alcove Site. From the trailhead you just head down the old stock trail about 1.3 miles through the sandstone cliffs, guided by the well-placed cairns. Once you arrive in the obvious wash you will be in Horseshoe Canyon. Turn right, which is upstream. Sometimes you will find some water flowing here, so it is good to check on canyon conditions through the park service before you set out, as flash flooding could be a problem.

After hiking about one-third mile up the wash, look on your left for a well-worn path that heads about thirty feet toward the cliff walls. Here, behind the vegetation, you will find your first site, known as High Gallery. The next three sites are Horseshoe Shelter, Alcove Site and then the best of all, the Great Gallery. These last three will all be located on your right and are easier to find.

In the past it was accepted that these panels were as old as eight thousand years, but recently scientists from Utah State University concluded that the rock art was no more than two thousand years old. Many other scientists, however, still believe they are older.

Be aware that from the park's main entrance near Moab, Utah, the drive to the trailhead takes more than two-and-one-half hours, including thirty miles on a gravel road. If you are coming from Las Vegas and want to visit The Maze or Horsehoe Canyon, yet also want to see the main areas of the park, organize your trip to visit this remote section on the way to or from the main park.

A four-wheel-drive, high-clearance vehicle, with good off-road tires, is recommended for the last thirty miles to the trailhead, for one often encounters deep sand and/or rutted sections along the road. Be sure to bring the *National Geographic Trails Illustrated Map* named "Maze District, Canyonlands National Park."

Dry camping is allowed before the trailhead, as this is land managed by the BLM, but no camping is allowed in Horseshoe Canyon within the park's boundary. There is a vault toilet. Bring all your own water. Call or visit the Hans Ranger Station and ask about road conditions for this specific area of the park: (435) 259-2652 between 8 a.m. and 4:30 p.m. only. Make after-hours calls to this number only for Maze-area emergencies. The Hans Ranger Station is located about twenty-seven miles, or one hour's drive, on a rough gravel road, from the Horseshoe Canyon Trailhead.

Horseshoe Canyon At A Glance

Best Season: April–May and September–October.

Length: 6.5 miles roundtrip.

Difficulty: Moderate.

Elevation gain: 780 feet.

Trailhead elevation: 5,344 feet.

Warning: Remote area, no services available.

Jurisdiction: Canyonlands National Park.

Directions: From Las Vegas take Interstate 15 north for 242 miles to Interstate 70. Go east and drive about 149 miles and go right to Utah Route 24 west. Follow about 24 miles and go left on the signed Horseshoe Road (just south of Goblin Valley State Park.) Drive about 30 miles, staying left at the obvious fork in the road after about 24 miles. (The right fork leads to the Hans Ranger Station in the Maze District of Canyonlands.) Stay left, drive about 5 miles, and go right on Horseshoe Canyon access road, then drive in about 1.7 miles to camping area and trailhead.

The Three Gossips formation,
seen along the scenic drive.

Arches National Park

Located just five miles from Moab, Utah, this park boasts more than two thousand natural sandstone arches, the largest concentration in the world.

For a formation to officially be deemed an arch, its opening must be at least three feet across. For the most part, arches are formed by water and ice erosion when combined with underground salt movement and extreme temperatures, all factors found in Arches. A visit here, though, is not all about the arches, as you will find other amazing natural formations such as spires, natural windows, balanced rocks, and pinnacles. If you had only enough time to drive the thirty-six-mile Scenic Dive through the park, you would be treated to a feast for the eyes. There are plenty of pullouts to see some wonderful formations.

For the Scenic Drive tour, leave the visitor center driving east about 2.5 miles to the Park Avenue Viewpoint. Here you can see some great scenery of steep cliff walls, balanced rocks, and other inspiring formations, or you can take the 2.5 mile roundtrip paved trail deeper into the park.

The next logical stop along the drive would be at Balanced Rock, located on your right about nine miles from the visitor center. This rock appears certain to fall at any second, but it has managed not to for many years.

Just 0.3 miles past Balanced Rock, be sure to go right and drive in about 2.5 miles to reach the Windows section of the park. This is one of my favorite places to take people, because they have to hike only short and easy trails to see North and South Windows and Double Arch.

The park was established in 1971, encompasses more than 76,359 acres, and has an elevation range from 4,085 to 5,653 feet. There are a variety of trails in Arches that range from easy to difficult — even wheelchair accessible trails — so you will find there is something for all ages and abilities.

About fifty species of mammals live in the park, as do twenty-one reptiles. More than 185 kinds of birds have been seen here, including the bald eagle and

Arches National Park is home to more than 2,000 natural stone arches including Double Arch. The southern span is the second largest in the park, at 144 feet across.

the Mexican spotted owl. In spring and fall you will probably see rock squirrels, chipmunks, lizards, and perhaps a few snakes during the day. At dusk and dawn, look for mule deer and coyotes. Many animals, though, are nocturnal, including kangaroo rats, mountain lions, and foxes.

The nearby town of Moab has complete services. For information on lodging, camping, restaurants, vehicle repair and other services, contact or visit the Moab Visitor Center, 25 E. Center Street, Moab, (435) 259-8825, *discovermoab.com*.

The park is open twenty-four hours a day, year-round. The Arches Visitor Center is open daily except Christmas, but hours vary seasonally. For hours and more information on the park, contact (435) 719-2299, *www.nps.gov/arch*.

Directions: From Las Vegas take Interstate 15 north and drive about 242 miles. Exit onto Interstate 70 east and travel about 182 miles. Exit south onto U.S. 191 and travel about 26 miles to Arches Visitor Center, located on your left.

82 Delicate Arch

DELICATE ARCH IS ONE OF THE MOST PHOTOGRAPHED ARCHES IN THE WORLD AND SERVES as a well-known emblem for Utah itself, even being featured on state license plates. It is the largest free- standing arch in the park. Measured at its midpoint, the opening of the arch is sixty-four feet high and forty-five wide.

There are three ways to view the arch. The close-and-personal way requires a three-mile roundtrip hike, but it can also be seen from either of two viewpoints.

The hike route is a moderate one but not good for children, as there are high drop-offs along the way. This arch is a wonderful place to be at sunset, but be aware it can be crowded, sometimes with more than one hundred people! If you want to see the arch without throngs of people, be sure to head out first thing in the morning.

If you are unable or unwilling to make the hike, you can still get a good look and good photos. The Lower Viewpoint is only about one hundred yards roundtrip and is even accessible to wheelchairs. With a little more effort, and a rocky uphill hike of 0.5 miles roundtrip, the Upper Viewpoint offers a good alternative.

Delicate Arch is 45 feet at its highest point.

Delicate Arch At A Glance

Best Season: April–June and September–November.

Length: Three miles roundtrip.

Difficulty: Moderate.

Elevation gain: 480 feet.

Trailhead elevation: 4,309 feet.

Warnings: Not good for small children as there are drop-offs. Extremely popular.

Jurisdiction: Arches National Park.

Directions: From the Arches Visitor Center drive 12 miles on the Scenic Drive and go right to Delicate Arch Road. Drive 1.2 miles to the parking area and Delicate Arch Trailhead. To reach the Upper and Lower Delicate Arch Viewpoints, drive one mile farther on Delicate Arch Road to the parking area and trailheads.

83 Landscape Arch

IF YOU ONLY HAVE TIME TO HIKE TO ONE ARCH IN THE PARK, THEN LANDSCAPE ARCH SHOULD be the one. This is the park's longest natural arch with a span of 290 feet base to base. This is a good hike for almost all ages, as it is fairly level.

The trailhead is located in the Devil's Garden parking area, and the 1.6-mile roundtrip trail is obvious to follow. The arch is now only about six feet thick at its center, very thin for its length. In 1991 a piece seventy-three feet long fell from its underside, followed by two more rock falls in 1995. With the continuing forces of weathering, erosion and gravity, it could possibly collapse in the near future. Come see it now. There used to be a spur trail that went underneath the arch, but the park has closed it because of potential rock falls.

In 2008, the Wall Arch, located very close by, collapsed. That arch was the twelfth largest in the park at the time, seventy-one feet wide and thirty-three high. No one witnessed the event since it happened at night.

Landscape Arch At A Glance

Best Season: April–June and September–November.

Length: 1.6 miles roundtrip.

Difficulty: Easy.

Elevation gain: Minimal.

Trailhead elevation: 5,242 feet.

Warning: No shade.

Jurisdiction: Arches National park.

Directions: From Arches Visitor Center head east on the Scenic Drive for about 16.5 miles. Continue onto Devil's Garden Road for 1.3 miles to parking area and Landscape Arch Trailhead.

Landscape Arch is North America's longest arch.

Grand

Canyon

National Park

Grand Canyon National Park, established in 1919, is one of the most famous places on earth. The Colorado River winds 277 river miles through it, and the canyon is as wide as eighteen miles, and one mile deep. Because of the extreme elevation differences in the park, there are also vast differences in the habitats that support different wildlife and vegetation. You will never see it all.

A visit here is what you make it. Although backpacking down into the canyon is a trip of a lifetime and I would highly recommend it, shorter day hikes can also be extremely rewarding.

The north and south rims are only about ten miles apart as the crow flies, but access between the rims is limited. The options to get from rim to rim are either twenty-four miles of strenuous hiking or a 215-mile highway trip.

Lookout Studio on the South Rim.

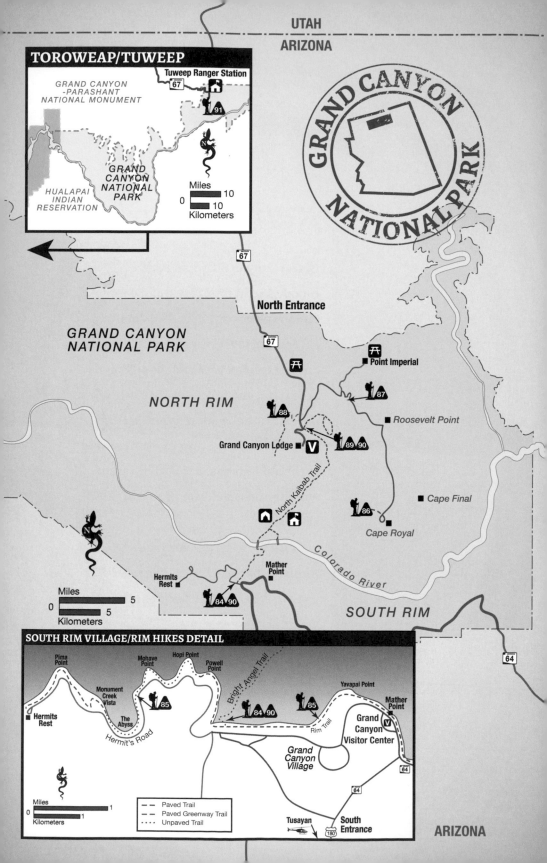

UTAH
ARIZONA

TOROWEAP/TUWEEP

GRAND CANYON
-PARASHANT
NATIONAL MONUMENT

Tuweep Ranger Station

67

91

HUALAPAI
INDIAN
RESERVATION

GRAND
CANYON
NATIONAL
PARK

N

Miles
0   10

Kilometers
10

GRAND CANYON
NATIONAL PARK

67

North Entrance

GRAND CANYON
NATIONAL PARK

67

Point Imperial

NORTH RIM

88

87

Roosevelt Point

Grand Canyon Lodge **V**

89 **90**

Cape Final

North Kaibab Trail

86

Cape Royal

Colorado River

Hermits
Rest

Mather
Point

84 **90**

N

Miles
0   5

Kilometers
5

SOUTH RIM

64

SOUTH RIM VILLAGE/RIM HIKES DETAIL

Pima
Point

Mohave
Point

Hopi Point

Powell
Point

Yavapai Point

Bright Angel Trail

Mather
Point

Monument
Creek
Vista

85

84 **90**

85

Rim Trail

Grand Canyon
Visitor Center **V**

Hermits Rest

The
Abyss

Hermit's Road

Grand
Canyon
Village

64

64

Miles
0   1

Kilometers
1

Tusayan

South
Entrance

180

- - - Paved Trail
- - - Paved Greenway Trail
····· Unpaved Trail

ARIZONA

Even so, it's worth visiting both rims; the experiences are different.

The South Rim is open year round, twenty-four hours a day, and has stores, a market, and many restaurants. Summertime temperatures usually range from the fifties to eighties with winter temperatures from the twenties to fifties.

Directions to South Rim: From Las Vegas take U.S. 93 south about 105 miles to Kingman, Arizona. Go east on Interstate 40 for about 112 miles to Williams. Exit onto Arizona Route 64 and drive north for about 60 miles to the entrance of Grand Canyon National Park. (928) 638-7888, *www.nps.gov/grca*.

The North Rim is far less crowded. Being about one thousand feet higher, it has cooler temperatures, ranging in summer from the forties to the seventies. The main road from Jacob Lake closes once the first snow falls, generally around late October to December, and usually doesn't open again until mid-May. Always call the park for road updates before heading there.

The North Rim has a general store, gas station and a few restaurants which are open only during the summer. The North Rim Visitor Center, near the Grand Canyon Lodge, is generally open from mid-May to mid-October from 8 a.m. to 6 p.m. daily.

Directions to North Rim: From Las Vegas take Interstate 15 north about 125 miles to Utah Route 9, the Hurricane/Zion National Park Exit. Drive about 12 miles and turn right onto Utah Route 59 east. This turns into Arizona Route 389 at the state border. Drive about 53 miles to Fredonia and turn right onto U.S. 89 Alt. for about 30 miles. Turn right at Jacob Lake onto Arizona Route 67, the Grand Canyon Highway. Continue about 45 miles to the Grand Canyon, North Rim Visitor Center and Lodge.

84 Bright Angel Trail

BRIGHT ANGEL TRAIL IS THE MOST POPULAR ONE IN THE PARK FOR BACKPACKERS HEADING down into the Grand Canyon and to the Colorado River. But it also makes an excellent choice for day hikes, as long as hikers don't overdo it. Spring and fall are the best times on this trail. Summers are too hot, and winter often brings snow and ice, especially near the rim.

The trailhead, which is 6,820 feet in elevation, is on the park's South Rim next to Kolb Studio, west of Bright Angel Lodge. Depending on the physical abilities of your group and how much time you have, there are a few general destinations you might use as planned turnaround points. Mile-and-a-Half Resthouse will make a moderate three-mile roundtrip hike; Three-Mile Resthouse, a six-mile moderate roundtrip hike; and Indian Gardens will be a strenuous nine-mile roundtrip.

When planning how far to go, keep in mind that it all will be uphill on your return. Return trips from the aforesaid turnaround points have elevation gains of 1,131 feet, 2,112 feet and 3,060 feet respectively. Under no circumstances should you try to hike to the Colorado River and back in one day. People have died trying. If there is snow or ice, do this trail some other time, or wear instep crampons. Hiking poles are a good idea no matter what the conditions.

I don't recommend this outing for children. Most kids will find the trail too strenuous. More important, there are extreme drop-offs, especially in the upper reaches.

Just a few hundred yards into the hike you will come to a man-made tunnel. On the downhill side of the tunnel be sure to look up on the cliff wall to the left, where you will see a shallow alcove. This is called Mallory's Grotto and you will see red pictographs painted on the rock. Some are thought to have been left by ancestors of the Havasupai Indians, who now live in the western Grand Canyon.

Prehistoric hunters and gatherers first wore the trail, and were followed by miners in the nineteenth century. In modern times, thousands have enjoyed it by backpacking or mule train. There isn't a bad view from the entire route and it is enchanting to travel down through millions of years of geologic history.

About three-quarters of a mile from the trailhead you will pass through another man-made tunnel and then the trail descends a series of steep switchbacks. Just prior to arriving at Mile-and-a-Half Resthouse you might encounter cooler temperatures and

Even in winter, hikers can be found on the South Rim trails.

a micro-climate that supports Gambel's oak and even some Douglas fir, rare for this area. But by the time you reach Three-Mile Resthouse you will be leaving much of the forest vegetation behind for desert scrub.

Mile-and-a-Half, Three-Mile and Indian Garden resthouses were constructed of native stone, by the Civilian Conservation Corps in 1935-1936.

Indian Garden is about halfway from the rim to the river and is the deepest point you should attempt on a day trip. This is a very pretty area with a ranger station, campground, picnic area and plenty of cottonwood trees that provide good shade and a place to rest before your return to the rim.

Water is available year-round at Indian Garden and seasonally, starting in May, at the upper resthouses, unless there happens to be a break in the pipeline, which happens from time to time. If you are depending on any of these water supplies to augment what you will carry,

Mule train descends the Bright Angel Trail.

be really sure to ask the park service, before setting out, if they're in order.

You might have to share the trail with mules for a short distance. If you come across them, unless one of the wranglers instructs you differently, proper etiquette calls for standing quietly off the trail on the uphill side, and staying put until the last mule passes you by at least fifty feet.

Bright Angel Trail At A Glance

Best season: March–June, and September–November.

Length: Three miles roundtrip to Mile-and-a-Half Resthouse, six miles to Three-Mile Resthouse, and 9.2 miles to Indian Garden.

Difficulty: Moderate to strenuous depending on distance traveled.

Elevation loss: 1,131 feet to Mile-and-a-Half Resthouse, 2,112 feet to Three-Mile Resthouse, and 3,060 feet to Indian Garden.

Trailhead elevation: 6,820 feet.

Warnings: Cliff exposure, slippery trail when wet or icy. Avoid in summer. Water availability uncertain. Trail shared with mules.

Jurisdiction: Grand Canyon National Park, South Rim.

Directions: Trailhead lies directly on the rim just west of the Bright Angel Lodge and next to Kolb Studio.

85 Rim Trail

THE RIM TRAIL IS ONE OF THE CLASSIC HIKES ON THE GRAND CANYON'S SOUTH RIM, AND an especially versatile one. It is relatively flat, and can be done in short segments or extended into an all-day excursion. It follows the rim for twelve miles, taking in the park's most popular viewpoints, including some from which you can see all the way down to the Colorado River. If you get tired or run out of time, you can hop on one of the free shuttle buses to return to the main area of the park.

One popular way to do this trail is to take the shuttle from the Village Route transfer station, located just west of the Bright Angel Lodge complex, all the way out to Hermit's Rest, the farthest west point of the Rim Trail and the end of the main road. While here, be sure to visit the viewpoints that lie west of Hermits Rest itself, the historic building constructed in 1914.

Then start hiking your way back toward the transfer station. This first part of the hike is also known as the Hermit Road Greenway Trail. It is two trail segments with a shuttle stop between, and totals less than three miles one-way, with six overlooks.

All the fourteen segments between shuttle stops are fairly short, and range from three-tenths miles to one and seven-tenths miles. The Monument Creek Vista and the Abyss are the longest. The trail is paved the entire way except for the segment between Monument Creek Vista and Powell Point, which is three and eight-tenths miles.

Rim Trail At A Glance

Best Season: May–June, and September–November.

Length: Short segments, or up to twelve miles one-way, from Hermit's Rest to Pipe Creek Vista.

Difficulty: Easy, if done in short segments.

Elevation gain/loss: Two hundred feet for entire trail.

Trailhead elevation: 6,636 feet at Hermit's Rest.

Warnings: Snow and ice in winter, steep drop-offs in some segments. Lightning; do not hike when thunderstorms threaten. No potable water available except at Grand Canyon Village area and Hermit's Rest.

Jurisdiction: Grand Canyon National Park, South Rim.

Directions: Private vehicles are not allowed on Hermit's Rest Road March–November; access is by free shuttle buses which stop at all viewpoints from Pipe Creek Vista to Hermit's rest. Before leaving home, download South Rim Transit Map to check schedule during days and hours you plan to visit.

Sunset at South Rim of Grand Canyon National Park.

North Rim

Lying on the Arizona Strip and thus accessed mainly via rural Utah, the Grand Canyon's North Rim has always drawn fewer visitors than the South Rim, which lies nearer large populations and has been more consciously developed for tourism.

While many people travel to the North Rim to embark on trips down into the canyon, there is plenty to keep you occupied along the rim. If you can hike all the short but sweet overlook trails, as well as the trails listed here, you will get a great idea of the diversity the North Rim has to offer.

Geography makes the North Rim a different experience from the South Rim, and in summer, an especially pleasant one. Because its elevations are higher, from about eight thousand to eighty-eight hundred feet, the North Rim is better for camping and hiking, with summer daytime highs averaging in the seventies and nighttime lows in the forties. This side of the park also gets twice as much precipitation as falls on the South Rim, resulting in lush vegetation and superb summer wildflower displays. You will find open grassy meadows, small ponds, aspen groves, and dense forests of ponderosa pine, white fir, Englemann spruce, and blue spruce.

The main draw of the park is spectacular canyon views, and its rim trails, such as the paved half-mile roundtrip Bright Angel Point Trail, display them wonderfully. But some are so popular that they don't provide much solitude; after admiring those vistas, be sure to explore some of the excellent, lesser-known trails away from the rim.

After checking out the visitor center and Grand Canyon Lodge area, the hub of the North Rim, most visitors take the drive out to Point Royal along Cape Royal Road. There are plenty of signed overlook trails, such as the Cape Royal Trail (six-tenths mile roundtrip) and the Roosevelt Point Trail (two-tenths mile roundtrip). Both are well worth your time, but to enhance your experience, this is an area to seek the differences of paths less traveled.

View towards the South Rim from behind the Grand Canyon Lodge. Right: Visitors can take it easy on the terrace of the North Rim's Grand Canyon Lodge.

86 Cliff Spring Trail

THE UNSIGNED CLIFF SPRING TRAIL IS LOCATED ON YOUR left about half a mile along your return from Point Royal. This trail is only one mile roundtrip and makes its way along a highly vegetated, yet somewhat steep canyon. Your destination is an enormous, natural rock overhang, perhaps seventy-five yards long, complete with a small spring, seeps, and hanging gardens. Along the way you will pass a well-preserved prehistoric food storage granary, just one among thousands of ruins that have been documented in the park. Ancestral Puebloans lived on the North Rim between the years of A.D. 1050 and 1150, scientists calculate.

~~~~~~~~~~~~~~~~~~~~~~~~~

Cliff Spring Trail At A Glance

Best season: June–September.

Length: One mile roundtrip.

Difficulty: Moderate.

Elevation loss: 250 feet.

Trailhead elevation: 7,754 feet.

Warnings: Cliff exposure, slippery terrain.

Jurisdiction: Grand Canyon National Park, North Rim.

Directions: From the North Rim Visitor Center take Route 67 north for about 2.9 miles. Go right onto Fuller Canyon Road (to Cape Royal) and drive 5.3 miles. Go right onto Cape Royal Road and drive 13.7 miles to small parking pullout on left. Signed trailhead is located across the road.

Hiker walks in a natural rock overhang.

Directions from Cape Royal: From parking area drive north on Cape Royal Drive for about 0.5 miles and park on right in small parking pullout. Signed trailhead is across the street.

87 Greenland Lake Trail

ANOTHER GREAT HIKE ALONG THIS ROAD, ESPECIALLY FOR YOUNG children, is the short and easy trail that brings you down to Greenland Lake. Formed in a natural sinkhole, the lake is surrounded by grasses, evergreen trees, and mature aspens. Once you reach the lake, look to the right and pick up the faint path that travels around to the other side, where you will find a small wooden cabin tucked in the woods.

Greenland Lake Trail At A Glance

Best season: June–September.

Length: Half-mile roundtrip.

Difficulty: Easy.

Elevation gain/loss: Minimal.

Trailhead elevation: 8,472 feet.

Warning: Trail to cabin often has downed trees and overgrown vegetation.

Jurisdiction: Grand Canyon National Park, North Rim.

Directions: From the North Rim Visitor Center take Route 67 north for about 2.9 miles. Go right onto Fuller Canyon Road (to Cape Royal) and drive 5.3 miles. Go right onto Cape Royal Road and drive 2.6 miles to parking pullout on right.

Greenland Lake was formed in a natural sinkhole.

88 Widforss Trail

CLOSER TO THE MAIN AREA OF THE PARK, ONE-QUARTER MILE SOUTH OF CAPE ROYAL ROAD, and about one mile off the main drag, you will find the Widforss Trail. The entire hike is ten miles roundtrip but only has 650 feet cumulative elevation change. It's a pleasant, moderate outing that encompasses both forest and canyon scenery. In one ponderosa grove you will even find a pine that has a thirteen-foot circumference. This would be rare outside national parks, as most big trees were cut for lumber years ago. Other highlights include Crinoid fossils in the Kaibab limestone and wild turkeys, which are frequently sighted along the trail.

Widforss Trail At A Glance

Best season: June–September.

Length: Ten miles roundtrip.

Difficulty: Moderate.

Elevation gain/loss: 650 feet.

Trailhead elevation: Eighty-one hundred feet.

Jurisdiction: Grand Canyon National Park, North Rim.

Directions: From North Rim Visitor Center drive north on Route 67 about 2.7 miles and go left. Follow gravel road 0.6 miles around Harvey Meadow and go left into parking area.

Jim Owens, game warden in the early 1900s for the U.S. Forest Service, used this cave as a shelter. It can be found at the edge of Harvey Meadow near the Widforss Trailhead.

89 Uncle Jim Trail

THE UNCLE JIM TRAIL WAS NAMED AFTER "UNCLE JIM" OWENS, A GAME WARDEN FOR THE U.S. Forest Service here in the early 1900s. He is best known for killing more than five hundred mountain lions to help save the deer population. Of course, with most of the mountain lions gone, the deer population soared out of control and many of them starved. For some time he lived in an improved cave, and you can find it tucked into a cliff at the far north end of Harvey Meadow near the Widforss Trailhead.

The Uncle Jim Trail travels through a thickly forested area of aspen, fir, and ponderosa. At the halfway point of the hike you will get excellent views from the rim down to the North Kaibab Trail switchbacks. The North Kaibab Trail is used by those backpackers hiking down to Phantom Ranch and the Colorado River or those doing a couple-day backpack on the Rim to Rim Hike. If you happen to be on the trail at the right time, you will also be able to see mule trains heading down into the canyon on their one-half-day inner canyon trips.

To those who want to camp yet crave solitude, I recommend bypassing the expensive, congested, and noisy North Rim campground. Instead, head out a few miles past the park's main entrance, explore the gravel roads in the Kaibab

Uncle Jim's Trail, named for a game warden in the early 1900s, on the North Rim of the Grand Canyon.

National Forest, and find a spot that meets your needs. There are plenty of places for dispersed camping, and they are not only free but afford lots of privacy.

The main rules for dispersed camping are simple. Camp in a previously used spot, at least one-quarter mile from water sources, two hundred feet from a main roadway, and at least twenty feet from the forest road. Don't camp in wilderness areas and follow principles of "Leave No Trace."

To get complete dispersed camping rules, and also to inquire about any fire restrictions and impending weather, the wise camper will stop first at the Kaibab Plateau Visitor Center in Jacob Lake, which lies on your way to the park.

The North Rim, via the Grand Canyon Highway from Jacob Lake to the rim, is usually accessible from mid-May to mid-October, depending on snowfall. All visitor services are closed in winter.

Uncle Jim Trail At A Glance

Best season: June–September.

Length: Five miles roundtrip. A loop begins after 1.25 miles into trail.

Difficulty: Moderate.

Elevation gain: Two hundred feet.

Trailhead elevation: 8,274 feet at North Kaibab Trail parking area.

Warnings: Shared with mules for first mile. Be prepared for trail being slippery with mud and manure.

Jurisdiction: Grand Canyon National Park, North Rim.

Directions: From North Rim Visitor Center drive two miles north and go right into North Kaibab Trail parking area. Trailhead is located by mule corral in northeast corner of parking area.

90 Rim to Rim

THE TWENTY-FOUR-MILE RIM TO RIM HIKE IS A CHALLENGING ONE AND THE LOGISTICS ARE complicated, but with a little planning it could be an experience of a lifetime. You will need to be in tip-top shape physically, understand the dangers of desert hiking, and know what you need for supplies and hydration. You'll have to obtain from the park service all the sometimes-hard-to-get permits for camping in the canyon, arrange transportation from your hiking destination back to your home or to the trailhead where you left your car, and also reserve lodging or campsites for the nights before and after your hike.

As the name suggests, you will be hiking from one rim to the other. You can start at either rim but I feel starting from the North Rim is better, since the temperatures are cooler there, it is less crowded, and, because the North Rim is higher, the greatest elevation change will be in the downhill hike on the first day rather than the uphill hike on the last.

Bright Angel Creek at Phantom Ranch in the inner canyon.

So you can see the sights in the canyon along the way and not overdo it, I would allot four nights for this excursion. One night at the rim before the hike, so you can hit the trail early in the morning; two nights in the canyon; and one night to rest after your hike when you return to the North Rim by shuttle, to pick up the auto you presumably left there. You could camp just one night in the canyon, but if you do, you won't have time to take in many of the wonderful sights, including the several waterfalls here that require side trips.

You should start your outing as early as possible; dawn is ideal. Therefore be sure to make camping or lodging reservations near the trailhead for the night before. Assuming you are leaving from the North Rim, head over to the North Kaibab Trailhead, at an elevation of 8,241 feet. You can park your car there, if there is room, or take the five-minute shuttle from the village or campground. The trail then descends more than fourteen miles down, and fifty-eight hundred feet in elevation, to Phantom Ranch and Bright Angel Campground, near the Colorado River. With your camping permit, which you have secured in advance, this is where you will camp.

Phantom Ranch's cantina sells drinks and snacks. If you have reserved them in advance, you can also get a hot meal that afternoon and even a picnic lunch made for the next day's segment. They're pricey but well worth it, as they are nutritious and well-balanced meals suited for hikers.

After you pack up and leave the campground the next morning, you will make the short walk down to the Colorado River and over the Silver Bridge. This bridge will take you to the 9.5-mile Bright Angel Trail that goes up to the South Rim. You can hike up to the South Rim directly, but in the past I have secured a camping permit at Indian Spring Garden Campground, about halfway up this trail. It is a pleasant place to spend the afternoon and evening; take in a ranger program and

Footbridge over the Colorado River

cool off in the creek. Consider taking the three-mile roundtrip to Plateau Point, a superb place to be at sunset.

For the final leg of the hike I recommend starting at first light again, as there is no shade and it is all uphill. From Indian Garden it will be 4.8 miles, with an elevation gain of 3,060 feet, to the South Rim. After a few miles you will be sure to encounter hikers heading on day trips a ways down the canyon and back. You will also probably run into a mule train descending the trail for Phantom Ranch. When a mule train is approaching in a straight uphill/downhill section, you stand to the side that has the most room to get off the trail, unless the wrangler instructs you differently. On switchbacks, which constitute much of the trail in and out of the canyon, it is almost always the uphill side, if possible. Mules have the right of way, and you should remain quiet and not resume hiking until the mule train is fifty feet past you.

Once on the South Rim, at an elevation of 6,860 feet, most hikers take the Trans-Canyon Shuttle back to the North Rim and their vehicles. Passengers gather at the Bright Angel Lodge. Through mid-October the shuttle departs promptly at 8 a.m. and 1:30 p.m. and arrives back at the North Rim at 12:30 and 6 p.m. respectively. Then, through Oct. 31, it departs once daily at 8 a.m. Shuttles are also available from the North Rim to the South Rim. Reservations are required for all trips, but as long as you book in advance, they will accommodate you; visit *www.trans-canyonshuttle.com* or call (928) 638-2820.

Make reservations and obtain those hard-to-get permits as far ahead as possible. For instance, if you plan on hiking in June next year, you will need to place a permit request in January. Be totally flexible on your dates. Permits are occasionally available for one or two people only, on a walk-in basis, at the Backcountry Desk on either rim. All information on obtaining backcountry permits, fees, details on the North Kaibab Trail and Bright Angel Trail, and the campgrounds can be found at *www.nps.gov/grca* or by calling (928) 638-7875. Remember that the North Rim more or less goes into hibernation every winter, and services there, such as lodging, food, and a general store are available only through Oct. 15. They usually reopen by mid-May. Once it snows in the fall, the access road isn't plowed.

Rim to Rim At a Glance

Best Season: End of May to mid-October.

Length: Twenty-four miles point to point.

Difficulty: Strenuous.

Trailhead elevation at North Rim: 8,241 feet.

Trailhead elevation at South Rim: 6,860 feet.

Colorado River Elevation: Near Phantom Ranch, 2,450 feet.

Warnings: High temperatures within the canyon, no timely rescue.

Jurisdiction: Grand Canyon National Park, North and South Rims.

Directions to North Kaibab Trailhead: From the North Rim Visitor Center, drive two miles north and go right into parking area.

91 Toroweap/Tuweep

TOROWEAP, ALSO KNOWN AS TUWEEP, LIES ON THE NORTH RIM IN A VERY REMOTE AREA of the Arizona Strip. The quickest way to get there from Southern Nevada involves driving a ninety-mile gravel road from St. George, Utah. The road is usually in good shape for most of the drive, but it can have washboard, be muddy, or even be washed out in places. The final few miles you will have to drive over uneven sandstone, making it very slow going. Allow three hours from St. George, Utah for this drive.

The reward, though, is one of the finest sights in the park, looking down three thousand feet to the Colorado River, with views both upstream and down. Be aware that the rim is not a good place to bring children, or anyone uncomfortable with heights or unsteady on their feet. There are no guardrails or other safety measures in place, and people have fallen to their deaths here.

While the view is what people come to see, the drive itself offers some must-see places. About sixty miles into the trip, directly off to the right side of the road is the

Mt. Trumbull (Bundyville) one-room schoolhouse, where you can go inside and peek around. It's a rebuilt replica of the original school that burned down in 2000.

From there you will be driving uphill about twelve miles to the Mt. Trumbull area itself, the highest elevation of the drive at 6,525 feet. As you continue, there is a wonderful side trip. It is the Nampaweap Petroglyph Site, a short one and one-half mile roundtrip hike that takes you to the largest petroglyph site found yet on the Arizona Strip. The site contains rock art from Archaic, Ancestral Puebloan and Paiute traditions.

To get there from Mt. Trumbull, drive 3.4 miles and go right on BLM 1028. Follow it for 1.1 miles and go left to signed parking area and Nampaweap Trailhead.

Looking upstream along the Colorado River from Toroweap Overlook.

Once back on the main road, drive about 4.5 miles to a major junction where you will go right onto County Road 115. Drive about 14.1 miles to the overlook. Here you can see downstream to the river below and probably see some rafts, although they will look tiny. Be sure to bring binoculars. If you walk to your right about five minutes from the parking area, you will get a fine view upstream, including that of Lava Falls, one of the toughest rapids on the river to negotiate.

If you have traveled to Toroweap before, be warned that new campground rules are more restrictive. You now must have a camping permit, only available in advance (visit *www.nps.gov/grca/* for more information) and not available at the campground itself or the Tuweep Ranger Station. You must arrive at the site before sunset. You no longer may have a campfire, but camp stoves are allowed. Also the Tuweep Airstrip is currently closed to private planes, and overflow camping is no longer allowed at the airstrip.

Vehicles traveling to the campground must have high clearance, and if you haul a trailer, you are limited to a total length of twenty-two feet for towing vehicle and trailer combined

Toroweap At A Glance

Best Season: October–May.

Elevation: 4,545 feet at Toroweap Overlook.

Warnings: No water, gas, food, lodging, or cell service in Toroweap and surrounding area. Requires high-clearance vehicle with two spares, extra gas for side trips.

Nampaweap Petroglyph Site, the largest concentration of petroglyphs yet found on the Arizona Strip.

Jurisdiction: Bureau of Land Management and Grand Canyon National Park, Tuweep.

Map: Arizona Strip Visitors Map. Available at the Interagency Information Center, 345 E. Riverside Dr. St. George, Utah, *www.nps.gov/para* or (435) 688-3200.

Directions: From Las Vegas take Interstate 15 north about 120 miles to St. George, Utah and exit to Southern Parkway, the St. George Municipal Airport Road. Follow for about 3.3 miles and exit right to South River Road. Go right to reach the Arizona state line and the start of BLM Road 1069. This route will become County Road 5 while en route to Toroweap. Follow for about 70 miles, until the road ends at a junction. Here you will go right onto County Road 115. Drive about 7.5 miles to the Tuweep Ranger Station and another 6.6 miles farther to the Toroweap Overlook. From the parking area you can walk 50 yards or so to the main viewpoint.

The road to Toroweap. Below: The Mt. Trumbull (Bundyville) one-room schoolhouse (a rebuild/replica of the original school that burned down in 2000).

Other Arizona

Approaching Monument Valley from "Forrest Gump" location.

Highlights

Many think of Arizona as a place to visit only during the famously mild winters of its desert regions. But in fact, Arizona offers a variety of climates and outdoor experiences suitable for every month of the year.

Arizona is rich in colorful history, at places like Lee's Ferry and Chloride, and even prehistory, for there one can visit dwellings that have stood eight hundred years at places like Wupatki and Walnut Canyon. There are natural formations like the towering monoliths of Monument Valley and the graceful, water-carved wonders of Antelope Canyon.

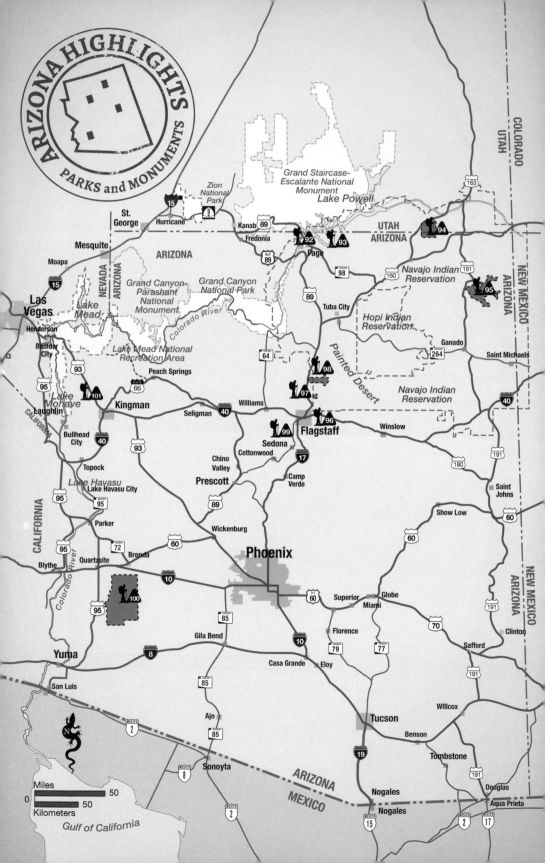

Even some of the routes between these charming places are experiences in their own right; much of the roadside romance of Historic Route 66, bypassed on interstate highways by travelers whose only priority is getting there fast, remains for those who will take time to delight in whimsy and mid-century Americana.

There was room in this book to detail only a few of Arizona's highlights; there are many more. There are more than thirty state parks; for a complete list, look at *azstateparks.com*. Members of twenty American Indian peoples reside in Arizona, and typically welcome visitors to specific areas of lands they control, such as the increasingly famous Grand Canyon Skywalk on Hualapai lands. And even Arizona's small cities like Prescott and Flagstaff, where residents live lives quite similar to those of Americans elsewhere, retain historic buildings and museums that make them charming, unique places to spend a day or two, or rest up a night before heading out on one of the hikes below.

92 Lee's Ferry and Lonely Dell

THIS PLACE MAKES A SUPER RELAXING, REMOTE SIDE TRIP IF YOU ARE COMING FROM PAGE, Arizona or traveling to there from the North Rim of the Grand Canyon. It is isolated for the most part and you will be able to find lots of solitude; whether it is sitting by the river, visiting the Lonely Dell Historic Ranch, or taking a remote day hike upstream into lower Paria Canyon.

It is one of the few places in Glen Canyon National Recreation Area where you can access the Colorado River. There are small parking areas near the river with footpaths to get to water's edge. Lee's Ferry is the place where river runners launch their rafts for the trip downstream through the Grand Canyon. Fishermen also launch small motorboats, then head upstream for world-class trout fishing in the fifteen-mile stretch between here and Glen Canyon Dam.

The Lonely Dell Ranch Historic Site, maintained by the National Park Service, is located at the confluence of the Colorado River and Paria Canyon. To see the entire ranch it will be about a one-mile walk around the property. You will be enchanted by the orchards, cabins, stone ranch house, outhouses, and a cemetery.

Depending upon where you access the river at Lee's Ferry, the ranch is located about one mile north.

Despite its charm, the 160-acre ranch comes with some dark history. John D. Lee, a prominent Mormon leader, was sent here by his church in 1872 to establish a ferry enabling travelers to cross the Colorado River. A polygamist, he built cabins for two of his many wives at the ranch. Besides a residence for his families, its remote location helped him, for a while, to avoid arrest by federal authorities for his part in the infamous Mountain Meadows Massacre, which had taken place in 1857, just east of Cedar City, Utah.

At Mountain Meadows, Mormon militia and their Indian allies attacked a wagon train of non-Mormon emigrants. About 120 people, including all the party's adults, and all children over the age of seven, were savagely murdered. A U.S. attorney finally prosecuted and convicted Lee for his part in the atrocity, and in 1877 a firing squad executed Lee at the site of the massacre. No other participants were ever convicted. One of his wives, Emma, maintained the ranch after Lee's death until another family took over the ranch and ferry operations. The ferry operated until about 1928, when it sank. Fortunately the Navajo Bridge was being built and opened seven months later, so the ferry was no longer needed. The property was acquired by the National Park Service in 1974.

The Colorado River at Lee's Ferry, at sunset.

From the north side of the Lonely Dell cemetery you can drop down into the Paria River drainage and head up the canyon. This makes a pleasant hike; you can travel as far as you feel comfortable, then return. Do not hike the drainage if it has rained or rain threatens.

The only accommodation at Lee's Ferry is a campground, but gas, groceries and showers are available at the small town of Marble Canyon, just five miles away.

There is no visitor center at Lee's Ferry. For more information contact Glen Canyon National Recreation Area, (928) 608-6200, *www.nps.gov/glca*. Also useful is the Navajo Bridge Interpretive Center, (928) 355-2319.

Lee's Ferry and Lonely Dell At a Glance

Best Season: April–June and September–November.

Length: Varies.

Difficulty: Easy.

Elevation gain: Minimal for short day hike.

Trailhead elevation: 3,150 feet at Lonely Dell Ranch.

Two utility buildings are well-preserved at the Lonely Dell Ranch Historic District.

Warning: Flash flooding in Paria Canyon.

Jurisdiction: Glen Canyon National Recreation Area.

Directions: From Las Vegas take Interstate 15 north about 125 miles to Utah Route 9, the Hurricane/Zion National Park Exit. Drive about 12 miles and turn right onto Utah Route 59 east. This becomes Arizona Route 389 at the state border. Drive about 53 miles to Fredonia and turn right onto U.S. 89A for about 30 miles to Jacob Lake. Stay left to continue on U.S. 89A and drive about 41 miles, then go left onto Lee's Ferry Road. Drive about 5 miles to Lee's Ferry area.

93 Antelope Canyon

THERE ARE HUNDREDS OF EXTRAORDINARY SLOT CANYONS IN THE SOUTHWEST. Unfortunately many of the finest are extremely difficult to reach, and once you get there, you need good technical skills to explore. But on the Navajo Indian Reservation just outside Page, Arizona, a couple are easily accessed, yet may be the most stunning slots you will ever see.

The two are only a few miles apart along Antelope Creek, a usually dry wash which drains into Lake Powell. Upper Antelope Canyon is known to the Navajo as Tse bighanilini, meaning "The place where water runs through rocks." Lower Antelope Canyon is called Hasdeztwasi or "Spiral Rock Arches."

You probably won't have any solitude in these canyons as they are tremendously popular, and you will also need to have an authorized guide to take you, but their natural beauty is so incredible it is well worth these caveats. Shaped primarily by water and wind, these corkscrew passages of Navajo sandstone are a feast for the eyes.

Each slot is visited as a separate outing. If you can only visit one, I think Upper Antelope Canyon is best, especially if you have children along. The walking is easy and there are no staircases to climb, as there are in the lower canyon.

The time of day of your visit will determine how much natural light filters in; the best light is around midday. Midday light paints the canyon walls and floors in a rich palette of pinks, oranges, reds and purples.

The majority of tours start in Page, where visitors head out with their guide in a four-wheel-drive vehicle. If you're heading for Upper Antelope, once you are off the main road your guide will drive you south, up the wide sandy wash for a few miles, and park. When you first arrive you might not even notice where you will enter the canyon, as the sandstone fracture before you appears to lead nowhere.

Many Navajo consider these canyons to be spiritual places, and it won't take long to see why. When you enter, try to leave all your troubles in the parking lot. Relax and immerse yourself in the splendor of this magical place.

Once in the canyon most guides will point out the well-known formations such as The Bear, The Weeping Eye, and The Dancing Flame. Some guides will also share the beauty of their culture with interested listeners, which is a lot more appealing than reading it in a book.

Corkscrew passage through sandstone in Upper Antelope Canyon, on the Navajo Reservation.

This slot serpentines about two hundred yards or so before the walls open up on the south side. As you are looking up the canyon walls — more than a hundred feet high in some places — see if you can spot debris left over from floods. On one visit I found a juniper log wedged between two walls of sandstone some thirty feet above the canyon floor.

All narrow canyons can be extremely dangerous during and after heavy rains, as water from upstream can funnel into these narrow passageways, creating a powerful flow of water, mud, and debris. There doesn't even have to be rain directly overhead, as a downpour many miles away will channel water into the drainages.

In 1997, eleven tourists were killed in lower Antelope Canyon when an afternoon thunderstorm caught them off guard. There was no easy escape route. Since then, safety precautions have been put into place.

There are many outfitters available in Page to guide you through Antelope Canyon. The ideal way is to make a reservation beforehand, although many guides are often available by dropping in at their businesses. Fees vary. Visit *www.go-arizona. com/Page/Outfitter/* for further information.

Upper Antelope Canyon At A Glance

Best season: September–April.

Length: Four hundred yards roundtrip.

Difficulty: Easy.

Elevation gain: Minimal.

Trailhead elevation: 4,372 feet.

Warning: This is a guided hike only, with transportation to trailhead provided by outfitter. A variety of guides and outfitters operate from Page, Arizona.

Jurisdiction: Navajo Indian Reservation.

Directions to Page, Ariz.: From Las Vegas, take Interstate 15 north about 125 miles to Utah Route 9 (Exit 16, Hurricane-Zion National Park). Drive 12 miles and go right onto Utah Route 59 east. This 61-mile paved road turns into Arizona Route

389 when it crosses the state line, and then into U.S. 89A north when turning left in Fredonia, Ariz., just a few miles south of Kanab, Utah. From Kanab, drive east on U.S. 89 for about 70 miles to the Glen Canyon Bridge and Page.

94 Monument Valley

MONUMENT VALLEY NAVAJO TRIBAL PARK, LOCATED WITHIN THE SIXTEEN-MILLION-ACRE Navajo Reservation, has some of the most-recognized landscapes and rock formations in the world. That's because the park's buttes, mesas, arches and spires are some of the most photographed. This 91,696-acre park was only established in 1958, but the Dine', as the Navajo refer to themselves, have occupied this area for more than four hundred years. Before that, the Ancestral Puebloans lived here.

Although you can take a self-guided tour, or a variety of two-to-three-hour guided tours, by either off-road vehicle or horseback, I would highly recommend one of the full-day guided tours. The best tour I have taken included not only the highlights of Monument Valley but also Mystery Valley, adjacent to the park. In Mystery Valley you will be treated to some out-of-the-way places boasting the best-preserved archaeological sites in the region, besides incredibly diverse natural formations you can't see on your own, as they are off limits to non-Navajo people. The guide will bring you to a dozen or so different locations, where you head out on short hikes to see the archaeological sites and formations.

The seventeen-mile self-guided driving tour does serve some people best, though, especially if they are short on time. Many of the park's most famous sights are along this route, such as the different views of The Mittens, The Totem Pole spire and some of the park's best arches. It heads out directly behind the park's View Hotel, heads south and then makes a large loop. The road is gravel and can be rough and sandy in places, but can usually be done in a high-clearance vehicle with good off-road tires, except during or after rain.

The east and west Mitten Buttes look like someone's hands sticking up in the air, but to the Navajo they signify that spiritual beings are watching over the Dine'. The Totem Pole is a very thin, five-hundred-foot spire that rises like a chimney above the valley floor. You might have seen it used in a few television commercials for IBM and Jeep, or in a 1975 thriller movie, *The Eiger Sanction*, starring Clint Eastwood.

Many other popular films have used Monument Valley for a shooting location, including *How the West Was Won*, *Back to the Future III*, *Thelma and Louise*, and *Forrest Gump*.

General admission to the park is $20 for up to four people, and $6 per additional person. National Park passes are not honored here. The Scenic Drive is open from 6 a.m. to 8 p.m. May 1–Sept. 30, and from 8 a.m. to 5 p.m. Oct. 1–April 30. For a list of approved Navajo tour guides check out *www.mountainvalleyview. com* or *gouldings.com*. For more information on the park contact the Monument Valley Tribal Park at (435) 727-5870 or *navajonationparks.org*.

Monument Valley At a Glance

Best Season: April–October.

Length: Seventeen miles for self-guided drive tour.

Trailhead elevation: 5,213 at visitor center.

Warning: Very confusing, but if you are visiting Monument Valley and maybe staying at a motel or campground off the Navajo Reservation, or in nearby Utah, be aware that Arizona does not participate in daylight

An arch in Monument Valley.

savings time, but the Navajo Nation and Utah do. So when daylight savings time comes around, the state of Utah and the Navajo Nation are one hour later than Arizona and Nevada. In non-daylight savings months, Arizona, Utah and the Navajo Nation are on Mountain Standard Time, which is one hour ahead of Nevada.

Jurisdiction: Monument Valley Navajo Tribal Park.

Directions: From Las Vegas, take U.S. 93 south for 105 miles to Kingman, Ariz. Go east on Interstate 40 about 146 miles to Flagstaff. Take U.S. 89 north for about 63 miles and turn right onto U.S. 160 and follow for 82 miles. Turn left onto U.S. 163 and drive 24 miles to signed park entrance road and visitor center, located on the right. To reach the Scenic Drive from the visitor center, exit, go right onto Monument Valley Road and drive 3.6 miles.

The Mittens and Merrick Butte in Monument Valley Tribal Park.

95 Canyon de Chelly

CANYON DE CHELLY NATIONAL MONUMENT TAKES ITS NAME FROM JUST ONE OF THE THREE main canyons that make up most of its eighty-four thousand acres. Canyon de Chelly (pronounced "de-shay"), Canyon del Muerto, and Monument are surrounded by red sandstone cliffs which rise up a thousand feet in some places. Fertile farm land is here, and the Ancestral Puebloans left ruins of buildings throughout the canyons. Later the Hopi lived here before migrating to their present territory, and in historic times, the canyons have constituted the heart of the Navajo homeland. It is thought that this area has been continuously occupied by humans longer than any other on the Colorado Plateau, some five thousand years.

The monument was established in 1931, largely to protect the archaeological resources. It lies entirely within the Navajo Nation and is jointly managed by the National Park Service and the Dine' (Navajo) people.

Because of the rich soil and reliable water sources, many Navajo still make their home in the canyons, where they farm and raise cattle, sheep and goats. At elevations between fifty-five hundred and seven thousand feet, the monument has many mature deciduous trees including cottonwoods. Wildlife includes mountains lions, bears, wild turkeys, and many raptors.

You can take the eighteen-mile North Rim and sixteen-mile South Rim scenic drives to visit one or all the ten overlooks, but the best way to see the canyons is a close-range view, only available on a Navajo-guided tour. On these you will be able to visit dozens of ruins, petroglyphs, pictographs and the wonderful natural sandstone formations. With the guides, you can tour by motor vehicle, horseback, or hiking, and within these options, tours of different lengths are available.

If you want to go into the canyon without a guide, you may take only one route, a self-guided, three-mile hike from the White House Overlook, (found along the South Rim Drive) down to the White House Ruin in the canyon. It is a steep hike that loses about 550 feet in elevation. The two-section dwelling was constructed partly on the valley floor and partly in an alcove above. It is thought to have been occupied about one thousand years ago by Ancestral Puebloans.

The Canyon de Chelly Visitor Center is open 8 a.m.–5 p.m. daily, except major holidays. Although Arizona does not participate in daylight savings time, the

A horse and colt in Canyon de Muerte at Canyon de Chelly National Monument.

Canyon de Chelly, viewed from the south.

Navajo Nation does. So during daylight savings time, the state of Utah and the Navajo Nation are one hour later than Arizona and Nevada. In non-daylight savings months, Arizona, Utah and the Navajo Nation are on Mountain Standard Time, one hour ahead of Nevada.

No reliable cell phone service is available on the Navajo Reservation.

Canyon de Chelly is one of the more popular destinations for those touring the Southwest, so if you wish to take a guided tour during the busy season, April–October, reservations are recommended. Prices vary depending on which tour company you choose, and you will need to have a permit, which your guide will help you get. I have used Speaking Rock Tours many times and I was immensely pleased by every different tour as they catered to my specific interests, offering both vehicle and hiking tours. You can reach them at (928) 781-2016, *www.spiderrockcampground.com*. For a list of other approved guides or information on Canyon de Chelly, check out the park web site, *www.nps.gov/cach/*.

Canyon de Chelly At a Glance

Best Season: April–May, then September–October.

Length: Three miles roundtrip for White House Ruin hike.

Difficulty: Moderate.

Elevation gain: 550 feet.

Trailhead elevation: 6,205 feet.

Warning: Drop-offs on trail.

Jurisdiction: Canyon de Chelly National Monument.

Directions: From Las Vegas take U.S. 93 south for about 105 miles to Kingman, Arizona. Go east on Interstate 40 for 283 miles to U.S. 191 north. Drive about 74 miles to Chinle, Arizona. Turn right onto Indian Route 7 and drive about 2.7 miles to park entrance and visitor center located on your right. For the White House Overlook, drive 6 miles from the visitor center on South Rim Road and go left to signed access road. Follow for about 0.6 miles to overlook and trailhead.

96 Walnut Canyon

WALNUT CANYON NATIONAL MONUMENT IS LOCATED ONLY MINUTES FROM INTERSTATE 40, just east of Flagstaff, so that makes it a really easy place to stop, spend an hour or so looking at cliff dwellings, and then continue your travels. The walking route featured here is the Island Trail, the only way to get a close look at the twenty-five ruins which completely surround the base of the "island," a natural promontory of limestone.

These are prehistoric cliff dwellings built under alcoves by the people archaeologists call Sinaguans, who lived here from around the year 1150 to about 1300. They were hunter-gatherers and farmers who planted squash, corn, and beans in fields above the rim. Wildlife in the habitat include bighorn sheep, deer, mountain lions, ringtails and coyotes, but they are rarely seen by today's human visitors.

The monument is a small one, just thirty-six hundred acres, and was established in 1915 to preserve the cliff dwellings found along a six-mile section of Walnut Canyon. The protected area was first managed by the U.S. Forest Service but was transferred to the National Park Service in 1934.

If you don't have the time, ability, or energy for the Island Trail, be sure to at least check out the Rim Trail. It travels about 0.7 miles roundtrip past two excellent overlooks into Walnut Canyon, from which you can see other cliff dwellings fairly well if you bring binoculars. The Rim Trail also brings you past a pit house and pueblo ruin located near the picnic area, slightly away from the rim.

Walnut Canyon National Monument and the visitor center are open daily, 8 a.m.–5 p.m. MST from June to November, but open at 9 a.m. the rest of the year. They are closed Christmas. There are no services here, but nearby Flagstaff has complete services. (928) 526-3367, *www.nps.gov/waca*.

Walnut Canyon At a Glance

Best Season: May–October.

Length: One mile roundtrip for Island Trail.

Difficulty: Moderate.

Elevation gain: 185 feet.

Trailhead elevation: 6,690 feet.

Prehistoric cliff dwellings at Walnut Canyon National Monument were built by the people archaeologists call Sinaguans, who lived here around 1150-1300.

Warnings: The Island Trail closes one hour before the monument closes. It is a paved trail, but steep. If you have not been traveling in the area for a few days and are unaccustomed to this high elevation, it will seem like a strenuous hike.

Jurisdiction: Walnut Canyon National Monument.

Directions: From Las Vegas take U.S. 93 south for 105 miles to Kingman, Ariz. Go left to enter Interstate 40 and drive for about 156 miles, passing through Flagstaff, Ariz. About 7.5 miles past the city, take exit 204 and drive south 3 miles on the signed road to Walnut Canyon National Monument and visitor center.

97 Sunset Crater

SUNSET CRATER VOLCANO NATIONAL MONUMENT IS LOCATED IN THE COCONINO NATIONAL Forest, just nineteen miles south from Wupatki National Monument, along the Sunset Crater-Wupatki Loop Road. Because of their close proximity to each other, and the prehistoric relationship between the two, they are usually visited on the same trip.

The park encompasses 3,040 acres and includes its namesake, Sunset Crater. The crater was formed as a vent on top of a volcano, and is about one thousand feet high, with the highest peak at an elevation of about 8,029 feet.

The last volcanic eruption is thought to have been between A.D. 1040 and 1100, and to have lasted a few months or years. Sinaguan people were living and farming in the area at the time. No evidence has been found that any died in the eruption, perhaps because there were enough warning earth tremors that the people fled in time. But their homes were destroyed, crops and forests were burned, and meadows covered with molten lava gradually hardening to stone. The country was rendered uninhabitable for a five-mile radius, and those driven from their homes are thought to have relocated at Wupatki and Walnut Canyon. Ash was scattered over sixty-four thousand acres, which had a profound effect on the landscape that is now Wupatki National Monument.

It is worth taking one of the short trails to see the volcanic rock up close. While reaching the peak of Sunset Crater is closed to hikers, there are other trails that offer a feel of the landscape. The Lava Flow Trail is an easy one-mile loop, and then

Sunset Crater was formed as a vent on top of a volcano, and is about 1,000 feet high.

there is the moderately strenuous Lenox Crater Trail. The latter is fairly steep, but it's only about one mile roundtrip. The views alone are worth the effort. To the north are the San Francisco Peaks, with Humphrey's Peak, the highest point in Arizona, at 12,633 feet elevation. You will also get great views of Sunset Crater itself and the Bonito lava flow, just north of the scenic drive.

The opportunity to see the natural crater, as it remains today, was almost lost back in 1929. Producers of the Hollywood movie *Avalanche* needed a scene of a major landslide, so they decided to create one by dynamiting the crater walls. After locals caught wind of this plan, they raised enough fuss to prevent the destruction. That incident was part of the reason President Herbert Hoover in 1930 proclaimed the Sunset Crater National Monument. The park officially added the word "Volcano" to its title in 1990.

The visitor center is open daily except Christmas. Hours are 9 a.m.–5 p.m., MST, from November to mid-May; it opens at 8 a.m. the rest of the year. Sunset Crater Volcano National Monument. (928) 526-0502, *www.nps.gov/sucr*.

Sunset Crater At a Glance

Best Season: May through October.

Length: Trails from 0.25 to one-mile roundtrip.

Difficulty: Easy to moderate.

Elevation gain: Minimal to 285 feet on Lenox Crater Trail.

Trailhead elevation: 6,960 at visitor center.

Warning: Snow in winter.

Jurisdiction: Sunset Crater Volcano National Monument.

Directions: From Las Vegas, take U.S. 93 south for 105 miles to Kingman, Ariz. Go east on Interstate 40 about 146 miles to Flagstaff. From Flagstaff, take U.S. 89 north for 12 miles, turn right on the Sunset Crater-Wupatki Loop Road and continue 2 miles to the Sunset Crater Visitor Center.

98 Wupatki National Monument

A VISIT HERE IS OFTEN DONE IN CONJUNCTION WITH NEARBY SUNSET CRATER VOLCANO National Monument. Not only are they conveniently close together, but the volcanic eruption that created Sunset Crater also had a big impact in the lifestyle of the people who lived, then and later, in what is now Wupatki National Monument.

Established in 1924, the monument encompasses thirty-five thousand acres with more than 2,500 documented archaeological sites. One of the most impressive ruins you can see anywhere in the Southwest lies near the park's visitor center. This is Wupatki Pueblo itself, from which the whole monument takes its name. It has been associated with the Cohonina, Sinagua, and Kayenta people.

Wukoki Pueblo is one of the best preserved pueblos in the park. It is thought the dwelling was occupied between 1120 through 1210.

It was built, as many pueblos in the region were, upon the base of a natural sandstone outcropping. The pueblo was at first a small one, perhaps occupied as early as A.D. 500, but after the nearby volcanic eruption, somewhere around A.D. 1040 to 1100, things changed dramatically.

A one-half-mile paved trail brings visitors to the Wupatki Pueblo, located behind the visitor center at Wupatki National Monument in Arizona.

The eruption caused ash to blanket the area, creating better agricultural opportunities, by enriching the soil and keeping moisture in. By the late twelfth century, thousands of people were living in the area. The residents were primarily farmers raising corn, beans, and squash, but they augmented their diet with deer, pronghorn, and small game.

With the influx of so many people, this pueblo alone grew to three stories high and about one hundred rooms. This expanded pueblo was probably used from the 1180s to about 1225. No one knows for sure why it was abandoned, but theories suggest drought, disease, or social problems, or maybe it was a mix of all three.

Before visiting the pueblo itself, check out the visitor center's museum, which displays arrowheads, ceramics and other artifacts associated with the people who lived here. Interpretive exhibits will help you better understand the places you will soon see. Once you are ready to look at the pueblo, pick up a trail guide for your self-guided tour, so you don't miss any of the highlights.

The trail, which begins at the visitor center's back door, is a one-half-mile loop that takes you to both sides of the pueblo. But don't confine yourself to the loop, for down the hill are other interesting things to see. There are two rounded structures here, a community room and a ball court. The ball court is about one hundred feet long and sixty-four feet wide, with an opening on both ends. Other ball courts have been found in Arizona but this is the only one found so far that was built of stone.

My favorite place on the grounds is the natural blowhole. This geological feature was formed in a fracture of the earth. Depending on outside air temperature during your visit, a strong air current will be blowing either out of the hole or into it. In warmer weather it often blows out so strong that if you lean over it, your hair will fly up in the air as if you were using a strong hairdryer. Those with long hair will want to get a photo of themselves with their hair apparently standing on end. A metal grate covers the hole, so even children can safely enjoy this phenomenon.

Be sure to allow time to see some of the other archaeological sites in the park. One that shouldn't be missed is Wukoki Pueblo. About three miles from the visitor center, it is one of the best preserved of the ancient structures. It contains only a handful of rooms, yet towers three stories above the surrounding landscape. Artifacts found on the site suggest it was occupied from about 1120 through 1210 A.D.

The visitor center at Wupatki National Monument is open daily from 9 a.m. to 5 p.m., MST, except Christmas. (928) 679-236, *www.nps.gov/wupa*.

Wupatki At a Glance

Best Season: April through October.

Length: Varies.

Difficulty: Easy.

Elevation gain: Minimal.

Trailhead elevation: 4,900 feet at visitor center.

Jurisdiction: Wupatki National Monument.

Directions: From Las Vegas, take U.S. 93 south for 105 miles to Kingman, Arizona. Go east on Interstate 40 about 146 miles to Flagstaff. Then take U.S. 89 north 12 miles and go right on the Sunset Crater-Wupatki Loop Road. Follow about 21 miles and go left to Wupatki Visitor Center.

99 Slide Rock State Park

JUST SIX MILES NORTH OF SEDONA, ALONG THE OAK CREEK SCENIC DRIVE, IS THE FORTY-three-acre Slide Rock State Park, one of the state's most adored destinations. It is best known for the section of Oak Creek where those daring enough can slide down an eighty-foot water chute in the Coconino sandstone.

While most people come for the untainted water, the park also has a network of short hiking trails and some great historic features worth seeing.

Frank Pendley arrived in the canyon back in 1907, and then officially received the land in 1910, under the Homestead Act. He planted apple orchards in 1912 and designed an irrigation system to transport water from Oak Creek. Pendley drilled, blasted, and built tunnels in the sandstone and then fashioned metal flumes to direct water to his apples and other crops.

The Pendley family farmed here until the 1980s and turned it over to the Arizona Parklands Foundation. The state of Arizona then acquired it and opened a park here in 1987. It is now jointly managed by the state park system and the Coconino National Forest. Apple orchards are still maintained and harvested, and the park holds an apple festival each fall.

You start a visit here by taking the paved Pendley Homestead Trail. This will take you by the original apple orchards, some newer semi-dwarf orchards, a small store, and the fruit picking barn. You will also pass the Pendley Homestead House, built in 1927 to replace the very modest previous home. About three-tenths miles from the parking area you will find some wide sandstone stairs to get you down to water's edge. There are some great, and relatively flat, sandstone areas for just sitting, relaxing or having a picnic.

If you are adventurous enough to do the water chute, be sure to watch others and their technique first, as you can get pretty banged up. The chute is about two and one-half to four feet wide and made slippery from algae.

There are some short trails that start from here. One, the Slick Rock Route, travels about three-tenths miles and takes you over a footbridge to the east side of the creek, where you can then walk upstream. You will come upon a stone cabin and a water wheel and the flume which Pendley used to generate electricity. Once you come to a high wall you can turn around.

The quarter-mile Nature Trail, located on a high bench, provides the best

Most visitors come to relax on the natural benches of Coconino sandstone and swim in the cool waters of Oak Creek.

views down into Oak Creek. Look for some of the interesting birds in the park including lazuli bunting, black-necked grosbeak, western tanager, and several types of hummingbirds.

Slide Rock State Park, 6871 N. Highway 89A, Sedona is open 8 a.m.–7 p.m. No entry after 6 p.m. Hours are subject to change. (928) 282-3034. Arizona State Parks, (928) 203-2900, *www.azstateparks.com.*

Slide Rock State Park At a Glance

Best Season: June–August.

Length: Varies.

Difficulty: Easy.

Elevation gain: Minimal.

Trailhead elevation: 4,930 feet.

Warnings: Arrive first thing in the morning for parking. No lifeguards.

Jurisdiction: Arizona State Parks and Coconino National Forest.

Directions: From Las Vegas take U.S. 93 south 105 miles to Kingman, Ariz. Go east on Interstate 40 for about 146 miles to Flagstaff. Take Interstate 17 south for about 2 miles and exit to Arizona 89A south. Continue about 17 miles to Slide Rock State Park.

Slide Rock State Park is best known for the section of Oak Creek where the daring can slide down an 80-foot water chute.

100 Palm Canyon/Kofa National Wildlife Refuge

SURE, THIS HIKE IS OUT OF THE WAY FOR most travelers, but if you are in the area, Palm Canyon, in the Kofa National Wildlife Refuge, is a place you should see. The Palm Canyon National Recreation Trail, designated in 2007, brings you to a rare site in Arizona: a naturally growing grove of native California fan palms (*Washingtonia filifera*). There are dozens of these palms at Kofa, all thriving in a microclimate within a steep canyon, located about one-half hour south of Quartzsite.

The entire wildlife refuge encompasses 665,000 acres. It was established in 1939 at the urging of Frederick R. Burnham, an American then famous for his exploits in the British military and one of the founders of the Boy Scout movement. Its main mission is to protect desert bighorn sheep. The herd here totals between four hundred and eight hundred animals.

Palm Canyon is located on the extreme northwest area of the refuge

Kofa is home to a rare sight in Arizona, a naturally growing grove of native California fan palms (*Washingtonia filifera*).

in a steep, narrow canyon consisting of rhyolite, a volcanic rock.

From the trailhead follow the trail, which is rocky but obvious and well-signed, up into the canyon. There is typical vegetation as commonly found in the Sonoran Desert, such as chollo, saguaro, ocotillo, ironwood, and palo verde. Once you reach the signed viewpoint to the palms, you will see a bush that resembles holly. This is the Kofa Mountain barberry, an endemic plant found only in southwestern

Arizona, which grows primarily in shaded, rocky canyons such as this one. Birds found in the canyon including thrashers, gnatcatchers, white-throated swifts, canyon towhees, and canyon wrens.

After hiking about one-half mile from the trailhead, you will see a small wooden sign that says "Palms" with an arrow pointing left to the north side of the canyon. You wouldn't think this would be necessary, but Palm Canyon itself is a steep, narrow side canyon, off the main canyon, and the palms are hard to see unless you know where to look. They are in the shade most of the time, except around midday.

These palms appear extremely healthy. The dead fronds that hang down below the top are nature's method of making way for the new. Lower fronds die and drape downward, forming a "petticoat" around the trunk. Eventually they fall to the ground where they decompose, enriching the soil to make good conditions for new palms to grow.

There is no visitor center near the remote location of the trail. The headquarters are located in Yuma, 63 miles south of here, but you can contact Kofa National Wildlife Refuge at (928) 783-7861 or www.fws.gov/refuge/kofa.

Palm Canyon At A Glance

Best Season: October–April.

Length: One-mile roundtrip to viewpoint.

Difficulty: Moderate.

Elevation gain: 250 feet to viewpoint.

Trailhead elevation: 2,141 feet.

Warning: Rocky trail with uneven footing.

Jurisdiction: Kofa National Wildlife Refuge.

Directions: From Las Vegas take U.S 95 south about 100 miles through Searchlight and into California. Go left onto Interstate 40 east/ U.S. 95 south for about 10.7 miles. Take exit 144, U.S. 95 south, toward Blythe. Drive for about 93 miles and merge onto Interstate 10 east. Drive about 21 miles to Quartzsite, Arizona.

From Quartzsite take U.S. 95 south about 18 miles and go left into Kofa National Wildlife Refuge. Drive about 7 miles on the well-maintained gravel road towards the large black mountain and parking area for Palm Canyon.

101 Chloride, Arizona

CHLORIDE, ARIZONA MIGHT BE THE SMALLEST TOWN YOU'VE EVER INTENTIONALLY VISITED, but it definitely will be unlike any of the others. That makes it, to city dwellers, the perfect destination for a revitalizing, one-day dose of Somewhere Else.

This former mining camp was founded in the 1860s at the base of the Cerbat Mountains just north of Kingman. At various times more than fifty mines operated at Chloride, and for a brief period in the early 1900s, the population soared to five thousand. Now it is small and quiet, with a couple of hundred residents.

One of the main reasons people visit Chloride is to see the complex of murals, painted in 1966 by artist Roy Purcell. These are no ordinary murals, such as those painted on the flat sides of buildings, but grace large granite boulders and cliff faces within a narrow, secluded canyon located just east of town.

Even without the murals, it would be worth the drive just to walk among Chloride's historic buildings and the quirky homemade sculptures that for some reason seem to occupy about half the yards in town.

Homes and yards are small, so it's easy to see buildings or art from the street. Like most mining towns of the nineteenth century, Chloride was laid out for the convenience of pedestrians, and the town retains this. The most pleasant way to see Chloride is to leave your car in the large parking lot near the center of town and take the self-guided walking tour. Start at the Mineshaft Market, 4940 Tennessee Avenue, which serves as an information center, and ask for the town map. Also ask the staff to mark highlights on that map, because otherwise you will never find all the choice places, as most buildings have no signs.

Not to be missed is the old and now-abandoned jail, built in the 1890s. One time when I visited, the front door was held in place by a nail, another time, the nail had been replaced with a flimsy ice cream stick. You are allowed to go inside and look around, but I'm not sure how safe that is; a large cable is wrapped around half of the building, seemingly to hold the place upright. If you go inside — just to say you've been in jail — you will find the bars and small toilets are still in place.

Other must-see buildings include the old train depot, bank, and even a gas station of antique vintage. Looking out at the surrounding mountains you will see abandoned buildings dotting the landscape, left over from the mining days. The Tennessee Mine was the largest in this area and produced $7.5 million from gold, lead, and zinc before it closed in 1947.

Tucked among the historic businesses and public buildings are modest homes, some upholding the Chloride tradition of yard art. As you stroll around you will

view projects exhibiting all levels of talent. Some still look like piles of trash, while others are carefully arranged and clever conversions of everyday objects into striking sculptures. Look for displays made from colorful bottles, worn cowboy boots, expired license plates, rusty farm machinery, and even bowling balls. Just about anything goes here.

After exploring the town proper you will want to visit the murals. To find them, head back to Tennessee Avenue and either walk or drive east for about one-half mile until the pavement ends. If you have a high-clearance four-wheel-drive vehicle you can keep driving, but it's a rough and rocky road, and in rainy weather

it becomes impassable. Instead of worrying about road conditions, it's almost easier to go on foot.

Because the murals are located in a bend of the canyon, you won't see them until you are upon them. They are painted on about two thousand square feet of boulders and cliff faces. Purcell originally painted the murals in 1966. Years of weather faded the colors so Purcell returned in 1975 to touch them up and vibrantly repainted them again in 2006, in honor of his seventieth birthday.

Purcell grew up in Utah but resided in Southern Nevada for decades, becoming well-known for his artwork, especially etchings. The Purcell Gallery of Fine Art is located next to Yesterday's Restaurant on Second Street in Chloride. His main gallery is located in Tubac, Arizona, where he now resides.

Purcell labeled the Chloride murals,

Purcell originally painted the murals in 1966 but repainted them in 1975 and 2006.

In 1966 Roy Purcell painted murals in a canyon east of town. This panel depicts the local Tennessee Mine.

"The Journey: Images From An Inward Search For Self." To fully understand the meaning of the murals you would have to make a trip into Purcell's subconscious mind fifty years ago.

The murals are meant to be read from right to left. One of the most pleasing panels is on the right, a charming rendition of the Tennessee Mine. The large panel to the left of this depicts chaos as an enormous claw can be seen destroying the mine. Farther to the left, order and harmony prevail again. It is all rather confusing, but the creative elements are enchanting. It would be doubtful you would again encounter anything quite so striking in the peaceful canyons of the desert West.

Chloride At A Glance

Best season: September–April.

Length: 0.5 miles roundtrip.

Difficulty: Easy.

Elevation gain: One hundred feet, if parking at pullout one-quarter mile before murals.

Trailhead elevation: Forty-five hundred feet at murals.

Warnings: Flash flood potential. Walking on rough gravel road requires appropriate footwear.

Directions: From Las Vegas take U.S. 93 South for 87 miles, into Arizona. Turn left at Mohave County Route 125 and go 3.7 miles to Chloride. To reach the Chloride Murals, from the town center drive up Tennessee Avenue, which turns into gravel after about 0.5 mile. Travel 200 yards farther, crossing over a wide rocky wash, and go right at the fork. Follow 1 mile farther, staying left at the fork. About 50 yards after the fork, look for the parking pullout on the right, which serves as the best trailhead. Without a high clearance four-wheel drive, and good off-road tires, it is best to walk from Tennessee Avenue.

The former mining camp of Chloride and its historic buildings are best seen at a pedestrian pace.

Acknowledgments

HIKING AND OUTDOOR EXCURSIONS HAVE SOMETIMES BROUGHT MORE ADVENTURE THAN planned, so I thank my family members and friends for returning to the trail with me, even after painful experiences and close calls. Over the years we have had close encounters with bears, mountain lions, rattlesnakes, and flash floods, and we've experienced extremely uncomfortable exposure to the elements. These encounters though, have enriched our relationships and have provided us rich stories and much retrospective laughter over the years. They might seem like tall tales to others, but they weren't.

I feel blessed by my Mom and Dad, who showed me at an early age that spending the maximum time outdoors, by land or sea, is the best life this earth affords. I have hiked thousands of miles throughout the United States and abroad, but there is nothing more satisfying, or as stunning, as hitting the trail and seeing the sights of the American Southwest.

This book would not have been possible without the endless energy and organizational skills of Mark Sedenquist and Megan Edwards of Imbrifex Books, which brought out this new and expanded edition. I must also thank Sue Campbell for her gorgeous book design, and Mike Johnson for creating the book's maps. I am forever indebted to editor A.D. Hopkins, who never missed an opportunity to encourage my efforts.

My most special thanks I offer to Pat Wall, for being patient and kind, and most of all, for believing in me.

CHOOSE YOUR PERFECT HIKE!

Since hikers' priorities vary so widely, we've selected some of those best-suited for particular interests and needs. These are the top five for each category, beginning with the best for each purpose.

Easy For Children or Adults with Limited Mobility

1 Calico Basin-Red Springs, Red Rock Canyon National Conservation Area **30**
45 Badwater, Death Valley National Park **191**
36 Corn Creek, Desert National Wildlife Refuge **149**
62 Riverside Walk, Zion National Park................................ **244**
85 Rim Trail, Grand Canyon National Park (South Rim).................**332**

Teen Favorites

74 Peek-a-boo and Spooky slot canyons, Grand Staircase-Escalante NM ...**291**
53 Rings Trail, Mojave National Preserve.............................**217**
56 Lava Tube, Mojave National Preserve **225**
63 Zion Narrows (out-and-back), Zion National Park **246**
49 Eureka Dunes, Death Valley National Park **202**

Solitude & Remote Adventure

80 The Maze, Canyonlands National Park..............................**314**
91 Toroweap/Tuweep, Grand Canyon National Park **344**
46 Telescope Peak, Death Valley National Park **193**
49 Eureka Dunes, Death Valley National Park **202**
48 The Racetrack, Death Valley National Park **199**

Waterfalls, Streams, & Wetlands

75 Coyote Gulch, Grand Staircase-Escalante National Monument **294**
77 Hackberry Canyon, Grand Staircase-Escalante NM...................**301**
47 Darwin Falls, Death Valley National Park..........................**196**
73 Calf Creek, Grand Staircase-Escalante National Monument.......... **288**
62 Riverside Walk, Zion National Park................................ **244**

Wildflowers

41 July: Alpine Lakes Loop Trail, Cedar Breaks National Monument **173**
43 July/August: Ruby Crest Trail, Ruby Mountains **180**

(continued on inside cover)